Recruiting, Retaining, and Terminating Employees

i

Published by
Ceridian Corporation
3311 East Old Shakopee Road HQW01E
Bloomington, MN 55425-1640
800-643-5999
www.hrcomply.com

ISBN 0-923-606-67-X

RRT 50-01

Foreword

Objectives and Philosophy

Gone are the days when an employer could rely on common sense alone when hiring, evaluating, disciplining, or firing employees. Federal and state employment laws impose legal obligation, and attendant risks, on virtually every employer. In addition to activities that are patently illegal, there are also a number of pitfalls for the unwary that are just plain bad business practice and should be avoided.

This book is intended to provide an overview of legal and practical issues you should consider as you prepare to make the employment decisions that need to be made each and every day. It should help you employ the best business practices and tools, and comply fully with the complex web of regulations that can trap even experienced managers and business owners. We have sought to provide you with only the most current and important information available. We have tried to do this by removing extraneous and less-relevant material and focusing on those things you need to know to do your job effectively and efficiently.

Therefore, we make some assumptions here. One is that you are not a lawyer and do not care to wade through the full law in all of its obscurity and unnatural English to find out the best way to deal with hiring, evaluating, disciplining or firing employees. A competing assumption, however, is that although you may not be a legal expert you are an intelligent and informed professional who is willing to do a little thinking to understand some important and complex material. Indeed some serious thought is required to adequately understand the hiring, retaining and terminating process and the applicable law as it currently exists — and considerable effort will be required to keep up with the law as it changes, which it is always doing.

About the Editors

Dr. Steven S. Nemerson (Editor-in-Chief)

A former Distinguished Professor of Law and Associate Dean. He earned a law degree in 1976 at Columbia Law School, where he was an editor of the Law Review. The City University of New York awarded him a PhD in 1973.

Richard A. Montgomery (Senior Legal Editor)

An attorney with extensive experience in the areas of federal and state labor and civil rights law. He is a member of both the Florida and Federal Bar. The Florida Coastal School of Law awarded him the degree of Juris Doctor in 1999. He received a Bachelor of Science degree in Justice Studies from Georgia Southern University in 1996. Mr. Montgomery served his country as a Reconnaissance Marine from 1991 – 94.

Samantha Dawn Yurman (Senior Legal Editor)

An attorney with special expertise in federal and state employment compliance law. She is a member of both the Florida and California Bar. Mrs. Yurman earned her Juris Doctor degree at California Western School of Law in San Diego, California. The University of Hawai'i at Manoa awarded her a Bachelor of Arts degree. Mrs. Yurman proudly attributes her successes to Ryan and Elvis Hayes, her husband and dog.

Jeannine Renée Burch (Production Editor)

A former journalist, Ms. Burch was the editor-in-chief of diverse international publications and co-authored significant articles on legal developments in newly emerging democracies. Ms. Burch earned a Bachelor of Science degree from the University of Illinois, College of Communications and Journalism.

Wendy L. Turanski (Production Editor)

Ms. Turanski became a published author while conducting research for the National Institute of Mental Health. She also serves as an expert reviewer for LifeWorks. Ms. Turanski earned her Master's degree from Temple University and her Bachelor of Arts degree from Concordia University – Ann Arbor.

Chapter
Table of Contents

Table of Contents

Chapter 3
The Hiring Process 35

Chapter 5
Employee Handbooks 99

Chapter 6
New-Hire Reporting 131

Chapter 7
Performance Evaluations 133

Chapter 8
Drug and Alcohol Testing in the Workplace ... 153

Chapter 9
Personnel Files 169

Chapter 10
Discipline 173

Chapter 11
Termination 185

Chapter 12

Alternative Dispute Resolution 205

Chapter 13
Telecommuting 221

Chapter 1

Job Descriptions

Introduction

Job descriptions play an important role in minimizing employee-related liability. Along with employment policies and employment contracts job descriptions define the employment relationship. Job descriptions often become critical evidence in employment disputes. In particular, job descriptions play an important role in disability discrimination cases and the determination of which employees are exempt from the requirements of the wage and hour laws. Thus employers need to take great care when preparing and updating job descriptions.

Roles of Job Descriptions

Disability Discrimination Cases

The disability discrimination laws protect only those disabled individuals who are qualified. Qualified individuals with disabilities are those who can perform the essential functions of a job, with or without reasonable accommodation. Virtually every disability discrimination case must look at the essential functions of the job to see if the complaining employee or former employee is protected as disabled under federal and state law. If the employer can show that the employee cannot perform any of the essential functions of the job even with accommodation, the employer wins. It is crucial to bear in mind; however, that one form of accommodation is reassignment to a vacant position for which the employee is qualified — with or without accommodation. Therefore, an employee with a disability who cannot be accommodated to perform all of the essential functions of a job may still be qualified if accommodated by reassignment to another vacant job the employee can safely and satisfactorily perform.

Determining the essential functions of the job can involve many factors, however job descriptions are an obvious starting point. The Americans with Disabilities Act (ADA) expressly recognizes that a written job description will be considered evidence of the essential functions of the job in ADA cases. Employers have won ADA cases where courts have held that an employee could not perform the essential functions of the job shown in the job description.

Conversely, other employers have lost ADA cases because their job descriptions did not include important job duties the employee could not perform. It is difficult for an employer to argue that a job duty is an essential function when that duty is not included in the job description prepared by the employer. These cases underscore the importance of carefully preparing job descriptions. As discussed below, job descriptions need to clearly state that the employee might be asked to perform duties not listed in the job description.

Exemption from Wage and Hour Laws

An employee's job description also plays a role in determining whether an employee is exempt from the overtime compensation and minimum wage requirements of the wage and hour laws. Even an employee who is paid a salary like an exempt employee is not exempt unless the employee has exempt duties involving the level of responsibility required by the U.S. Department of Labor Regulations.

Just as in disability discrimination cases, a court, or administrative agency likely will find that the employee's job description provides significant evidence of the employee's job duties. In Department of Labor investigations and court cases involving exemption issues, employees often minimize the importance of their duties so that they will be found to be nonexempt and be eligible for overtime compensation. Job descriptions — provided they are current and accurate — may be the only written record available to an employer to refute the employee's statements.

Performance Standard

Almost any employment dispute where the employer has found the employee's job performance to be inadequate will require a similar determination of the employee's actual job duties. Judges and juries are much more likely to find in the employer's favor where the employee had clear notice of the job expectations and failed to meet them. There is no better place to begin providing this notice than the job description. Employers who are unable to prove that the employee had notice of the employer's expectations may have a more difficult time resolving the dispute.

Preparation of Job Descriptions

To help minimize liability, an organization should follow these guidelines in preparing job descriptions:

♦ **Use the Employee.** No employer should let employees write their own job descriptions. However, obtaining an employee's input in writing the job description will make it very difficult for the employee to later allege that the job description does not accurately reflect the duties.

♦ **Update Regularly.** Employees who do not review their job descriptions for a long time may allege that that the job has changed. To avoid this problem, employers should periodically distribute job descriptions to employees. Employees should be required to identify any changes in their job duties since the descriptions were last reviewed. The employees might be asked to conduct this review as part of the performance-evaluation process.

♦ **Include Essential Information.** Employers need to maintain a balance between too much and too little information in job descriptions, yet should include as many job duties and expectations as possible. Employers should be particularly careful to include any physical requirements for the job such as lifting, standing, walking, working frequent overtime, working weekends, rotating shifts, and exposure to particular conditions such as weather and chemicals.

The job description should also include unexpected job duties and should state that the employee may be asked to perform other duties as required by business needs.

Employers should be careful not to include job duties that the employee will not perform. The more duties in a job description that the employee does not perform, the less likely the employer can persuade a judge or jury that the job description is a reasonable measure of the employee's job responsibilities.

Overall, job descriptions should reflect the reality of the employee's job as closely as possible. Business needs may also change on a daily basis, so job descriptions should specifically provide for this flexibility in a properly drafted description.

♦ **Include Special Attendance Requirements.** Employers covered by the Family and Medical Leave Act (FMLA) must provide employees with 12 weeks of leave for serious health conditions per 12-month period. It may be impossible for the organization to function if certain positions are vacant for 12 weeks a year. If a particular job has unusual attendance requirements, the job description should include those requirements. However, an employee still might be entitled to be absent from work under the FMLA notwithstanding such requirements.

♦ **Include Unusual Job Stress.** One common type of disability discrimination involves job-related stress. Job stress should be addressed in the job description so that job applicants and employees have advance notice of special circumstances they may be required to handle.

♦ **Use Descriptions in the Application Process.** Employers will benefit most from job descriptions if they use them at the earliest possible stage — the application process. Applicants should be asked to review the job description for each job they are seeking and to certify by their signature that they are able to perform that job. This may prevent the employer from being surprised by an employee's disability. If the employee later asserts a disability that limits ability to perform the job and the disability was known to the employee at the time of application, the employer may be able to assert that the employee falsified the application. Note, however, that termination of an employee for this reason should be carefully reviewed. Intentional falsification will not always be provable or even the real reason. Some employees who have performed similar work for another employer may honestly believe they can perform the present job as well only to discover there are some differences, not readily discernible from the job description that render them a bad fit for the job. For example, the job may require operating a truck does not have an automatic shift, unlike the truck the employee used on a previous job. If the employee's disability precludes using the gearshift, the employee will not be able to do this particular job, but was not lying on the initial application.

♦ **Measures of Satisfactory Performance.** Performance evaluations should be in regard to particular functions where applicable or state that a specific job task must be performed "safely and satisfactorily" in order to include quantitative and qualitative dimensions of job tasks.

Chapter 2
Recruiting Employees

Introduction

A major responsibility and concern for all organizations is recruiting and hiring the best candidate for the job. In all recruiting and hiring efforts employers must comply with state and federal laws.

Furthermore, employers are prohibited from discriminating against an employee or applicant on any legally recognized basis including, but not limited to, the following:

- Race.
- National origin.
- Religion.
- Age.
- Sex.
- Sexual orientation.
- Marital status.
- Pregnancy
- Disability.
- Military status.
- Veteran status.

Additional protected classes may be found in state fair employment practice laws.

Job Analysis

A job analysis is a questionnaire that aids employers in gathering the data necessary for developing job descriptions. The reason employers use job analyses is to first gather information about a job and then apply that information to create an accurate job description. Job analyses also assist employers with wage and salary administration, orientation of new employees, and training employees.

The following steps may assist an employer in the implementation of an efficient job analysis:

- An announcement of the analysis should be provided to all effected employees, stating the purpose of the analysis and stressing that employee input is vital.

♦ The gathering of further information is facilitated by an employer's observations of and interviewing of current employees. Employees may be asked to complete a summary of their duties and responsibilities; however, employees should not be expected to write the entire job description. An employee provided summary should focus on the tasks the employee performs and the percentage of the day, week, and/or month that is spent on each task. The employee's regular duties, not temporary duties, should be listed.

♦ The completed job analysis questionnaire should provide the employer with a synopsis of the employees' summary of duties, while allowing room for the insertion of any additional duties as necessary.

Note: Employers should always include employees in the job analysis process by asking them to complete a similar questionnaire. However, employers should be aware that employees are personally involved and may present a subjective rather than an objective picture of the job.

Job Descriptions

Job descriptions provide an employer with the most articulate explanation of what a position requires. A job description outlines the necessary skills, duties, responsibilities, training, and education for each job.

Moreover, job descriptions may be used as follows:

♦ During the hiring process to review the position with a potential employee.

♦ To acquaint a new employee to their position.

♦ To evaluate current employees' job performances.

Job description development follows a cycle starting with a position's analysis and continuing through its ongoing review. A well-written job description should include all of the following elements:

♦ Basic functions of the position.

♦ Responsibilities of the position with the primary purpose of identifying those tasks considered.

♦ Supervisory responsibilities, when applicable.

♦ Skills necessary for the position.

♦ Experience necessary for the position.

♦ Work environment identifying the physical surroundings.

♦ Education/training.

♦ To whom the position reports, in terms of organizational relationships.

♦ Date of the most recent update to the description.

Essential Job Functions

Essential job functions are those functions that any candidate or employee must be capable of completing to qualify for a position. A well-written job description will outline the essential tasks of a job position and establish a guideline for the position. For instance, determining the essential tasks of each position is a critical step to ensure compliance with the Americans with Disabilities Act (ADA). Accordingly, employers should review the position's guideline prior to interviewing any job candidates.

Benefits of Job Descriptions

It is essential to the recruiting process that an employer maintains a thorough job description for all positions. An accurate and suitable job description offers many benefits to the employer, employee, and applicant.

For example, a proper job description would meet the following criteria:

- ♦ **Defines basic responsibilities and essential job functions.** The definitions will effectively communicate job information to current and potential employees.

- ♦ **Establishes a basis for recruitment, selection, and hiring.** An employer will know what experience or skills a job requires prior to searching for the appropriate candidate. This knowledge allows an employer to write effective employment advertisement, post job notices accurately, and recruit the person most suitable for the position.

- ♦ **Protects against legal actions in hiring.** A job description may help prevent an interviewer from over-representing or under-representing the job position.

- ♦ **Assists in ADA compliance.** Organizations are required to identify essential versus nonessential job tasks when complying with the ADA.

  Note: Employers with 15 or more employees must comply with the ADA.

- ♦ **Forces the employer and employee to place emphasis upon data, resulting in clear, accurate performance reviews.**

- ♦ **Provides a tool for employee orientation that prepares employees to begin their position with optimal productivity.**

- ♦ **Measures and evaluates job performance.** Resulting in reduced turnover with clearly defined job expectations and performance evaluations based on those expectations.

- ♦ **Provides a management tool, exposing responsibility gaps and overlaps within the organization.** This is especially helpful during reorganization or downsizing.

Techniques

Upon completion of an accurate and thorough job description employers gain the vital knowledge of job criteria and required qualifications. The recruiting process then begins, using the two basic types of employee selection technique — inquiry and examination. Pre-employment inquiries (applications) tend to reveal an applicant's general background information.

Examinations and tests tend to gather more specific information, in an effort to predict future job performance. For example, many employers administer some type of formal pre-employment test to determine skills, honesty, intelligence, aptitude, and personality tests. Additionally, many employers also perform drug testing.

Pre-Employment Testing

Regardless of the type of test, employers must unilaterally apply testing to **all** employees consistently and uniformly.

If a test tends to screen out individuals with a disability, then the test must be job-related and consistent with business necessities to be deemed as legal. For example, regulations of the American with Disabilities Act (ADA) require that any abilities the test measures must be necessary to perform the essential functions of the job.

An employer may also need to make reasonable accommodations to provide applicants with equal opportunities to participate in the application testing process.

Performance and Aptitude Evaluations

Performance and aptitude tests should identify those candidates most likely to succeed. These tests determine an applicant's mastery of the skills required for the particular job. Such tests typically attempt to predict job performance by measuring an applicant's mental ability, job knowledge, simulated job performance, agility, or strength, as well as the applicant's motivation and desire.

Adverse Impact

Employers should always exercise caution when administering tests because some tests may adversely impact certain protected groups.

Adverse impact occurs when the test screens out individuals in protected groups, such as females, minorities, or the disabled, in greater proportion than others. However, adverse impact alone does not necessarily make a test unlawful.

Generally, if a test adversely impacts any protected group, an employer must validate the results of the test by establishing the following:

- ♦ The test is a neutral predictor of job performance.
- ♦ The testing criteria used directly relates to the qualifications for the job.

Note: A physical fitness or agility test must not involve the monitoring of an applicant's physiological or biological response. Monitoring physical responses to a physical fitness test qualifies the test as a medical exam, which is prohibited before an employment offer is extended.

Drug Tests

Employers may test applicants for illegal drug use before extending a job offer. However, employers may not test for alcohol or legal drug use, since the ADA defines alcohol or legal drug testing as protected medical examinations.

Existing drug testing programs may require a modification if testing is not restricted to the illegal use of drugs only. The service or clinic used for testing should comply with the ADA and state law.

Medical Information and Testing

Traditionally, employers sought medical information about applicants to assess the applicant's abilities to perform a job. However, as medical insurance, workers' compensation, and other costs associated with disabilities and other medical impairments have increased, employers have also sought such information in an effort to control or reduce such costs.

Note: A number of federal and state laws have been enacted to assist employers in the prevention of discrimination and privacy violations against disabled or medically impaired individuals resulting from overzealous medical screening.

Federal Laws

Employers must comply with the following federal regulations while performing any pre-employment tests:

♦ The Rehabilitation Act of 1973, which applies to some government contractors, prohibits employers from discriminating against all qualified individuals with a handicap and limits how employers can collect and retain medical information about applicants.

♦ The ADA states that employment offers can be conditioned on an applicant's satisfactory passage of a physical exam. However, nonjob-related disabilities uncovered during a physical exam may not be used to disqualify an applicant.

The ADA prohibits employers with 15 or more employees from discriminating against qualified individuals with a disability in hiring, firing, establishing compensation levels, and other privileges of employment. Additionally, the ADA prohibits an employer from performing any of the following:

- Asking applicants about their physical or mental limitations.

- Conducting medical examinations before making the applicant a conditional offer of employment.

- Limiting, segregating, or classifying a job applicant or employee in a way that adversely affects the person's opportunities or status.

♦ Importantly, certain employers are required to abide by the HIPAA privacy protections.

State Laws

Some states have laws that limit the types of medical information employers can seek from job applicants. These laws may prohibit employers from discriminating against disabled individuals or people diagnosed with certain conditions, such as the following:

♦ Acquired immunodeficiency syndrome/human immunodeficiency virus (AIDS/HIV).

♦ Cancer.

♦ Genetic diseases, such as sickle-cell anemia or Tay-Sachs.

These laws may also protect an individual's privacy in relation to specific conditions.

Other states have laws that expressly or implicitly mandate testing for communicable diseases for certain categories of workers. For example, several states require teachers to be tested for tuberculosis, and other states prohibit food industry employers from hiring an individual infected with communicable diseases.

Genetic Testing

Genetic tests determine whether individuals have genetic traits that make them susceptible to certain diseases. Employers may desire to perform genetic tests on applicants to identify those applicants who may succumb to conditions having high costs in terms of absenteeism, workers' compensation, disability, and medical insurance. The concern about invasion of privacy and discrimination in employment increases as scientific breakthroughs make it easier to identify genes linked to specific diseases. To address this concern, many states are considering and implementing legislation to prohibit or control the use of genetic tests in the employment process and to mandate the confidentiality of test results.

Extensive regulations, found in Executive Order 13145 and enforced by the Equal Employment Opportunity Commission (EEOC), prohibit discrimination against employees in federal employment based on protected genetic information or information about a request for or the receipt of genetic services. An employing department or agency may not discharge, fail or refuse to hire, or otherwise discriminate against any employee with respect to the compensation, terms, conditions, or privileges of employment because of protected genetic information with respect to the employee or because of information about a request for or the receipt of genetic services by such employee.

According to Executive Order 13145, protected genetic information is information about **any** of the following:

- An individual's genetic tests.

- The genetic tests of an individual's family members.

- The occurrence of a disease, or medical condition or disorder in family members of the individual.

However, information about an individual's current health status (including information about sex, age, physical exams, and chemical, blood, or urine analyses) is not deemed as protected genetic information.

An employing department or agency may not limit, segregate, or classify employees in any way that would deprive or tend to deprive any employee of employment opportunities or otherwise adversely affect that employee's status, because of protected genetic information with respect to the employee or because of information about a request for or the receipt of genetic services by such employee.

Note: In the interests of privacy, an employing department or agency may not maintain protected genetic information or information about a request for or the receipt of genetic services in general personnel files; such information shall be treated as confidential medical records and kept separate from personnel files.

Polygraph and Psychological Testing

The general purpose of conducting a polygraph test (lie detector) is to detect whether or not an applicant or employee was involved in an incident of workplace theft or other misconduct causing economic loss. As an alternative to polygraph tests, some employers use paper-and-pencil honesty tests aimed at assessing the honesty of applicants through questions about theft. These tests are essentially a form of a psychological test.

Applicants or employees who have been asked or required to take polygraph tests have sued employers in the following instances:

- Under federal and state laws that restrict or prohibit the administration of such tests.

- For violation of federal and state constitutional rights of privacy.

- For invasion of privacy under common law theories, including negligence, defamation, and infliction of emotional distress.

Polygraph Tests

Employee Polygraph Protection Act of 1988

With few exceptions, the Employee Polygraph Protection Act of 1988 (EPPA) protects most applicants and employees from employer-required polygraph examinations. However, the following are exceptions to the act:

- ♦ Applicants and employees for jobs in government, national defense, security services (such as armored-car, alarm, and guard), or manufacturing of controlled substances may be required to take polygraph tests.

- ♦ Private sector employees may be asked to take polygraph tests in conjunction with criminal investigations of theft, embezzlement, or business espionage or sabotage, as long as the employee had access to the property that is the subject of the investigation and the employer has a reasonable suspicion that the employee was involved.

Employers who administer polygraph tests must adhere to the following:

- ♦ Provide employees with information concerning their rights under the act.

- ♦ Refrain from asking questions about religion, race, sex, politics, or union or labor affiliations.

- ♦ Refrain from taking certain actions against employees solely on the basis of results of a test or the refusal to take a test.

- ♦ Respect the examinee's right to terminate the test at any time.

- ♦ Respect the examinee's right to not be asked degrading or unnecessarily intrusive questions or questions concerning religious or political beliefs or sexual preference.

Warning: Employers wishing to implement a polygraph testing policy should first consult an attorney.

Governmental Entities

When acting as an employer, the U.S. government, any state or local government, or any political subdivision of a state or local government is exempt from the EPPA.

Employers Authorized to Manufacture, Distribute, or Dispense Controlled Substances

Employers authorized by the Drug Enforcement Agency to manufacture, distribute, or dispense controlled substances may administer polygraph tests to a prospective employee who, if hired, would have direct access to controlled substances. *Direct address* under such circumstances signifies that the position requires involvement in manufacture, testing, storage, distribution, sale, or dispensing of controlled substances.

Employers Providing Security Services

Employers whose primary business purpose is to provide security services (such as armored cars, security protection, and security alarm) may administer polygraph tests to applicants. However, such tests may only be administered to those prospective employees who are being hired to protect facilities, materials, or operations having a significant impact on the health or safety of any state or the national security of the United States.

Psychological Tests

Some employers use psychological tests to assess an applicant's honesty or work habits. Psychological testing commonly takes the form of objective tests consisting of true or false questions, and often contains questions about private matters including religion, sexual practices and preferences, and bodily functions.

For legal and ethical reasons, psychological testing should be job related and narrowly tailored to serve a specific employer purpose. The provider of a frequently used test, the Minnesota Multiphasic Personality Inventory, cautions against uniform administration of the test and advises that only those in jobs involving safety or high stress be tested.

Employers performing psychological tests need to consider whether they will run afoul of the ADA or EEOC guidelines when performing testing. Psychological tests that are designed to reveal or assess an applicant's mental impairment or general psychological health may be deemed as medical examinations and cannot be given at the pre-offer stage. However, psychological tests designed to reveal or assess an applicant's honesty and work habits would not be deemed as medical examinations and may be given at the pre-offer stage. Similar analysis must be made with respect to each question on a psychological test.

Warnings Using Polygraph Alternatives

Employers should use extreme caution when administering personality tests that are in actuality a psychological evaluation. Personality and honesty testing may also raise privacy and discrimination issues and should be limited to assessing job-related traits.

Warning: A pre-offer test that identifies mental disorders would violate the ADA.

The ADA provides protections for mental disorders including major depression, bipolar disorder, anxiety disorders, schizophrenia, and personality disorders that substantiality limit one or more major life activities. Despite claims to the contrary, no guaranteed means exists to accurately assess honesty or personality.

However, if an employer must use an honesty or personality test an employer should refrain from using tests as follows:

◆ For which little or no validation research exists.

◆ Based on anonymously provided data or lacking data from real candidates.

◆ With validation studies designed, conducted, and published only by the test developer and not replicated by independent psychologists or agencies.

Pre-Employment Inquiry Guidelines

When employers make pre-employment inquiries, they must use caution to avoid any potential discrimination actions. The following section provides a general list of permissible inquiries based on federal, state, and local antidiscrimination statutes.

Please note that these are only general guidelines and employers should not interpret them as representing the law of any one state or municipality.

Age

Permissible inquiries: "Upon hire will you be able to demonstrate your age?" "Are you over 18 years of age?" "If you are under 18 years of age, are you capable of producing a work permit upon hire?"

Suspect inquiries: Age. Birth date. Questions which tend to identify applicants as 40 years of age or over, such as retirement or health concerns.

Arrest or Criminal Record

Permissible inquiries: Questions regarding prior convictions when accompanied by a statement that convictions will not prohibit employment, only considered in relation to specific job requirements. "Have you ever been convicted of a crime?"

Suspect inquiries: "Have you ever been arrested?"

Birthplace or Citizenship

Permissible inquiries: "Are you a citizen of the United States?" "If you are not a U.S. citizen, have you the legal right to remain permanently in the United States? Do you intend to remain permanently in the United States?"

Note: Statement that proof of the applicant's legal right to work in the United States will be required **after** being hired.

Suspect inquiries: "Of what country are you a citizen?" Inquiring into the birthplace of an applicant or the applicant's parents or family.

Education

Permissible inquiries: Questions regarding the extent of education, degree(s) received, names of schools attended, but only where such requirements are clearly related to the job.

Suspect inquiries: Inquiry as to how the applicant acquired the ability to read, write, or speak English language.

Fidelity Bonding

Permissible inquiries: Statement that fidelity bonding is a requirement of employment.

Suspect inquiries: "Have you ever been denied a fidelity bond or had one cancelled?"

Height or Weight

Permissible inquiries: Questions may be asked about an applicant's height or weight only if it is a bona fide occupational qualification, demonstrably related to safe and efficient job performance.

Suspect inquiries: Height. Weight.

Note: Employers generally should seek legal review or advice in determining whether a bona fide occupational qualification exists before making inquiries regarding a protected characteristic or status.

Hours of Work/Attendance

Permissible inquiries: "Are you able to work overtime?" Questions regarding ability to work the employer's normal work hours. Questions regarding tardiness and/or attendance record during previous employment.

Suspect inquiries: Questions regarding the number of sick days taken during previous employment.

Military Service

Permissible inquiries: Questions regarding relevant experience gained during military service

Suspect inquiries: Questions regarding the type of discharge, except honorable discharge. Questions regarding reserve duty obligations. Questions regarding service in foreign military.

Name

Permissible inquiries: "Have you ever used any other name?" "Is additional information, such as assumed name, necessary in order to check job references?"

Suspect inquiries: "What is your maiden name?" "Has your name been changed by court order?"

National Origin

Permissible inquiries: Where languages other than English are relevant to the job sought: "What languages, other than English, do you read or write?" "Can you speak, read, or write other languages?"

Suspect inquiries: Questions requiring applicant to identify national origin, ancestry, or nationality. "What is your first/native language?"

Notice in Case of Emergency

Permissible inquiries: Statement that the name and address of an individual to be notified in case of accident or emergency will be required upon hire.

Suspect inquiries: Name, address, and relationship of nearest relative to be notified in case of emergency.

Organizations/Activities

Permissible inquiries: "List all job-related organizations, clubs, or professional societies to which you belong — you should omit those which would identify your race, color, religion, sex, national origin, age, disability, or sexual orientation."

Suspect inquiries: "List all organizations, clubs, and societies to which you belong." Questions related to political affiliations or union memberships.

Photograph

Permissible inquiries: Statement that the employer may require a photograph after employment.

Suspect inquiries: Requiring an applicant to affix a photograph to the application. Requesting applicants, at their option, to submit a photograph. Requiring a photograph after an interview but before employment. Videotaping interviews.

Physical/Mental Disability

Permissible inquiries: Describing the various functions of the job and asking: "Can you perform the functions of the job for which you are applying?"

Suspect inquiries: "Do you have any physical or mental condition/disability that may affect your ability to perform the job applied for?" Questions regarding an applicant's general health, medical conditions, illness, or disabilities. Questions regarding receipt of benefits for disability or workers' compensation.

Qualifications/Previous Work Experience

Permissible inquiries: Questions related to previous experience and/or job skills that are relevant to the job applied for, names and addresses of former employers, dates of prior employment, and reason(s) for leaving previous employer.

Suspect inquiries: Questions containing inflated experience requirements that are not strictly job related.

Race or Color

Suspect inquiries: Questions requiring an applicant to identify race, complexion, color, color of skin, hair, or eyes. Questions requiring applicant to identify attitudes about working with, supervising, or being supervised by a person of another race.

Note: Data for OFCCP affirmative action compliance or Equal Employment Opportunity (EEO) recordkeeping should be recorded and maintained separately from the application.

References

Permissible inquiries: "List those persons willing to provide personal and/or professional references."

Suspect inquiries: Questions directed to applicant's former employer(s) or personal references that elicit information regarding an applicant's race, color, religion, creed, national origin, sex, age, or disability.

Relatives/Anti-Nepotism Policies

Permissible inquiries: Statement of the employer's anti-nepotism policy. Although this is not an inquiry, a statement informs the applicant that such a policy exists and that it may be a disqualifier. Question as to whether the applicant's spouse is employed by the potential employer.

Suspect inquiries: "Are you married?" "Do you have any children?" "Is your spouse employed?" "What is your spouse's name?"

Religion

Permissible inquiries: Statement of the employer's regular working hours, days or shifts and whether the applicant can work this schedule.

Suspect inquiries: Religion of the applicant. Any questions which tend to elicit information about an applicant's religious affiliation, for example. Questions regarding activity in church groups. Requirement that applicants include a member of the clergy as a personal reference.

Residence

Permissible inquiries: Address.

Suspect inquiries: "Do you own or rent your home?" "Do you have any foreign residences?"

Sex

Permissible inquiries: Applicant's sex but only if sex is a bona fide occupational qualification, demonstrably related to job performance.

Note: Employers should generally seek legal review or advice in determining whether a bona fide occupation qualification exists before making inquiries regarding a protected characteristic or status and should be aware that a bona fide occupational qualification is very difficult to prove.

Suspect inquiries: Sex of applicant. Questions regarding pregnancy, birth control, number and/or ages of children, child bearing, or child care plans. Questions inquiring whether an applicant's spouse will allow the applicant to travel.

ADA Pre-Employment Inquiries

The Americans with Disabilities Act (ADA) has a significant impact upon the hiring process, including the questions and information employers may ask applicants.

The Equal Employment Opportunity Commission (EEOC) has issued an ADA enforcement guide to provide guidance regarding specific inquiries that may be permissible or impermissible.

The EEOC regulations (located at 29 C.F.R § 1630.14(a)) state that an employer may make pre-employment inquiries into the ability of an applicant to perform job-related functions and/or may ask an applicant to describe or to demonstrate how — with or without reasonable accommodation — the applicant will be able to perform job-related functions.

The following section represents a general list of permissible and impermissible pre-employment inquiries (please note that this is a guideline only and not inclusive of all issues):

- An employer **may** do the following:

  - Ask about an applicant's ability to perform both essential and marginal job functions, although employers may not refuse to hire an applicant with a disability who cannot perform a marginal function.

  - Ask the applicant if they are able to perform a specific job function, such as "Can you lift 50 lbs?" or "Can you drive a truck?" if this function is required in performing job duties.

  - Demonstrate a job function and then ask if the applicant is capable of performing the function.

  - Ask an applicant to describe or demonstrate how they might perform the function.

  - Ask an applicant how much time off they took in a previous job (but not why), the reasons the applicant left a previous job, and any past discipline.

  Note: This request must be made of all applicants unless the applicant has an obvious disability that may prevent the performance of a particular function.

  - State attendance requirements, and ask whether the applicant can satisfy such requirements.

- An employer **may not** ask the following:

  - Whether an applicant has a disability that would prohibit the applicant from performing a job.

  - If the applicant has a specific disability.

  - Inquiries regarding the applicant's general, physical condition.

  - Questions about an applicant's temporary impairments, such as a broken bone, that could relate to possible long-term conditions.

  - Inquiries regarding potential leave for treatment, and/or when the applicant first became disabled, regardless of whether the applicant volunteers that they have a disability.

  - Question how many days the applicant was sick or absent on medical/disability leave from prior positions.

  - The applicant's workers' compensation history.

Application of the ADA and Reasonable Accommodation

The ADA regulations protect people who have a physical or mental impairment that substantially limits one or more major life activities. The scope of ADA protections is vast and wide. For example, the ADA offers protections for people who are deaf, people who have epilepsy, severe arthritis, people with a manic-depressive disorder, and major depression.

After an applicant is determined as having a disability, the employer must fulfill immediate responsibilities to maintain compliance with ADA regulations. Employers must consider whether the individual is qualified to perform the tasks of the job. A determination of job qualification automatically triggers ADA protections. However, the standard of disability and qualification creates an inherent tension because, regardless of any accommodation, a disabled individual may not be qualified for any job.

Another concern for employers is safety and whether a person with an emotional or mental disability is qualified for a job or poses a direct threat to workplace safety. According to the ADA, individuals are deemed a direct threat if they pose a significant risk to the health and safety of others that cannot be eliminated by reasonable accommodation. Additionally, the ADA allows employers to incorporate the direct theory in the qualification standards of a job position. For example, to qualify for a particular job, an applicant may be required to not pose a direct threat to the health and safety of others in the workplace.

A reasonable accommodation is capable of transforming an unqualified individual with a disability into a qualified individual. *Reasonable accommodations* are adjustments or modifications provided by an employer to enable people with disabilities to enjoy equal employment opportunities. The reasonable accommodation standard requires employers to treat every applicant or employee with a disability on an individual, case-by-case basis. Employers must respond to the disability-based workplace needs of the individual, as long as the accommodation does not impose an undue hardship on the employer's operations. Based on the employer's resources and operation of business, undue hardship occurs when the providing of a reasonable accommodation would result in significant difficulty or expense.

The ADA provides a list of examples of accommodations an employer may offer. However, an employer must be aware that the list is not intended to be all-inclusive. An employer for example may initiate the following reasonable accommodations:

- Make facilities accessible and usable by persons with disabilities.
- Restructure jobs.
- Provide part-time or modified work schedules.
- Reassign the person to a vacant position.
- Modify policies or training materials.
- Provide qualified readers and interpreters.

An employer is obligated to provide a reasonable accommodation only where the employer knows of the physical or mental limitations of an otherwise qualified individual. The EEOC has indicated that, generally, an individual must request an accommodation. For instance, there are two basic issues regarding ADA accommodation for persons with psychiatric disabilities:

- Disclosure.
- Participation.

To be provided with a needed reasonable accommodation, a person with a disability — psychiatric or otherwise — must request an accommodation and disclose the nature of the mental limitation or limitations to be accommodated. No consensus appears to exist as to how, when, what, or to whom information should be disclosed in the accommodation process.

Individuals with mental disabilities may be unable to communicate effectively due to their disability. Unlike a person with a physical disability, a person with a mental disability may be unaware of the nature or extent of the disability. Similarly, poor self-awareness or self-denial (which may be traits of the mental disability itself) may also make disclosure difficult. However, the failure by the employee explicitly to disclose a mental disability can prove fatal to that employee's ADA claim.

Questions Regarding Reasonable Accommodation

With exception, employers are prohibited from inquiring as to whether an applicant has a physical or mental impairment. Where it seems likely that an applicant has a disability that will require a reasonable accommodation, an employer may ask the applicant whether they will need a reasonable accommodation. However, employers must be particularly cautious in asking an applicant any questions regarding a disability because the ADA regulations are difficult and complicated.

Generally, employers should only inquire as to what is specifically required for the job and where any needed special equipment may be obtained. As an example, if an applicant applying for a job requiring extensive computer work discloses a severe visual impairment, the employer could ask about and discuss any visual enhancement equipment that may be fitted to the computer.

The following exceptions to the general rule exist where:

♦ The employer reasonably believes that the applicant will need reasonable accommodation because of an obvious disability.

♦ The employer reasonably believes that the applicant will need reasonable accommodation because of a disability that the applicant has voluntarily disclosed to the employer.

♦ The applicant has voluntarily disclosed to the employer the need for a reasonable accommodation to perform the job.

In these cases, the employer is permitted to ask whether the applicant needs reasonable accommodation and what type of reasonable accommodation is needed to perform the functions of the job.

Caution When Asking About Reasonable Accommodations

When an employer asks whether reasonable accommodation is needed and the applicant responds in the negative, the employer may not ask any additional questions about reasonable accommodation. However, the employer could ask the applicant to describe or demonstrate a particular job function.

If the applicant indicates that a reasonable accommodation is required, the employer may ask questions about the type of accommodation needed at that time or in the near future.

Employment Applications

A sample of an employment application is provided at the end of this chapter.

Generally, an employment application should be tailored to an open employment position and contain the following:

♦ A statement that the employer is an equal opportunity employer and will not discriminate.

♦ A statement that the application is not an offer of employment and that any employment with the organization is on an at-will basis, terminable at any time for any reason.

♦ An applicant certification stating that all information and answers provided on the application and during any interviews are true and accurate.

Note: This should include the applicant's acknowledgment that denial of employment (or if hired) termination of employment may occur if the applicant provides false information.

♦ A place for the applicant to provide general information, such as the following:

• Name.

• Address and telephone number.

• Confirmation of legal minimum working age.

• Position sought.

• Availability.

• I-9 statement regarding proof of legal authorization to work in the United States, if applicable.

♦ Work experience inquiry, such as the following:

• The name, address, and telephone number of previous employer(s).

• Dates of employment.

• Last wage/pay rate.

• Job titles and duties.

• Name(s) and title(s) of supervisor(s).

• Reason for leaving.

• Inquiry as to whether the applicant has ever been discharged from a position for making threats, fighting or any other incidents involving violence.

♦ A place to record educational background, such as the following:

• High school and college(s) attended.

• Number of academic years completed (without designating dates attended).

• Whether the applicant graduated and any degree(s) obtained.

• Any specialized licensing or vocational school(s).

- Military experience applicable to the job sought, such as the following:
  - Branch of service and rank.
  - Special skills or training.
  - An inquiry if the applicant was honorably discharged.
- Inquiries regarding other experience or certificates. The following inquiries may be included as relevant to the position sought:
  - Licensure or certification required.
  - Typing/word processing skills.
  - Computer skills.
  - Languages.
  - Professional affiliations.
- Personal and professional references.

Fees for Employment Applications

Employers are not permitted to collect fees from individuals applying for a job. This includes any form(s) of payment in order to perform the following:

- Apply orally or in writing.
- Receive, obtain, complete, or submit an application for employment.
- Provide, accept, or process an application for employment.

Employer Sources for Applicants

Employers have various avenues available for recruiting new employees, such as the following:

- Newspaper advertisements.
- Employee referrals.
- Educational institutions.
- Community organizations.
- Outside professional search firms.
- Computer data banks and the Internet.

Employers also have various nontraditional media to use for advertising vacancies. These channels include the following:

- Radio advertisements
- Television advertisements.
- Public-access cable channels advertisements or announcements.
- Billboard advertising.

- ♦ Bulletin board displays.

- ♦ Direct mail and door-hanger advertisements.

- ♦ Calling cards and point-of-sale messages.

In choosing a recruitment method, employers should consider whether the method chosen could discourage diversity among its workforce or have a discriminatory impact upon applicants. Employers that rely heavily upon referrals from current employees could sustain imbalances in the workforce if the existing workforce is not sufficiently diverse.

When possible, employers should use several recruitment sources. For example, an employer may advertise for employees in newspapers and through institutions and organizations that are likely to produce an applicant pool from many demographic groups.

In-House Recruitment Sources

Promoting from Within

Employers should first utilize the pool of current employees to fill all but the lowest entry-level jobs. Filling jobs with internal candidates improves employee morale and reduces hiring costs associated with advertising, applicant screening, new-hire orientation, and administrative processing.

Disadvantages

Of course, promoting from within results in a position remaining open — the opening left by the promoted employee. Internal recruitment can also lead to stagnation since the organization does not gain new perspectives from outside recruits. If the organization currently faces problems in diversity, internally hiring perpetuates current workforce characteristics and does little to promote affirmative action or diversity goals.

Policies and Procedures

Spelling out policies and procedures for internal hires is important in maintaining a constant standard for promotion. Some employers require internal candidates to have worked at least six months in their present position and have a satisfactory performance rating. In other situations, union contracts may impose restrictions, such as seniority requirements. In addition, employers must decide whether to keep internal applications confidential or require employees to notify their current supervisor before applying for job openings. Most organizations use some combination of job posting, nominations by supervisors, and skills inventories to find qualified inside candidates.

Job Posting

Job posting may be accomplished through the use of a print or computer bulletin board, internal job hotline, or employee newsletter to advertise vacant positions to employees. A typical job posting includes a description of the position, hiring requirements, an application, and instructions about application procedures and deadlines.

Nominations By Supervisors

Another way to promote employees is to circulate descriptions of job openings to supervisors who may have subordinates with the required skills. Supervisors are excellent sources for employee referrals because they have the vantage point in regard to the qualifications and skills of their employees.

Skills Inventory

Keeping a record of current employees' skills makes it easier for employers to find qualified internal candidates. All employees should complete a skill inventory form and update the record whenever an employee completes new training, obtains a degree, or otherwise enhances job skills.

Employer Application Files

Potential sources of candidates may be found in employment applications held by supervisors or in a central personnel file. Supervisors or a company's personnel department may have already performed some of the initial screening tasks and can provide additional information on the candidate. For recordkeeping purposes, applications should be kept for one year. However, company policy will dictate the length of time employment applications are considered active.

Employee Referrals

Employers have a choice of several styles when implementing an employee referral program. Some employee referral programs are informal and operate though word-of-mouth. Other employers have formal programs offering a reward or bonus to employees who refer qualified candidates. Employee referral programs often produce quality candidates since current employees know the internal operations and company culture. In addition, most employees will not refer someone unless they believe that person will represent themselves and the organization in a positive light. Importantly, employee referral programs need careful structuring to avoid internal problems.

Antinepotism Considerations

Antinepotism policies would eliminate the situation where employees refer relatives in an employee referral program. Employers should prohibit relatives from working in the same department or in positions that have direct reporting relationships to prevent favoritism, scheduling problems, and disciplinary issues.

EEO Considerations

Employee referral programs tend to perpetuate the characteristics of the present workforce because people tend to refer friends or associates who have similar interests and activities. This can occasionally be problematic. For example, if minority representation in the organization's current workforce does not parallel minority representation in the labor pool, an organization should avoid relying too heavily on employee referrals. On the other hand, an employer can boost its EEO program by soliciting referrals from minority and female employees.

Developing Referral Award Programs

Employers who use award referral programs need to carefully define and structure the program to prevent any problems after a candidate is hired.

The following guidelines may be helpful for employers that implementing a referral award program for employees:

- ♦ Determine if the award will be monetary or some other benefit, such as extra time off with pay, free merchandise or services, or an entry in a prize drawing.

- ♦ Accurately define the amount of the award in terms of cash value, days off, merchandise, or winning prize form a drawing.

- Provide a specifically detailed writing of the program's terms to reflect all differing reward amounts.

- State the dollar value in the proper amount — either net or gross — depending on the employer. Referral bonuses are considered taxable income.

- Pay the award on a specific date, decided in advance, and provided to all employees. For example, the date should be at the time of hire, after completion of a probationary period, or some other landmark.

- State whether the award depends on how long the referred employee stays at the job.

- Check for any limitations on referrals, such as a policy against hiring family members, before implementing an award policy.

- State within the policy if the award is only for full-time hires or whether part-time, temporary hires, and temp-to-hire are also eligible.

- State the conditions employees must meet to receive an award for a proper referral. Complications arise when a candidate for the position forgets to put the referring employee's name on the application form or when more than one person claims to have referred the same candidate.

- State whether a referral is considered to be a recommendation in favor of the applicant.

- State whether the employees will suffer any consequences for referring an applicant who, once hired, proves to be a poor performer. A policy statement relieving the referring employee of responsibility for the applicant's performance may reduce such fears and help increase the number of employee-based referrals. However, this policy may also lower the quality of referrals.

- State whether an employee must still be working for the employer to claim the referral award.

- Specify who is eligible for awards. Some employers feel that recruiting good people is a job requirement for managers, rather than a task deserving an award. An organization also risks the possibility that a manager might abuse the system by claiming a referral for everyone individual hired.

Outside Recruitment Sources

Employers looking to fill a position may use a number of sources outside the organization, such as the following:

- Classified ads in the help-wanted sections of local newspapers are one of the most widely used recruitment tools.

- Professional journals and trade associations.

- Electronic media, radio, television, and the Internet.

- Public and private employment agencies, job fairs, colleges and universities, and unions and trade groups.

Employment Advertisements

Help Wanted Ads

Help-wanted ads may take the following two forms:

- ◆ **Open Ads.** Ads which give the employer's name and address. Typically used to recruit semiskilled industrial workers, lower-paid clerical employees, and other candidates whenever giving the organization's name would not adversely affect the business.

- ◆ **Blind Ads.** Ads which omit the organization's name and ask applicants to submit their résumés to a box number or other neutral address. Useful when an employer expects many responses, wants to avoid sending acknowledgments to every applicant, or prefers to keep competitors or others from learning about hiring plans.

Employers may place help-wanted ads in metropolitan dailies, weekly newspapers, trade or association newspapers and magazines, professional journals, or specialized magazines. Each avenue of advertising has advantages and disadvantages.

Newspapers

Most job ads appear in daily newspapers, particularly Sunday editions, which usually have the largest circulation. Local weekly papers and free shoppers are an inexpensive option when a job opening requires skills widely available in the area labor pool. When the job demands specialized or unique skills, employers are at an advantage by placing ads in out-of-town newspapers, particularly in larger dailies circulated nationwide at airports and newsstands, or in smaller papers circulated in areas with promising labor pools.

Specialized Publications

Most trade magazines, association newspapers, and professional journals have classified sections that offer an excellent way to target sales, technical, or professional people with industry experience. A disadvantage of these specialized publications is the delay in getting an advertisement to its audience because most of these publications are published monthly or less often. Additionally, compared with mass-market newspapers, professional and trade journal advertising is relatively expensive and attracts fewer applicants.

Hazards of Classified Advertising

Poorly worded ads may violate discrimination laws or create an implied contract of employment. Employers must review ads prior to publication to ensure that the advertisement is in compliance with Title VII of the Civil Rights Act. Compliance requires that advertisements avoid any reference to race, color, religion, sex, or national origin... Furthermore, compliance with the Age Discrimination in Employment Act (ADEA) requires that ads avoid reference to age. Employers should review the ads to eliminate words such as "young and energetic salesman," "waitress," or "repairman," and replace them with terms such as "mature" or "experienced." Statements that imply permanent or guaranteed employment, such as annual salaries, should also be avoided.

Checklist for Effective Employment Advertisements

Employers seeking to draft effective employment ads should include the following information in all advertisements:

- ◆ The name of the job and descriptive job title in the headline or first line of copy, s. For instance, the term "trainee," could apply to any occupation, while "real estate appraisal trainee" is sufficiently descriptive.

- Stress placed upon the organization's and/or the job's strong points. A short phrase that tells applicants what makes the organization a good place to work. Examples of these phrases include "corporate culture that values employee input," "excellent working conditions," "chances for improvement," "liberal fringe benefits," and "steady employment."

- Clearly stated job qualifications. The advertisement should detail minimum acceptable education, training, and experience, as well as any special skill requirements, such as typing, stenography, familiarity with certain machinery, or ability to drive a car.

- Factual information about the job. For example, specified working hours and days, job location, overtime, whether travel is involved, or any other special requirements.

- Details of when, where, and how prospective applicants may apply. A statement as to whether applicants may phone for appointments and/or mail, email, or fax résumés. Hours should be supplied when and employer is holding an open house or job fair.

- The salary of the position. Employers should consider whether to offer a specific figure, give a range, mention a top-starting figure, or include a noncommittal statement, such as "salary commensurate with experience." On the contrary, an employer may ask applicants to state salary requirements or present earnings.

- Compliance with EEO requirements. All job titles must be gender-neutral, and all listed requirements must be job-related. Federal contractors must include an EEO statement; however in any employment advertisement, all employers would benefit from stating that they are an equal employment opportunity employer.

How to Design an Employment Advertisement

Employers may use the following guidelines to design an employment ad:

- Experiment with formats and track applicant response to different ads. Experiment with varying amounts of white space around the copy, differences in size and kind of type, and unusual arrangement of elements. Creative headlines may cause an advertisement to stand out in a column of uninteresting type. Newspaper staff is also available to assist employers with simple graphics, such as adding a company's logo, a border, or stock artwork.

- Determine whether to use display advertising or help-wanted advertising. Employers should consider buying space in sections of the paper other than the help-wanted classifieds to reach people who might not be job hunting. Ads displayed on the business pages or the general news pages are able to use illustrations and graphic techniques that are impossible in standard classified sections. Display ads are particularly effective when recruiting professionals or higher-salaried employees.

- Select the correct advertisement size. The size of the advertisement depends on the labor market, as well as the type and number of other ads the publication carries. When other ads fill several columns, an individual advertisement running four lines is not apt to get noticed unless it is distinctive. One large advertisement may become more distinctive than multiple, smaller ads. Additionally, in stating the organization's name and address once, rather than multiple listings, an employer may save in both space and reduce the ad's cost.

Sample Advertisement

Accounts Payable Clerk: Data entry experience required; minimum one-year experience; must generate weekly payment reports. Credit experience preferred. Thirty-five hours; parking, medical insurance, advancement opportunity. Salary to $350/week. Call Office Manager, M-F, and 9-5. 567-1234. EOE

Commercial Employment Agencies

Hiring an outside employment agency may be more efficient than using in-house staff for advertising, screening, testing, and initial interviewing. In most cases, an employer pays the agency's fees, however some employment agencies charge job seekers instead. Contingency-fee arrangements typically range from a low of 10 percent of a successful applicant's starting salary for a clerical position to 20 to 35 percent for an executive or professional position. Most agencies will only receive payment upon the successful placement of a candidate. Additionally, agencies may offer a prorated refund of a fee if the placement of the person is not successful. When choosing an employment agency, an employer should inquire as to whether the agency specializes in particular fields, fee amounts, services included, and payment schedules. Agencies must not discriminate or make false representations regarding the employer's company. Employers should also question the agency about how candidates are sought and whether the agency has faced discrimination or other employment law charges.

Public Employment Agencies

State employment agencies associated with state unemployment compensation offices and the U.S. Employment Service offer an inexpensive way to find job candidates. These agencies have access to many job seekers and charge no fees. State employment agencies often supply professional, technical, and managerial candidates to employers. Within a specific timeframe, state agencies enter any job not locally filled into a nationwide database to facilitate the employment process. This nationwide database expands the span of applicants beyond the local labor pool. For example, people willing to relocate may send résumés through a local office to a distant employer. Jobs listed in the national system tend to fall into the professional and highly skilled categories since less-skilled jobs are more likely to be filled from the local labor force. The on-line version of the national job system, America's Job Bank located at *www.ajb.org,* contains more than 100,000 job openings from 25,000 organizations, and is available free to employers and job seekers. Employers should ensure that a written agreement with a public agency details all the terms of the employer's relationship with the agency.

The written agreement should include the following information:

- ◆ **Services.** Explaining the exact services that the agency will perform. Specifying that the agency will seek as many qualified candidates as possible and thoroughly checks references and credentials before referring candidates.

- ◆ **Expenses.** A list of recruitment expenses the employer will pay and how the agency will document expenses.

- ◆ **Equal employment opportunity.** A clause stating that the employer and the agency are committed to equal employment opportunity. In addition, a clause stating that the agency will reimburse any damages paid by the employer because of discrimination or other actions by the agency.

- ◆ **Limits to agency's authority.** Clarify that the agency has no authority to make promises or enter contracts on the employer's behalf, especially as to job duration or conditions for termination.

- ◆ **Payment terms.** State either that the agency is the exclusive agency for the position or that the employer will owe no fee if it hires an applicant from another source. A guarantee that any fees paid will be rebated if a referred employee does not perform satisfactorily for a minimum length of time, usually 90 days.

- ◆ **Other.** A guarantee that the agency would not, within a specified period, attempt to hire away anyone whom the employer has hired through the agency.

Schools, Colleges, and Universities

Effective recruiting sources for employers looking to fill entry-level positions are local vocational and technical schools. Sources for part-time employees, full-time employees, and interns are high schools, community colleges, and universities. Enlisting the placement office's assistance in posting job openings and scheduling interviews makes schools a convenient and inexpensive recruiting source. Methods of establishing or improving an organization's standing with placement offices include the following:

♦ Keeping the placement office informed about the types of jobs the organization needs to fill and the requirements for those jobs. Employers should let the office know how the recruitment effort is progressing and notify the school when a position is filled.

♦ Informing students where they stand in the application process and what screening procedures they will be expected to undergo, such as physical examinations, drug tests, and interviews with company executives or supervisors.

♦ Participating in career day events, offering plant tours to students, encouraging knowledgeable employees to speak to classes or sit on curriculum steering committees, and trying to sponsor scholarships or work-study programs.

♦ Offering frank answers to questions about job requirements and the corporate culture. An organization that only selects students from the top 10 percent of a class should be prepared to explain why. In addition, an initial explanation should be offered if the company policy is to routinely hire a number of students and then only employ the top two at the end of an evaluation period.

♦ Providing the placement office feedback on an employees or interns job performance. Such communication may help the school determine what types of courses are most useful and what weaknesses could be improved upon.

♦ Placing all contract terms in writing.

Internships

An unpaid intern from a local school can be an excellent source for future employees. Students typically work 12 to 15 hours per week for 13 to 16 weeks. They receive school credit for their work and are ideal for peak operation times or special projects. However, employers should be cautious when employing unpaid interns who may be considered employees according to the Fair Labor Standards Act (FLSA). Such unpaid interns would actually be eligible for minimum wage and overtime consideration. Compliance with the FLSA requires that an unpaid internship program provide a legitimate learning experience. If interns replace employees or perform duties typically performed by other employees, they may be considered employees and must be compensated for their time.

Religious Organizations

Religious organizations often know of people who are seeking employment through their own organizational channels. For further applicants, religious organizations may consider advertising for openings in weekly bulletins or posting advertisements on a bulletin board placed in a conspicuous place.

Job or Career Fairs

Career fairs offer employers exposure to numerous job seekers without the expense of bringing each candidate to the office or plant for an interview. Colleges, professional associations, or groups of employers generally sponsor career fairs.

Employers may meet candidates at job fairs in one or more of the following ways:

♦ An outside sponsor advertises the upcoming career fair, solicits résumés in advance, and sends résumé packets to participating employers prior to the fair. Employers can then contact promising candidates whom they wish to interview at the fair.

♦ Career fair sponsors rent a large hall for the fair and solicit employers to buy a booth or table where they may meet candidates and distribute recruiting information. The sponsor handles advertising and attracting job seekers to the fair but does not provide advance résumés.

♦ Career fairs may also take the form of a social function, such as cocktail parties or luncheons. These more relaxed settings offer employers a chance to promote an organization's opportunities and meet candidates on a more informal level.

♦ Governments, trade schools, outplacement agencies, or consortiums of companies that are downsizing often sponsor job fairs where local companies can recruit at low or no cost.

A booth rental at a career fair may cost anywhere from $2,000 to $5,000, depending on the level of services provided and the number of participating employers. Some career fair sponsors also factor into the price the number of job openings an organization has available. In these situations, organizations with many positions to fill would normally receive a discount.

Union Referrals

A trade union may often point an employer to applicants with the right training and experience in industries employing skilled workers. Union hiring halls, common in the construction and long shoring industries, are essentially employment agencies that match workers with jobs. Bargaining contracts sometimes require employers to hire either solely or primarily from union-referred applicants. However, employers generally retain the right to decline unqualified union referrals. Additionally, an employer is free to ask a union for applicants regardless of whether required to do so by a bargaining contract.

Employers may be held liable for a labor union's discriminatory acts if the employer knew or should have suspected illegal referral practices. Consequently, employers should monitor a union's hiring hall activity. Discriminatory activities by a hiring hall include the following:

♦ Refusing to refer applicants who do not belong to the union or who incurred the union's disfavor.

♦ Allowing only union members to take training courses for skills tests required to meet an employer's specifications.

♦ Giving referral preference to former union officers or executive committee members who have no role in administering the bargaining agreement.

♦ Adopting different standards, other than a service fee for nonmembers' share of hiring hall costs, for referring nonmembers than for referring members.

Radio and Television Advertisements

Radio and television announcements serve to boost a company's image as a good place to work and prompt prospective candidates to apply. However, broadcast media, radio, and television lack a distinct marketplace of job seekers.

Limits on Information

Due to time restrictions, broadcast advertisements provide the viewer/listener with a limited amount of information. Information presented on the air is fleeting.

When the advertisement is aired listeners may not have time or tools prepared to record vital information. The vital information is most often the name, address, contact person, and phone number of the organization.

Costs

Broadcast time is usually expensive, especially in metropolitan areas or on national networks. However, radio and television spot announcements may prove worthwhile for specific situations, such as reaching applicants in areas with poor newspaper coverage, recruiting experienced people who are unlikely to be job hunting or looking in want ads, or advertising an open house to attract applicants.

Advertising with television and radio stations that are aimed at minority audiences may also help an organization meet affirmative action goals.

Other Media Outlets

Some nontraditional media that might be creatively used in recruitment advertising include the following:

♦ Billboards, effective for simple messages.

♦ Direct mail and door-hanger ads reach people who are not actively job-hunting. With the use of specialized mailing lists, recruiters have progressed from simple letters to more expensive and sophisticated mailings, such as video or audio presentations or interactive computer diskettes.

♦ Point-of-sale messages, such as fast-food tray liners, restaurant table cards, cash register displays, or printed messages on receipts or bills can be useful if customers of these businesses would make qualified applicants.

♦ Posters and bulletin board displays with pull-off mini-application forms can be an inexpensive way to reach the local labor pool.

Internet and Computer Data Banks

Many universities, professional associations, executive search firms, employment agencies, and other commercial companies maintain databases of candidate résumés and job vacancies that are accessed via the Internet. The Internet offers an effective and easy way to list available positions to a national and global audience.

The Internet has various advantages including a vast pool of potential candidates, extensive search capabilities, reduced paperwork, and inexpensive advertising opportunities for an organization. Posted information can be updated as often as necessary while employers are capable of quickly and efficiently narrowing their search.

Note: Internet recruiting is best for high-level technical or executive posts and college graduate recruiting.

Retiree Job Banks

Those employees who leave an organization due to retirement may serve as a valuable pool of well-qualified candidates who are already familiar with the company's culture and policies. By having employees fill out forms specifically describing their skills, interests, and willingness to be recruited for later projects, managers are able to compile a list of former employees whom the organization may wish to recall in the future.

Since some employees may wish to work part-time instead of retiring altogether, forming a database of retirees with special skills needed may be the quickest way to recruit employees for short-term projects.

Additional Information

Reminders

When recruiting applicants employers should adhere to the following guidelines:

♦ Avoid using shortened job titles such as "JPO" (junior press operator) in advertisements. Job titles are appropriate only when clearly spelled out for potential employees.

♦ Write the job description from an overall viewpoint so that it can be used in several departments.

♦ Always keep statements brief and use appropriate action words.

♦ Identify essential-tasks and nonessential tasks of all jobs.

♦ Prioritize responsibilities and avoid minor duties that are only performed occasionally.

♦ State specific tasks and frequency, quantity, and production quotas, if applicable.

♦ Be clear and direct so that duties are interpreted uniformly.

♦ Use positive statements instead of statements that reflect past discipline to help recruit applicants.

♦ Avoid negative statements such as, "Will not tolerate tardiness."

♦ Specify reporting relationships in terms of job title instead of an individual's name.

Contact Information

Equal Employment Opportunity Commission
1801 L Street, NW
Washington, DC 20507

Telephone: 202-663-4900
Toll-Free: 800-669-4000
TTY: 202-663-4494
Toll-Free: 800-669-6820
Internet: *www.eeoc.gov*

Job Accommodation Network
P.O. Box 6080
Morgantown, WV 26506-6080

Telephone (Toll-Free): 800-526-7234 or 800-ADA-WORK
Fax: 304-293-5407
Email: jan@jan.wvu.edu
Internet: *www.jan.wvu.edu*

Note: Calls are answered from 8 a.m. to 8 p.m. Eastern Time, Monday through Thursday, and on Fridays from 8 a.m. to 7 p.m. Machines answer after-hours calls.

Employment Application
(Sample)

PERSONAL INFORMATION — Complete **all** applicable information

Name (Last, First, MI):	

Position(s) applied for:	Are you willing to work: ___ Full Time ___ Part Time ___ Temporary ___ Weekends ___ Evenings ___ Nights

Street Address:	City:	State:	Zip:
Home Phone:	Business or Cell Phone:	Have you previously been employed by our company? __ Yes __ No Where?	

Are you legally authorized to work in the United States? __ Yes __ No	When could you start employment?

Have you ever applied for employment with our company? __ Yes __ No When? Where?

EMPLOYMENT HISTORY — List below last three employers, starting with the most recent one first

Present or Last Position:	Name of Company:	From Mo/Yr:	To Mo/Yr:
Street Address:	City:	State:	Zip:
Duties:	Reason for Leaving:		
Starting Annual Salary:	Final Annual Salary:	Bonus:	Commission:
Name of Supervisor:	Title and Department of Supervisor:	Phone Number of Supervisor:	

Next Previous Position:	Name of Company:	From Mo/Yr:	To Mo/Yr:
Street Address:	City:	State:	Zip:
Duties:	Reason for Leaving:		
Starting Annual Salary:	Final Annual Salary:	Bonus:	Commission:
Name of Supervisor:	Title and Department of Supervisor:	Phone Number of Supervisor:	
Next Previous Position:	Name of Company:	From Mo/Yr:	To Mo/Yr:
Street Address:	City:	State:	Zip:
Duties:	Reason for Leaving:		
Starting Annual Salary:	Final Annual Salary:	Bonus:	Commission:
Name of Supervisor:	Title and Department of Supervisor:	Phone Number of Supervisor:	

EDUCATION INFORMATION

High School or GED:	Address:	City:	St:	Degree:	Subjects Studied:	
College:	Address:	City:	St:	Degree:	Major:	GPA:
College:	Address:	City:	St:	Degree:	Major:	GPA:
Graduate School:	Address:	City:	St:	Degree:	Major:	GPA:
Other:	Address:	City:	St:	Degree:	Major:	GPA:

GENERAL

Additional Space (if needed)

If applying for a clerical position, what business equipment can you operate? (For example, computers, copiers, etc.)	
If applying for a secretarial position: Do you have stenographic skills? __ Yes __ No Words/Minute	If applying for a secretarial position: Do you have any typing skills? __ Yes __ No Words/Minute
In what computer software programs are you proficient? [Name the package(s).]	

PLEASE READ THE FOLLOWING STATEMENTS CAREFULLY

- In consideration of my employment, I agree to conform to the policies and procedures of the company. I understand that in accepting this application, the company is in no way obligated to provide me with employment, and that I am not obligated to accept employment if offered. Furthermore, if employed, I understand that I am employed at will and that my employment and compensation can be terminated with or without cause, and with or without notice at any time.

- I certify that the facts contained in this application are true and complete to the best of my knowledge. I understand that any falsified statements on this application or omission of fact on either this application or during the pre-employment process will result in my application being rejected, or, if I am hired, in my employment being terminated.

- I also understand that any offer of employment is conditioned on the completion of pre-employment tests and documentation. I will, upon request, sign all necessary consent forms.

Date:	Signature:

Note: This is a generic sample policy and does not necessarily reflect the employment laws in any or all of the 50 U.S. states. Before establishing any company policy, one should review the applicable state laws or seek guidance from legal counsel.

Chapter 3
The Hiring Process

Background Checks

Federal Laws and Regulations

Under the Federal Fair Credit Reporting Act, employers using credit histories to make hiring decisions and to monitor employees are required to make certain disclosures. As a result, the act imposes restrictions on an employer's use of this form of background check on applicants and employees to determine qualifications for employment.

The act distinguishes between consumer and investigative consumer reports. The requirements for notice and disclosure differ, as do the kinds of information that may be reported. Employers must comply with the specific requirements for each type of report if they are used in the employment process.

The term *consumer report* means any written, oral, or other communication of any information prepared by a consumer reporting agency bearing upon an individual's credit worthiness, credit standing, credit capacity, character, general reputation, personal characteristics, or mode of living, if the report is used or is expected to be used to determine employment qualifications.

A *consumer reporting agency* is defined as any person, firm, or corporation that regularly engages in the practice of assembling or evaluating credit or other background consumer information for the purpose of furnishing consumer reports. The employer need not in all cases disclose intent to seek a consumer report for an employee or job applicant.

Employers are not required to notify individuals when a consumer credit report has been requested, but must give written notice when requesting a more extensive investigative consumer report. However, if the employer reaches any adverse employment decision, such as demotion or failure to hire, as a result of information contained in a consumer report, that fact must be communicated to the employee or applicant.

An employer seeking background information through this process faces additional reporting and disclosure requirements. Whenever an employer requests an investigative consumer report, the employer must make a written disclosure of its request to the subject employee or applicant within three days after making the request. This notice must state that the individual has the right to know the "nature and scope" of the report.

In addition, if the employer reaches any adverse employment decision based on information contained in the report, the employer must automatically disclose to the subject employee or applicant the nature and scope of the background investigation. This disclosure must be made within five days of the employer's receipt of the report.

Consumer reports **may not** contain any of the following information:

♦ Cases under Title 11 U.S. Code or under the Federal Bankruptcy Act that from the date of entry of the Order for Relief or the date of adjudication predate the report by more than 10 years.

♦ Suits and judgments that from the date of entry predate the report by more than seven years or until the governing statute of limitations has expired — whichever is the longer period.

♦ Paid tax liens that from the date of employment predate the report by more than seven years.

♦ Accounts placed for collection or charged profit and loss that predate the report by more than seven years.

♦ Records of arrest, indictment, or conviction of a crime that from the date of disposition, release, or parole, predate the report by more than seven years.

However, the prohibition on reporting the listed types of adverse information **does not apply** when the report relates to the following:

♦ A credit transaction involving, or which may reasonably be expected to involve, a principal amount of $150,000 or more.

♦ The underwriting of life insurance involving, or which may reasonably be expected to involve, a face amount of $150,000 or more.

♦ The employment of any individual at an annual salary that equals, or may reasonably be expected to equal, $75,000 or more.

Although employers are permitted to use both investigative consumer reports and noninvestigative consumer reports, much of the information included in such reports provides little assistance in making employment decisions. For example, the type of debts that may ordinarily tempt employees to engage in dishonest activities may not be reported (for example, gambling debts or other debts related to illegal drag use or other clandestine activities).

Additionally, since the percentage of minority group members in the United States with poor credit ratings is significantly higher than the percentage of nonminorities with unsatisfactory credit histories, the EEOC has advised and courts have held that consideration of credit histories in taking adverse employment actions can disproportionately affect minority applicants in violation of Title VII of the Civil Rights Act. When such an adverse impact results, the employer must demonstrate that this selection criteria is justified by business necessity. To avoid claims of discrimination against members of minority groups, employers must make credit checks in a consistent, evenhanded manner. Otherwise, applicants or employees could complain that the use of such information in making adverse employment decisions represents disparate treatment on the basis of their race, sex, or other protected personal characteristics.

Some inquiries that typically appear on investigative consumer reports cannot lawfully be asked before the commencement of employment. For example, inquiries related to the following subjects **should not** be a part of the credit checking process:

♦ Citizenship.

♦ Age.

♦ Arrests.

♦ Marital status.

♦ Number of dependents.

♦ Type of military discharge.

Pre-Employment Check

The amount of background employers obtain depends on the type of job and the potential harm an employee in that position could pose. At minimum, applicant screening for most jobs should involve certain steps.

Review the Résumé for Work History Gaps

A checkered work history could reflect poor performance, imprisonment, alcohol or drug abuse, or other problems that affect someone's reliability. On the other hand, the applicant may have been in school or in some other innocent nonwork pursuit. **Always** give applicants an opportunity to explain any gaps.

Verify Previous Addresses

This procedure allows the organization to determine that the applicant lived where the individual claimed and was not in custody. Employers should record and document sources used to check prior addresses.

Confirm Credentials

Employers should check with educational institutions to verify that any degrees listed were received. They should also contact professional accreditation groups or government licensing boards to confirm information about an applicant's credentials.

Obtain Consent to Contact Former Employers

A signed authorization and release eases a past employer's fear of defamation for giving a poor reference. Employers should beware of hiring any applicant who refuses or shows reluctance to give this consent.

Follow-Up Professional References

Checking with past employers serves the following two important purposes:

- ♦ Past employers can at least confirm employment dates, job descriptions, and salaries.

- ♦ Managers usually are not hesitant to discuss former employees with excellent records.

Specific Position Checks

When the position involves contact with the public or issues of trust, employers should try to perform both credit and criminal checks. Legal restrictions apply to both types of checks, but investigating an applicant for possible financial or criminal misconduct minimizes the risk of later facing a negligent hiring suit.

Consider a credit and/or criminal check with the following types of employees:

- ♦ Delivery and repair workers.

- ♦ Building managers.

- ♦ Security guards.

- ♦ Television installers.

- ♦ Exterminators.

- ♦ Others who gain access to a dwelling by virtue of their employment.

- Child care employees.

- Health care employees.

- Teachers.

- Real estate agents.

- Bartenders and bouncers, who must deal with unruly customers.

Checking References

The main source of references traditionally has been a candidate's former employers. Reference checks are a valuable way for employers to communicate with one another about an applicant. However, in recent years concerns about defamation lawsuits have received a great deal of publicity and made many former employers reluctant to cooperate.

When an applicant's former employer refuses to give any information, employers should document that they have attempted to check the applicant's prior work history to prevent or combat any later claims of negligent hiring. Therefore, employers must be knowledgeable of their rights as well as the rights of the applicant.

Getting References to Talk

To address concerns over lawsuits, some states have passed laws providing immunity from lawsuits to former employers who supply even negative references, unless they knowingly and maliciously falsify information. Employers who wish to verify whether or not their state has such a law should contact the Division of Employment before giving any references.

Even in states without a law providing immunity for truthful references, contacting former employers can still prove useful. At minimum, most companies will confirm a former employee's name, dates of employment, positions held, compensation, and other pertinent employment factors.

Employers should use the following strategies to obtain performance-related information:

- Require all applicants to sign a form giving consent to contact former employers and releasing anyone providing truthful references from liability. Consider modifying the organization's job application to include such a consent and waiver statement.

- Have job candidates obtain letters of reference or copies of performance evaluations. Unfortunately, this strategy still requires follow-up to verify authenticity.

- Remind former employers that failure to disclose serious problems about an ex-employee can leave them liable for negligent referral.

- Ask applicants for the names and/or direct-dial numbers of former supervisors. Even in companies with policies requiring routing all reference inquiries to human resources, supervisors pleased with former employees are often willing to bend the rules.

Common Questions for Interviewing and Evaluating References

Often the type of questions a potential employer asks a reference will determine the willingness of the reference to talk. Employers should develop questions that will yield the desired results and ask them consistently. A sample of a **Reference Check Form** is included at the end of this chapter.

What to Ask References

The following are samples of inquiries for references:

- ♦ What work and management style does the applicant display?
- ♦ How often was the individual tardy or absent?
- ♦ What is this person's reputation among colleagues, both inside and outside the organization?
- ♦ Describe the applicant's character and work attitude.
- ♦ Does this person have career potential?
- ♦ What type of "company culture" best suits this person?
- ♦ How well equipped is this person to handle specific aspects of the job such as deadline pressures, attention to detail, and people skills?
- ♦ Would the reference be willing to hire or rehire the applicant?

Evaluation of Reference Information

Upon contacting references, an evaluation should be made as follows:

- ♦ Does the information furnished by the reference and the applicant match?
- ♦ How long has the reference known the applicant?
- ♦ How well does the reference know the applicant?
- ♦ Was the reference in a position to evaluate the applicant's work?
- ♦ Was the applicant's former job comparable to the current job opening?

Waiver to Check References

Employers intending to check an applicant's references should require the applicant to sign a waiver allowing confirmation and investigation of all information the applicant submits on the application. A sample of this **Waiver to Check References** is included at the end of this chapter.

Conducting Credit Checks

Utilizing credit checks for employment purposes is regulated by the FCRA.

An organization must be able to prove that an applicant's financial condition is relevant to the job before conducting a credit check. Employers that are not able to prove relevance could face discrimination charges, since requiring a clean credit history tends to screen out disproportionately certain minority job applicants.

The Federal Bankruptcy Act also bars refusing to hire someone solely because the applicant or someone associated with the applicant has filed for bankruptcy, was insolvent before filing for bankruptcy, or failed to pay a debt dischargeable in bankruptcy.

Despite these limitations, credit checks are appropriate for certain positions, such as ones involving handling of money or spending authority over large amounts of money. If an applicant is denied employment for reasons relating to the credit report, the applicant must be informed of this fact and furnished with the name of the credit agency that issued the report.

Types of Credit Checks

To check on a person's financial status, employers may request two types of credit checks:

♦ A consumer credit check deals with a person's creditworthiness, credit standing or capacity, work habits, and mode of living, as reported by consumer reporting agencies. Consumer reporting agencies include organizations such as Equifax, TRW, and Trans Union, which regularly assemble or evaluate information when making reports to third parties.

♦ Investigative consumer reports go beyond a mere evaluation of credit worthiness and may include personal interviews with a person's neighbors, friends, or associates to obtain information on the person's character, general reputation, personal characteristics, or mode of living.

Consumer Credit Reports

Consumer reports are written, oral, or other communications of a consumer-reporting agency, which bear upon the following attributes of a consumer:

♦ Credit worthiness, standing, and capacity.

♦ Character.

♦ General reputation.

♦ Personal characteristics.

♦ Mode of living.

Note: These elements are used to establish employment eligibility.

Responsibilities to Applicants and Employees

If employers use consumer reports for employment purposes, they must take the following steps:

♦ Make a clear and conspicuous written disclosure to the applicant or employee that a consumer report may be obtained. This disclosure must be made before the consumer report is obtained or requested from a CRA. The disclosure must consist of a separate document and cannot be incorporated into an employment application.

♦ Obtain the applicant/employee's written authorization before requesting the report. Despite the "separate document" requirement, the disclosure and authorization may be combined in the same document.

♦ If the employer decides to take any adverse action based in whole or in part upon the consumer report, the employer must comply with a two-step process notifying the applicant/employee of the adverse action.

Samples of a certification from a company to a consumer reporting agency, a disclosure statement, and an authorization form, and letters before and after adverse action are included at the end of this chapter.

Before a CRA can provide a consumer report; the employer must certify the following to the CRA:

♦ The employer will distribute the required written disclosure and obtain authorization.

♦ The information being obtained will not be used in violation of any federal or state equal opportunity law or regulation.

♦ The employer will comply with the adverse action requirements.

Requirements When Adverse Action Taken

An ***adverse action*** is defined as a denial of employment or any other decision that adversely impacts any current or prospective employee. When adverse action is taken as a result of obtaining a consumer report, employers must go through a two-step process regarding the adverse action.

First, before the adverse action is taken, the employer must provide the applicant or employee with the following:

- A copy of the credit report obtained for the CRA.

- A summary of the consumer's rights under the act.

Note: After providing these documents, the employer must wait before taking the adverse action. The Federal Trade Commission (FTC) has approved a five-business-day waiting period.

Second, after the adverse action is taken, the applicant or employee must be provided the following:

- Notice of the adverse action taken.

- The name, address, and toll-free telephone number of the consumer-reporting agency that furnished the consumer report.

- A statement that the CRA did not make the decision to take the adverse action and is unable to provide the consumer the specific reasons why the adverse action was taken.

- Notice of the consumer's right to obtain a free copy of the consumer report from the CRA within 60 days.

- Notice of the consumer's right to dispute the accuracy or completeness of any information in the consumer report furnished by the CRA.

Summary of Rights

When an employer takes an adverse action, the applicant is entitled to know the rights regarding the adverse action that led to the decision. The following is a summary of rights under the FCRA:

The Federal FCRA is designed to promote accuracy, fairness, and privacy of information in the files of every "consumer reporting agency" (CRA). Most CRAs are credit bureaus that gather and sell information about you (such as if you pay your bills on time or have filed bankruptcy) to creditors, employers, property owners, and other businesses. The complete text of the FCRA is located at 15 U.S. Code 1681-1681u. The FCRA gives you specific rights, as outlined below. State law may provide for additional rights. Consumers can contact a state or local consumer protection agency or a state attorney general's office to learn of these rights.

You must be told if information in your file has been used against you. Anyone who uses information from a CRA to take action against you, such as denying an application for credit, insurance, or employment, must tell you, and give you the name, address, and phone number of the CRA that provided the consumer report.

You can find out what is in your file. At your request, a CRA must give you the information in your file, and a list of everyone who has requested it recently. There is no charge for the report if a person has taken action against you because of information supplied by the CRA; however, you must request the report within 60 days of receiving notice of the action. You also are entitled to one free report every 12 months upon request if you certify that (1) you are unemployed and plan to seek employment within 60 days, (2) you are on welfare, or (3) your report is inaccurate due to fraud. Otherwise, a CRA may charge you up to eight dollars.

You can dispute inaccurate information with the CRA. If you tell a CRA that your file contains inaccurate information, the CRA must investigate the items, normally within 30 days, by presenting to its information source all relevant evidence you submit, unless your dispute is frivolous.

The source must review your evidence and report its findings to the CRA. The source must also advise national CRAs, to which it has provided the data, of any error. The CRA must give you a written report of the investigation and a copy of your report if the investigation results in any change. If the CRA's investigation does not resolve the dispute, you may add a brief statement to your file. The CRA must normally include a summary of your statement in future reports. If an item is deleted or a dispute statement is filed, you may ask that anyone who has recently received your report be notified of the change.

Inaccurate information must be corrected or deleted. A CRA must remove or correct inaccurate or unverified information from its files, usually within 30 days after you dispute it. However, the CRA is not required to remove accurate data from your file unless it is outdated or cannot be verified. If your dispute results in any change to your report, the CRA cannot reinsert into your file a disputed item unless the information source verifies its accuracy and completeness. In addition, the CRA must give you a written notice telling you it has reinserted the item. The notice must include the name, address and phone number of the information source.

You can dispute inaccurate items with the source of the information. If you tell anyone such as a creditor who reports to a CRA that you dispute an item, they may not report the information to a CRA without including a notice of your dispute. In addition, once you have notified the source of the error in writing, it may not continue to report the information if it is, in fact, an error.

Outdated information may not be reported. In most cases, a CRA may not report negative information that is more than seven years old (ten years for bankruptcies).

Access to your file is limited. A CRA may provide information about you only to people with a need recognized by the FCRA, usually to consider an application with a creditor, insurer, employer, property owner, or other business.

Your consent is required for reports that are provided to employers, or reports that contain medical information. A CRA may not give out information about you to your employer, or prospective employer, without your written consent. A CRA may not report medical information about you to creditors, insurers, or employers without your permission.

You may choose to exclude your name from CRA lists for unsolicited credit and insurance offers. Creditors and insurers often use file information as the basis for sending you unsolicited offers of credit or insurance. Such offers must include a toll-free phone number for you to call if you want your name and address removed from future lists. If you call, you must be kept off the lists for two years. If you request, complete, and return the CRA form provided for this purpose, you must be taken off the lists indefinitely.

You may seek damages from violators. If a CRA, a user, or a provider of CRA data violates the FCRA, you may sue in state or federal court.

Investigative Consumer Reports

The FCRA requires employers to inform the applicant or employee that the employer intends to obtain an investigative consumer report. The notice and other requirements are more burdensome for investigative consumer reports than for consumer reports.

An employer should not obtain an investigative consumer report under the act **unless** the employer performs the following:

♦ Provides a written disclosure that an investigative consumer report may be made, including a statement to the effect that the consumer may request additional disclosures regarding the nature and scope of the investigation, as well as a written summary of rights under the statute.

♦ Certifies to the consumer-reporting agency that it has made the above disclosures and that it will comply with any requests for additional disclosures.

When the applicant or employee requests additional disclosure within a reasonable time, the employer must completely disclose the nature and the scope of the investigation. The disclosure must be in writing and given to the applicant or employee no later than five days after the date on which the request was received or the report was first requested, whichever is later in time. A sample of an investigative report disclosure statement is included at the end of this chapter.

Consumer Reports with Medical Information

CRA's are prohibited from providing consumer reports which contain medical information for employment purposes without the specific prior written consent of the consumer who is the subject of the report. This means that the applicant or employee must explicitly consent to the release of the medical information in addition to authorizing consent to obtain a consumer report.

Investigating Criminal Records

Prohibitions against inquiring about applicants' criminal records can create a dilemma for employers who need to make reasonable investigations of applicants to avoid liability for negligent hiring. Employers should, therefore, consider broadening their pre-offer investigations to include searches of public records on felony and misdemeanor convictions. To do so, employers should obtain certified copies of all conviction records (instead of relying on oral information) and should check all jurisdictions where an applicant lived or worked. If a search turns up a criminal conviction, however, employers must consider the relationship between the conviction and the applicant's fitness for a particular job before rejecting an applicant because of any particular conviction.

While this information is generally available to the public, searching through public records is a time-consuming task. Investigative services and other document and information retrieval services may be helpful, but costly. For that reason, it is advisable to devise guidelines as to when such information is necessary. Such guidelines should be applied consistently and uniformly to avoid any appearance of discrimination or unfair treatment of certain job applicants.

It is also recommended that an organization notify applicants that a conviction record search is required, if that is to be the case, and check any state law restrictions that may apply.

Consider Business Necessity

Even when records show an applicant has been convicted of a crime, consider whether business necessity justifies rejecting the applicant.

Under EEOC guidelines for weighing business necessity, an employer must consider the following:

♦ The nature and gravity of the offense(s).

♦ The time that has passed since the conviction or completion of sentence.

♦ The nature of the job in question.

State Laws

States may have additional requirements for consideration, such as age at the time of the offense, evidence of rehabilitation, and responsibility for protecting property, personal safety, or general public.

Besides limiting employers' use of arrest records, many states bar employers from basing decisions on expunged or sealed conviction records. A few states go even further and prohibit employers from asking about or refusing employment based on certain types of convictions.

For example, California bars employers from even asking applicants about convictions for possession of marijuana that are more than two years old. Massachusetts prohibits employers from rejecting applicants based on misdemeanor convictions more than five years old or a first conviction for drunkenness, simple assault, speeding, affray, minor traffic violations, or breach of peace.

Positions Where Checks are Allowed

For certain positions, however, federal or state laws require criminal record checks. Most states, for example, require checking criminal convictions before hiring anyone into a position that involves working with minors. Federal law also requires checking child care center employees for convictions. Certain states also require fingerprinting and conviction record checks of applicants for positions involving public trust, such as employees of financial institutions, security guards, or health care employees. Employers filling these types of jobs should check with the applicable state regulatory agency to find out the state law.

Refusals to Hire on the Basis of Conviction Records

An employer may lawfully refuse to hire an applicant on the basis of a conviction record if such refusal is justified given the nature, timing, and other factors of the offense as it relates to the job. It is important to make such decisions on a job-related, case-by-case basis, and not to have a blanket policy against hiring persons convicted of crimes. For example, one court held that a refusal to hire a hotel bellman who had been convicted of theft was justified because the crime of theft was related to the bellman's job which involved access to and custody of personal property of hotel guests.

In contrast, another court held that a refusal to hire a bus driver who had been convicted of burglary was unjustified because the crime of burglary was unrelated to the driver's job, because six years had passed since the conviction, and because prior employers and parole and police officers had given the applicant good recommendations.

Sexual Harassment

Concerns for Employers

Employers are faced with new concerns determining the application of the Fair Credit Reporting Act (FCRA) to sexual harassment investigations.

A recent Federal Trade Commission (FTC) opinion letter suggests that outside organizations utilized by employers to assist in their investigations of harassment claims should be considered consumer-reporting agencies. The letter does not have the force of law, but the courts could possibly treat it with deference.

Therefore, it appears that the reports prepared by outside organizations performing harassment investigations for employers are most likely "investigative consumer reports" within the meaning of the FCRA. As a result, employers would have to follow all the requirements for preparing an "investigative consumer report" or they may be found in noncompliance with the FCRA.

Until the courts rule otherwise, or Congress amends the FCRA, employers must beware of the risk of liability for violating privacy in the workplace laws when they hire outside investigators to conduct workplace investigations. Employers should protect themselves and always follow the consent and notice requirements of the FCRA.

Note: Often outside counsel conducts investigations in anticipation of litigation only. The employer does not rely upon the outside investigation for any other purpose. These limited investigations by outside counsel should still be protected by the attorney-client privilege and not be subject to the FCRA amendment requirements.

However, this strategy requires the employer to use company employees to do its own separate investigation in other matters — to discipline employees and/or to assert an affirmative defense in future litigation. Obviously, this defeats the purpose for which employers often hire outside counsel or consultants to perform a thorough and neutral third-party investigation.

Liabilities

State or federal actions and private lawsuits are available to enforce compliance with the act, as well as any state provisions that may apply.

Available damages include actual damages, the cost of bringing the action, including attorney's fees, and, in the case of willful noncompliance, punitive damages. Further, any person who knowingly and willfully obtains a consumer report under false pretenses may face criminal prosecution including fines and/or imprisonment for not more than two years.

Recommended Action

For compliance with the FCRA and any applicable state laws, employers should ensure that any use of background information from the FCRA's satisfies the consent and notice requirements. Specifically, employers should pay close attention to employment applications and other documentation used in the interviewing and hiring process.

Employment forms should be developed for consumer report disclosure and authorization. In addition, when an employer obtains releases from employees, the employer should stipulate that the release takes effect immediately and lasts throughout the term of employment. Thus, future background checks will already be covered.

Background Checks Conclusion

The law imposes numerous and hefty requirements on employers who use consumer reports in their employment decision-making.

Specifically, employers will have to make a written disclosure to and obtain written permission from applicants and employees before obtaining consumer reports. Moreover, employers will have to provide copies of the credit reports along with a summary of consumers' rights before taking any adverse employment action based on the report. Although these requirements are easily met, liability for not complying can be costly. Therefore, employers should take the time necessary to become familiar with the FCRA.

Finally, employers should remember that various states have also enacted additional laws governing the use of consumer reports. Employers should make sure they comply with state law requirements.

Interviewing

Introduction

The employment interview vital to the hiring process. In order to hire the most qualified applicant, human resource professionals must conduct effective interviews.

Successful interviewing requires preparation, good listening, and a thorough understanding of the job and the minimum qualifications of candidates. The interviewer must also be aware of federal and state legislation that prohibits certain questions during the interview.

Goals of the Interview

A hiring interview has three goals as follows:

- ◆ To assess the applicant.

- ◆ To describe the job and working conditions.

- ◆ To create goodwill for the organization, whether or not the applicant is hired.

Elements of Good Interviewing

Meeting these goals requires the following interpersonal abilities, preparation, objectivity, and good recordkeeping skills on the interviewer's part:

- ◆ Interpersonal skills put a job candidate at ease and elicit the most accurate responses.

- ◆ Preparation helps an interviewer cover all job-related questions and avoid saying things that might violate anti-discrimination laws, create an implied employment contract, or misrepresent the job.

- ◆ Objectivity is perhaps the most challenging demand placed on a job interviewer. Unfortunately, interviewers usually rate an applicant based on shared personality traits or appearances. These are not the things that help predict future job performance.

- ◆ Good recordkeeping supplies the information needed to compare different candidates and documents the screening process in case a rejected applicant claims discrimination.

Interview Types

Interviews fall into two categories: structured and unstructured.

Structured Interviews

Structured interviews rely upon a pre-planned agenda. The interviewer knows ahead of time what to ask the applicant and tries to stick to the agenda. Some interviewers will ask the questions in order. Others will take a more relaxed approach, while still addressing all of the pre-planned questions.

Structured interviews generally provide the interviewer with the information needed to make the hiring decision. They also provide a defense against discrimination because all applicants are asked the same questions.

Unstructured Interviews

Unstructured interviews do not rely upon a prepared agenda. Instead, the applicant sets the pace of the interview. This style of interviewing does not always provide the interviewer with necessary information. In addition, the lack of structure makes it difficult to compare and rank applicants because they so not respond to the same questions.

Note: In a panel interview, more than one person interviews the applicant. Generally, the interviewers take turns asking questions. Panel interviews can be either structured or unstructured.

Interview Questions

Interview questions should accomplish the following goals:

- Determine an applicant's qualifications and general character.

- Expose undesirable traits.

- Clarify information.

- Provide other job-related data.

- Reveal inconsistencies.

Develop Job-Related Questions

Employers should develop sound interview questions by looking at the job description and decide what the job demands in each of these following areas:

- Determine what skills and abilities the job requires, such as the following:

  - Work experience.

  - Education.

  - Technical skills.

  - Communication skills.

  - Analytical skills.

  - Specialized training.

- Consider behavioral factors, such as the following:

  - Motivation.

  - Interests.

  - Goals.

  - Drive and energy.

  - Reliability.

  - Loyalty.

  - Stress tolerance.

- ♦ Address corporate culture with items, such as the following:

  - Team orientation.

  - Independence.

  - Social effectiveness.

  - Interpersonal style.

Employers should design questions that will elicit information about the candidate's job qualifications in each of the noted areas. These questions can form a standardized questionnaire used in each interview. To customize the questionnaire, employers should review an applicant's résumé for points covered on the questionnaire and individualize inquiries to elicit more information.

Questioning Techniques

The best interviewers employ a flexible questioning technique to elicit pertinent, accurate information. Employers should vary the questioning technique according to needs. A technique that is appropriate in one instance may yield false, incomplete, or misleading information in another. The best interviewers use some combination of the following 12 techniques as the situation demands.

Close-Ended Questions

Close-ended questions are most commonly asked in interviewing. They are also the most commonly abused. The following is an example of an ineffective closed-ended question: "Can you work under pressure?" Only "Yes" and "No" are the possible answers. The interviewer has no information and no way of evaluating any one candidate against another.

Even though a closed-ended question is inappropriate in the above usage, it is useful as a questioning technique when looking for commitment: "Can you start on Monday?" A closed-end question also helps interviewers when they are refreshing their memory or verifying information from earlier in the interviewing sequence: "You were with Xerox for 10 years?" Interviewers can also use the close-ended technique to get the ball rolling when they have a series of questions on the same subject.

Open-Ended Questions

Open-ended questions often yield better results than close-ended. Open-ended questions do not lend themselves to monosyllabic answers; instead, the question demands an explanation. Consider the following open-ended question: "How do you succeed in working under pressure?"

As a rule, this style of question is preferable to closed-ended questions, and is guaranteed to keep the candidate talking and the interviewer listening. These questions often start in the following ways:

- ♦ "I'm interested in hearing about . . . "

- ♦ "I'm curious to learn . . . "

- ♦ "Would you share with me . . . ?"

Past-Performance Questions

This technique has developed into a whole style of interviewing. Past-performance, or behavioral, questions are based on the premise that past actions can predict future behavior, that an employer can expect an individual to do at least as well or as badly on the new job as on the last.

Past-performance questions are open-ended, but they request specific examples of past behavior. They elicit conversation and are usually prefaced with something like the following:

- "Tell me about a time when . . . "

- "Share with me an experience when . . . "

- "Give me an example of . . . "

Ask past-performance questions early in the interview, so that an interviewee will realize early on that detailed examples about the past are expected. Used appropriately, past-performance questions discourage attempts to "pull the wool over the interviewer's eyes."

Negative-Balance Questions

Interviewers often commit the fallacy of assuming that a candidate strong in one area is equally impressive in all areas. This is not always the case. To avoid this fallacy, try the following:

- "That's very impressive. Was there ever an occasion when things didn't work out quite so well?"

- "Now can you give me an example of something in this area you are not so proud of?"

Negative Confirmation

When interviewers have sought and found negative balance, they may feel content that they are maintaining their objectivity and move on, or that the answer they receive may be disturbing enough to warrant negative confirmation.

For example, an interviewee tells the interviewer about a situation when the individual felt that it was necessary to go around or behind a supervisor to achieve a goal. A manager should be troubled because if such behavior is common, the person may not be desirable to hire. Consequently, negative confirmation should be sought with perhaps the following: "You know, that's very interesting. Let's talk about another time when you had to . . ."

Successive examples will help interviewers confirm negative traits and perhaps save them from a poor hire. On the other hand, they might find that the negative situation was an aberration — a one-time thing — and nothing to worry about.

Reflexive Questions

Reflexive questions are great top-closers that move the conversation forward. They help interviewers calmly maintain control of the conversation no matter how talkative the interviewee.

When an applicant starts to ramble about various experiences, the interviewer can easily interrupt with a reflexive question that will allow the interviewer to proceed with other topics.

An interviewer may accomplish this by adding phrases such as the following to the end of a statement:

- Don't you?

- Couldn't you?

- Wouldn't you?

- Didn't you?

- Can't you?

- Aren't you?

For example, the interviewer might say, "With time so short, I think it would be valuable to move onto another area, **don't you**?" The candidate's reflex is to agree, and the conversation moves on.

Mirror Statements

Use this subtle form of probing in conjunction with that most effective tool — silence. To employ this technique, the interviewer mirrors or paraphrases a key statement and follows it by closing the mouth, nodding, and looking interestedly at the interviewee. Interviewers should use mirror statements to capture the essence of a candidate's answer and to get more detail. First, repeat the substance of key comments: "So, whenever you arrive two hours early for work, you leave work two hours early to make up for it?" Then sit and wait for the interviewee to expand on the mirror statements.

Loaded Questions

Loaded questions easily lead to abuse and power games by the interviewer. They place the interviewee in a double bind, having to decide between equally unsuitable options. For instance, the following is a loaded question: "Which do you think is the lesser evil, embezzlement, or forgery?"

Obviously, the interviewer should avoid absurd, loaded questions. However, carefully balanced judgment-call questions may have a place in a good interview. The technique may allow the interviewer to probe the interviewee's decision-making approaches. For example, the interviewer may want to recall a real-life situation where two divergent approaches were both carefully considered. Next, frame the situation as a question:

- ♦ "I'm curious to know what you would do if . . . "

- ♦ "What would be your approach to a situation where . . . "

Half-Right Reflexives

Use this question style to smoke out "yes-men," the incompetent, the oddballs who resist giving information, and the competent but incurably tongue-tied. To employ the technique, make a partially correct statement and ask the interviewee to agree.

This technique creates enlightening insights. For instance, this example of a half-right reflexive always generates fascinating responses: "I've always felt that customer service should commence only after the bill has been paid, haven't you?"

Leading Questions

Here, interviewers lead the listener toward a specific type of answer. These questions often arise accidentally when the interviewer explains what type of organization the interviewee will be joining. For instance, the interviewer might proudly exclaim, "We're a fast-growing outfit here, and there is constant pressure to meet deadlines and satisfy our ever-increasing list of customers," then ask, "How do you handle stress?" The interviewee knows that to retain any chance of landing an offer, the person must answer a certain way and consequently does so.

Leading questions are often useful, but like closed-ended questions the interviewer must use them appropriately. As information verifiers, they encourage the candidate to expand on a particular topic, for example, "We are an organization that believes the customer is always right. How do you feel about that?"

However, the technique should be used only after establishing a candidate's belief or performance in a particular area. In any case, leading questions should not be used early in the interview or confuse them with the somewhat sophisticated half-right reflexive.

Question Layering

A good question poorly phrased will lose its bite and give the interviewer incomplete or misleading information. However, question layering can probe an answer thoroughly and on many levels.

Returning to the earlier example: wanting to know whether a potential employee can work under pressure. Many interviewers would simply ask, "Can you work under pressure?" While the intent is good, the question style is wrong for the following two reasons:

♦ The question requires only a yes or no answer, which tells the interviewer nothing.

♦ It leads the interviewee toward the type of answer the individual knows the interviewer wants.

Instead, interviewers should take a leaf out of a good reporter's notebook. The reporter uses all the styles we have discussed, but in ways that peel back different layers of truth until a topic has been examined from every angle. In other words, the reporter asks the following:

♦ Who?

♦ What?

♦ When?

♦ Where?

♦ Why?

♦ How?

Similarly, the interviewer does the same by joining the closed-ended question with some of the other questioning techniques.

Consider the following sequence of questions to see how much more relevant information an interviewer can glean:

♦ "Can you work under pressure?" (Close-ended.)

♦ "Tell me about a time when you had to work under pressure." (Open-ended.)

♦ "So, it was tough to meet the deadline?" (Mirror statement.)

♦ "How did this pressure situation arise?"

♦ "Who was responsible?"

♦ "Why was this allowed to occur?"

♦ "Where did the problem originate?"

The previous demonstrates seven different angles to the same question, each revealing a different aspect of the personality, performance, and behavior of the candidate. This technique makes the possibilities for questions theoretically endless, depending only on how thorough the interviewer wants to be.

Note: The interviewer should not feel that a candidate's first answer to any of the questions must be accepted. Look closer and check for cracks. When the interviewer feels an answer is lacking, pursue it by layering the questions. Keep asking until satisfied.

Additional Input Questions

Three Techniques

Interviewers can use these following three techniques to stretch a question:

♦ If the interviewer wants to hear more — whether dissatisfied with the first answer or so fascinated with the answer that the interviewer wants to hear more — say, "Give me some more detail on that. It's very interesting," or, "Can you give me another example?"

♦ The interviewer may hear an answer and add after it, "What did you learn from that experience?" This is an excellent layering technique that can give insight into judgment and emotional maturity.

♦ Perhaps the best technique for gathering more information is simply to sit quietly, looking at the interviewee and saying nothing. If the conversation lulls, the interviewee thinks, "Well, the interviewer is not saying anything, so I must be expected to say something else. I must not have finished my answer to proper satisfaction." Even if the interviewer may find the silence difficult to manage at first, it can pay substantial dividends in the long run.

Additional Questions

Employers should try to include questions that go beyond a candidate's technical competence or knowledge. The interviewer should probe for qualities needed to succeed at the job, including the following:

♦ The ability to work under pressure.

♦ Organizational skills.

♦ Willingness to put in the extra time and effort necessary to complete a project.

Relevant and job-related questions might target the following:

♦ Incomplete information on application form.

♦ Work experience or education.

♦ Geographic preferences and feelings about relocation.

♦ Normal working hours.

♦ Willingness to travel.

♦ Reasons for leaving previous job.

♦ Personal attributes that could contribute to job performance.

♦ Job-related achievements.

♦ Signs of initiative and self-direction.

♦ Indications of work habits.

♦ Specialized knowledge or expertise.

♦ Meaning of former job titles.

Improper Interview Questions

Do not solicit information that employers are legally barred from considering in the hiring process.

For example, under Title VII of the Civil Rights Act of 1964 and similar state laws, hiring decisions cannot be based on an the following:

♦ Race.

♦ Religion.

♦ Creed.

- Sex.

- Marital status.

- National origin.

- Ancestry.

Other laws prohibit questions about military background, age, disability, or union membership. Generally, do not ask about the following:

- Medical or mental health history.

- National origin and citizenship status.

- Height, weight, or physical characteristics.

- Disability.

- Membership in professional or civic organizations that would reveal national origin, race, gender, religion, or any of the other protected classes under fair employment practice laws.

- Military service history.

- Marital status.

- Sexual orientation.

- Age.

- Previous address.

- Names of relatives.

- Receipt of unemployment insurance, workers' compensation, or disability benefits.

- Foreign languages (unless required by the position).

- Child care situation, family planning, or number of children.

- Religion or religious beliefs.

- Past rejection for bonding.

- Salary history.

Structuring the Interview

All too often, interviewers use a job applicant's résumé as a guide for structuring the interview. The résumé is essentially a PR sheet, giving only information the applicant wants to reveal. Following the résumé allows the candidate to control the interview, not the interviewer. To avoid this tendency, try to use the following format to structure the interview:

Set the Atmosphere

After greeting the candidate, make small talk to help him or her relax. Comfortable and secure candidates feel comfortable revealing truthful and sensitive information. Ask about the person's hobbies, interests, travel, or city of residence. Remember to avoid sensitive areas like children, marital status, or church activities. Then begin the formal interview by asking a transition question, such as, "What do you know about the organization?" or "How did you hear about this opening?"

Give an Overview

Tell the candidate how the interview will proceed and what will be covered — job experience, education, interests, and so on. Explain that after discussing the candidate's background, the interviewer will ask for information about the job, explain the organization, and answer any questions the candidate might have.

Cover Candidate's Work Experience and Education

Ask prepared questions first, following up any responses that deserve further inquiry. Have the candidate cover the experiences in chronological order. For instance, when exploring work experience, begin with the first job; when discussing education, begin with high school. This background review helps paint a picture of tendencies over time. People also tend to rehearse statements about their current positions but are less prepared, and more spontaneous, when it comes to discussing old jobs.

Note: Take good notes on any discussion of job qualifications to document the screening process.

Candidate's Interests and Self-Assessment

After covering education and work experience, ask a few questions about a candidate's activities and interests to get a broader perspective of a personality. Then ask for a self-assessment. Give the candidate a chance to summarize personal and professional strengths, as well as to talk about "developmental needs" or qualities that the individual might want to change or improve.

Review the Job

Do not discuss details of the job until the interview has covered a candidate's qualifications; otherwise, an applicant may exaggerate certain skills required by the position. Review the organization, the job, salary, benefits, location, and any other pertinent data. Be careful to limit comments to the specific facts about the job as it currently exists.

Warning: Statements made during job interviews can create an implied employment contract and could lead to a lawsuit if some remark later proves untrue.

Close the Interview

In the final portion of the interview, give the candidate an opportunity to ask questions about the organization and the job. Explore any doubts or reservations the individual might have. Thank the candidate for the time spent on the interview, review the next steps in the hiring process, and give an estimate, if possible, as to when the organization will make its decision.

Note: Leave a way out for possible rejection by explaining that the organization has other candidates to interview before selecting a person.

Uniformity of Interviews

Employers can help avoid exposure to lawsuits by creating a list of acceptable questions and rigidly following them. Employers have the option of asking all of the questions on the list or choosing only those that pertain to a particular job. Regardless of the questions asked, employers must make sure all questions are strictly job-related, nondiscriminatory, and do not invade the applicant's privacy. The interviewer should review the entire list of questions prior to the interview and clearly mark those questions most related to the available position. Each applicant should be asked only those questions identified by the interviewer. When more than one interviewer is interviewing applicants, the employer must make sure each interviewer has the same listed of marked questions. Interviewers must be instructed not to deviate from the pre-marked questions.

Pre-Employment Interview Training

Employers need to train individuals to conduct pre-employment interviews without incurring complaints of discrimination. Managers and supervisors must have a clear understanding of what is required by the Equal Employment Opportunity (EEO) rules and regulations.

People in personnel departments must have this understanding as a matter of course. However, every manager and supervisor who interviews job candidates before hiring must be trained. Apparently innocent questions, asked in good faith, can leave the organization open to costly and time-consuming charges of discrimination.

Employers should design a pre-employment interview training tool. Training should provide a better grasp of the intent of the equal-employment-opportunity regulations. It will enable managers and supervisors to conduct an effective, nonbiased selection interview.

Interview Training for Managers

Even experienced managers make interviewing mistakes. They ask illegal or inappropriate questions, or they spend the interview talking about themselves and the organization, never bothering to learn anything helpful about the candidate. Novice interviewers can be even worse representatives for an organization, playing favorites, hiring personal friends, or hiring on a whim. Managers must learn the "do's" and "don'ts" of interviewing, either one-on-one, or in a group session. This will result in more effective interviewing and, consequently, better hiring decisions.

When designing an interview training program for managers, companies should consider the following:

- ♦ Handling introductions and ascertaining personal objectives.
- ♦ Overview of previous good and bad interviewing experiences.
- ♦ How to clarify the needs for the hiring department, such as the following:
  - Job skills.
  - Motivation.
  - Behavioral fit.
- ♦ How to identify and meet the hiring department's expectations as follows:
  - Timing.
  - Number of applicants.
  - Advertising needs.
  - Pre-screening activities.
  - Testing requirements.
  - Background investigation agencies.
  - Decision-making process.
  - Other expectations.
- ♦ Developing an appropriate selection process using the following:
  - Establish the minimum requirements.

- Application.
- Résumé.
- Cover letter.
- Phone calls.
- Reception observation checkpoints.
- Testing.
- Number of interviews.
- Presentations, tours, and demonstrations.

◆ Developing interviewing guidelines as follows:

- Identifying key behaviors for success.
- Developing legally defensible behavioral interview questions.

◆ Discussing candidate evaluation and presentation to department.

◆ Decision-making process; consultation versus go or no-go.

◆ Extending an offer or advising of nonselection.

◆ Other issues and concerns.

◆ Program evaluations.

Legally Interviewing Disabled

Employers with 15 or more employees must comply with the ADA. The ADA protects persons with disabilities from discrimination in hiring and treatment on the job. The EEOC recently issued new interviewing guidelines that spell out the kinds of questions an interviewer can and cannot ask job applicants.

Sample Questions an Interviewer Can Ask

According to the EEOC guidelines, the following questions are acceptable during an interview:

◆ "Can you perform the essential functions of this job . . . with or without reasonable accommodation?"

◆ "Describe how you would perform the essential functions of the job?"

◆ "Can you meet the attendance requirements of this job?"

◆ "How many days of leave did you take last year?"

Sample Questions an Interviewer Cannot Ask

The following questions **may not** be asked while conducting an interview:

◆ "Do you have (name of disease)?"

◆ "Do you have a disability that would interfere with your ability to perform the job?"

◆ "How many days were you sick last year?"

The following example will illustrate both the incorrect and the correct ways to elicit information:

The applicant for a telephone sales job is obviously blind.

Do not say, "I imagine that with your blindness you'd have some difficulty filling in our call forms and keeping track of the results of your calls. In what ways do you think your blindness would interfere with your sales job?"

Instead, questions should be phrased something like this: "This job requires that you ask questions from our telemarketing script and record the results of your calls. How would you perform these essential functions of this job with reasonable accommodation?"

The following three keys facilitate legal interview questioning:

- ♦ Avoid any inquiry or comment that requires an employee to reveal or talk about an illness or disability.

- ♦ Focus questions and comments on job-related topics.

- ♦ Focus on the positive: "How will you perform . . . ?" As opposed to "Is there anything that prevents you from . . . ?"

Checklist for Conducting a Hiring Interview

The person conducting the interview should be well prepared and knowledgeable on the company's interviewing and hiring practices. When conducting the interview, the interviewer should use the following outline:

Establishing Rapport

- ♦ Help the candidate relax with brief casual conversation.

- ♦ Maintain appropriate eye contact.

- ♦ Listen sympathetically.

- ♦ Avoid direct criticism.

- ♦ Reassure the candidate after an awkward disclosure by commending the openness, honesty, and willingness to face up to a problem.

- ♦ Remain neutral; do not speak approvingly of questionable conduct.

Controlling the Interview

- ♦ Keep the purpose of the interview clearly in mind.

- ♦ Decide in advance what questions to raise in light of the job requirements and the candidate's résumé.

- ♦ Keep to the planned agenda and allocate time appropriately.

- ♦ Politely return to the original question if the candidate's answer was evasive.

- ♦ Persuade the candidate to elaborate on suggestive or incomplete responses by:

  - Asking follow-up questions.

  - Repeating or summarizing the candidate's statements in a questioning tone.

  - Maintaining silence.

  - Make smooth transitions from one topic to another.

Documenting the Interview

- Pace the interview well.

- Take notes for reliable recall.

- Note dress, behavior, or facial expressions, if relevant.

- Wait until after the candidate has left to write down any evaluative judgments.

- Note points to follow up on later in the interview.

Interview Conclusion

A good interview does not guarantee a successful hire. However, a sound interviewing technique can help an employer find the right person for a particular job; it can also help weed out unsuccessful candidates.

Interviewers should be as thorough as they can be, within the limits of the law, when interviewing a potential employee. If the interviewer is thorough and accurate when conducting the interview, the risks resulting from the interviewing process are reduced.

Note: A sample of an employment interview form is at the end of this chapter.

Hiring Employees

Many employers spend a great deal of time and money dealing with employees that should not have been hired in the first place. This problem exists because the only measure of a hiring program's success is the speed by which an available position is filled. A truly efficient hiring program, however, hires people who do the job required without producing problems.

Successful hiring programs contain the following elements:

- **Job Specification.** Define what the job really requires in terms of the required education, experience, physical capabilities, and interpersonal skills.

- **Recruit Diversity.** Diversify the external sources of applicants to achieve the business benefits of diversity; include sources that specifically target women and minorities.

- **Selection.** Interview only applicants who meet the minimum requirements established for the job; establish and document objective procedure for further winnowing of the applicant pool if there are too many qualified applicants to interview.

- **Application.** Require that every applicant complete and sign an application for employment, even if the applicant has a typed résumé.

- **Nondiscriminatory Interviews.** Avoid asking questions that directly elicit or may indirectly elicit information prohibited by the EEOC; avoid personal questions that may be perceived as inappropriate and/or invasive.

- **Job-Related Interviews.** Develop a uniform list of job-related questions for each position to ensure consistency in questions and phraseology; focus on past experiences, job requirements, expectations for the future, as well as how applicant would handle specific workplace situations.

Note: Some sample questions can be found in the section entitled **Interview Questions.**

- **Multiple Interviewers.** Involve multiple persons in the interview process; ensure demographic diversity among the multiple interviewers.

- **Nondiscriminatory Hiring.** Avoid either the consideration or discussion of EEOC characteristics or customer preferences related to the same in the decision-making process; consider and document only legitimate, articulable, job-related factors.

- **Hire Diversity.** Be aware that in the selection process the human tendency is to be comfortable with similarity and unconsciously uncomfortable with difference; and that differences in style, perspective and community contacts are beneficial to the business.

- **Reference Checking.** Perform a reference check before extending a job offer; document the attempt, even if no response is received.

Types of Hiring

Under the pressures of operating a business, many managers treat hiring decisions more casually than they do other business decisions of similar magnitude. Often, they have concluded from their past experiences that hiring is mostly a matter of luck. However, hiring effective employees does not have to be a gamble.

Hiring managers use three quite different approaches for hiring employees, which produce vastly different results as follows:

- Warm-body hiring.

- Ritual hiring.

- Performance-based, high-impact hiring.

Warm-Body Hiring

Warm body hiring occurs when managers simply hire the first person available. This may occur when the following applies:

- The manager lacks the time to do a careful job.

- Few applicants are available.

- The job is not considered important enough to deserve a careful job of screening applicants.

- The manager has simply given up.

With warm-body hiring, an employer is essentially hiring randomly. Some hires will be good; some will cause problems. The vast majority will be quite mediocre, which gives an employer no advantage over business competitors.

Ritual Hiring

Many hire people the way that they were hired, or that they have seen others hired. According to the familiar ritual: casting a jaundiced eye over an application blank, conducting a 20-minute interview with some time-honored questions ("Now tell me about your weaknesses." "Where would you like to be in five years?"), and somehow divining who to hire. This is a comforting ritual, but ritual is not much more likely than warm-body hiring to predict future job performance. If an employer happens to use a ritual that's job-related, the employer will probably end up with more effective hires than with warm-body hiring. However, if the ritual is not job-related, the employer will be systematically hiring the wrong people and the results could easily be worse than random, warm-body hiring.

High-Impact Hiring

High-impact hiring offers a performance-oriented alternative to warm-body and ritual hiring.

High-impact hiring includes five critical steps as follows:

♦ **Analyzing performance.** The foundation of high-impact hiring is a thorough understanding of what an employer expects the new employee to do on the job and how this performance adds value to an organization. The cause of most hiring mistakes is not that managers are incapable of understanding people. Rather, hiring mistakes occur because managers have not taken the steps they could to truly understand the performance required for the job. Performance analysis provides the basis for determining the critical attributes (such as skills, knowledge, or attitudes) that differentiate effective employees from the rest.

♦ **Anticipating turnover.** Panic hiring when employees unexpectedly leave is a common cause of warm-body hiring. Anticipating hiring needs and strategies before turnover occurs allows an employer to avoid panic hiring through such strategies as continuous hiring, succession planning, and redesigning jobs.

♦ **Recruiting high-potential applicants.** A fundamental rule is that an employer cannot hire employees who are better than the applicants recruited. A thorough performance analysis enables employers to move beyond scattershot networking and advertising to a planned repertoire of recruiting efforts that build a pool of high-performing candidates.

♦ **Developing a comprehensive set of hiring tools.** To hire for performance, an employer needs to use a combination of assessment procedures that accurately assess the attributes needed to be successful on the job. Depending on the job, this combination may include the following:

- Structured interviews.
- Ability.
- Personality and integrity tests.
- Work samples.
- Effective background and reference checks.

Using valid, job-related hiring tools differentiates a performance-based high-impact approach from a ritual approach, and also ensures that hiring can pass legal muster.

♦ **Making effective hiring decisions.** Make the hiring decision based on a systematic review of applicants' capabilities for performance. Basing decisions on "gut feel" or on nonperformance-based hiring rituals will transform even the best hiring system into an expensive, ineffective, and potentially illegal hiring ritual.

Selecting a High-Performance Employee

Employers are continuously faced with the challenge of finding effective and successful employees. There are many different techniques and practices for the hiring process. The process outlined below is designed to serve as a guide for hiring a candidate who will be successful within the employer's organization.

Developing a Profile

This involves two determinations by an employer. First, the employer must determine what the candidate must do to be considered a success in the position. Next, the employer must determine the knowledge, skills, and abilities necessary to meet the specific expectations.

Recruiting

Employers should ask for referrals from each new employee hired and recruit 365 days a year.

Screening

It is better for employers to read résumés in chronological order. Reading résumés in chronological order allows the employer to follow the candidate through a career and be better able to detect patterns and trends. Employers should also conduct a brief phone screen before inviting any candidate in for an interview.

Gathering Data — An Effective Interview

The employer should ask specific questions with a planned purpose. The candidate should be asked for specific examples of behavior with follow-up questions for clarification.

Data Verification

The candidate should have the responsibility of getting references and not the employer. Employers need to ask pointed and specific questions in order to verify the data.

Evaluating a Candidate

Employers can use a simple matrix to evaluate all the candidates. In situations where additional questions are raised, employers can add to the evaluation using data gathered in the interview.

Review the Hiring Decision

A major factor in a successful screening process is the involvement of more than one person. The actual hiring decision should be made by or subject to the approval of more than one manager. Higher levels of management and/or human resource managers should scrutinize the hiring recommendations, and require explanations and justifications for the decision. Any discrepancies between the recommendation and qualifications required for the position should be questioned, as should vague or inconsistent justifications.

The recommending supervisor or manager should also be able to justify the preferred candidate's selection over other final or interviewed candidates. If the manager's decision cannot withstand the employer's internal scrutiny, the decision most likely will not be able to withstand challenge by a plaintiff's attorney or client.

Employment Offer Letters

An employer may want to provide a written offer of employment which verifies the terms agreed to by the employer and the prospective employee. The offer letter usually outlines that the individual has accepted the offer for a particular position and will start work on a specific date. The offer letter also sets forth the agreed upon salary and describes any benefits.

When writing an offer letter, care should be taken to ensure that no promises of continued employment are made which might inhibit the employer's ability to later terminate the individual. As an example, the offer letter should never indicate that the individual will "always have a job with XYZ Company" or that a person is being hired for a "permanent" position or a specified period of time. Employers should have their offer letters reviewed by an experienced human resources professional or attorney because of the numerous and potential pitfalls involved. A sample of an offer letter is at the end of this chapter.

Employment Rejection Letters

Employers may want to provide unsuccessful applicants with a rejection letter that explains why the applicant did not receive an offer. The rejection letter usually outlines that the individual did not meet the company requirements for hire or that the organization has decided to go with another candidate. The rejection letter is not mandatory for the employer and is usually done as a courtesy to the applicant for his or her time during the interview process.

When writing a rejection letter, care should be taken not to promise a continued review or that the resume will remain on file unless specific time periods are included. These types of promises may result in future problems for the employer. Employers should have their rejection letters reviewed by an experienced human resources professional or attorney because of the numerous and potential pitfalls involved. A sample of a rejection letter is at the end of this chapter.

Employment Agreements

Employers can use written employment agreements to gain certain protections and benefits. Provisions implemented through agreements include future employment restrictions and mandatory arbitration. Employment agreements are often used for professional or executive positions to define terms and conditions of employment, including job duties, termination rights, length of employment, compensation, and benefits. These agreements may or may not modify the presumptive employment-at-will relationship. Employers must carefully draft employment agreements to ensure the agreement is enforceable and does not create contractual rights and obligations that the employer is not willing or able to meet. A poorly drafted agreement can create more problems than having no agreement.

When determining whether to use an employment agreement for a particular job position or applicant, employers should consider the following:

♦ The extent to which the employee will engage in the use of confidential information and the competitiveness of the business.

♦ The uniqueness or status of the position, and the extent to which job duties, compensation, and benefits need to be specifically clarified in relation to the employer's general policies.

♦ The need to manage litigation costs and expenses for employment-related claims through mandatory arbitration or alternative dispute resolution methods.

♦ The demographics of the workforce and industry customs and practice. (Do similar positions customarily utilize employment agreements?)

I-9 Form for Employment

New employees and the employer must complete an attestation under penalty of perjury. The employee must attest that the individual is authorized to work and is not an illegal alien. The law requires employers to attest that they have reviewed the documentation supplied by the employee and that the documents appear genuine.

Employers do not guarantee that the documents provided by employees are genuine; employers merely attest that the employees' documents have been examined and appear to be in order. If the employee refuses to sign the form, the individual should not be employed.

Note: Form I-9 must be completely filled out; simply attaching photocopies of the documents is no longer an acceptable practice. See a sample of Form I-9 at the end of this chapter.

Filling Out the Form I-9

The following are some points to keep in mind when completing Form I-9:

♦ An applicant should not be asked to complete Form I-9 prior to the offer of employment. Form I-9 provides information on citizenship, national origin, and visa status that could serve as a basis for a claim of discrimination if the applicant is not hired.

♦ Section 1 of Form I-9 must be completed and signed by the employee on the date the employee begins work. Any translator or person preparing Sec. 1 for an employee must also sign the form.

♦ The employer should immediately review Section 1 to make sure that it was properly completed and that the employee makes any necessary corrections.

♦ When reviewing the documents provided by the employee for Section 2, the employer should review the information provided in Section 1 against the documents produced by the employee for consistency. The employee should be given an opportunity to correct Section 1 if there is a discrepancy. The employer is not expected to be an immigration expert but should have a sufficient understanding of the immigration system to know whether a proffered document is consistent with an employee's claimed status.

♦ Do not ask for any document to substantiate the information in Section 1.

♦ Section 2 of the form must be completed within three business days of the commencement of employment.

♦ A Form I-9 should be completed for every employee and for each independent contractor who could be perceived as being the equivalent of an employee. The burden of I-9 compliance can be shifted by contract to an entity providing individual contractors. A Form I-9 does not need to be completed for truly independent contractors, for example, contractors who spend only a few hundred hours per year working for the employer and who work off-site.

♦ Do not ask for any particular document for Section 2. The employee should be given a Form I-9 (see copy attached) and asked to provide either one document on List A or one document on each of Lists B and C.

♦ The employer should accept any document specified on Form I-9, provided that it appears genuine and relates to the employee.

♦ Do not ask for an INS document to confirm the expiry date of work authorization.

♦ Do not consider the expiration date of work authorization in making the hiring decision.

♦ Review the documents that are provided to make sure that they are on list of approved documents for Section 2.

♦ The employer is not required to be a document expert. The INS Handbook does not contain every variation of every document that can be submitted. If a document is one of the approved documents, and does not appear to have been tampered with or to be forged, the employer should accept it.

♦ The employer is not required to make copies of the documents that are produced for Section 2. While there are certain advantages to not making copies of these documents, on balance it seems preferable to make copies and keep them paper-clipped to the I-9. Retaining a copy of the documents tends to negate the inference that the documents produced were obvious forgeries and permits errors in completing the I-9 to be remedied during an audit. If copies are made, they must be retained and attached to the relevant form I-9.

♦ Be particularly careful when an employee shows a filing receipt instead of an actual document. There are four situations in which a filing receipt is acceptable as follows:

  • The filing receipt indicates that the employee has applied for a replacement List A, B, or C document because the original was lost, stolen or damaged (the actual document must be submitted within 90 days after the date of hire).

  • The filing receipt is a temporary I-551 stamp (green card) in the employee's passport or on a Form I-94 (the actual Form I-551 must be submitted within 180 days following the date of hire).

  • The filing receipt takes the form of a refugee admission stamp on a Form I-94 (an employment authorization card, Form I-766, or a social security card must be submitted within 90 days after the date of hire).

  • The filing receipt is for an application to renew an H, L, E, O, or P visa with the same employer (the INS approval notice or new visa and Form I-94 must be submitted within 240 days after expiration of the present period of authorized stay). This is a tricky area (for example, certain Haitians were granted an automatic one year extension of their employment authorization documents in December 1998). An employer should contact a lawyer if there are any doubts about the validity or acceptability of the documents submitted.

  • Keep a tickler file for I-9s showing that employment authorization will expire at a certain date. The employee should be reminded of the need to renew an employment authorization at least 90 days prior to expiration of the current employment authorization. Given INS delays in producing Employment Authorization Documents, it would be wise to give employees even more advanced notice of the impending expiration of their documents.

  • Follow the same I-9 procedures for all employees.

  • Remember that the employer must retain the I-9 for the longer of three years from the date of hire or one year after termination of the employment relationship. A safer way of implementing this requirement is to keep Form I-9 for at least three years after the termination of employment. Keep in mind that the employer must have an I-9 on file for all current employees other than employees hired before November 6, 1986. Disposing I-9s, which are no longer legally required to be kept, frees the employer of potential liability for errors made in completing those forms.

Documentation

The list of acceptable documents is provided on the back of the Form I-9. List A sets forth documents which establish both identity and employment eligibility. However, several documents in List A have been eliminated including the following:

♦ Certificate of U.S. Citizenship (INS Form N-560 or N-561).

♦ Certificate of Naturalization.

- Unexpired Re-Entry Permit (INS Form I-327).

- Unexpired Employment Authorization Document issued by the INS which contains a photograph (INS Form I-688B).

The acceptable documents remaining are as follows:

- U.S. passport (unexpired or expired).

- Unexpired foreign passport, with I-55 stamp or attached INS Form I-94 indicating unexpired employment authorization.

- Alien Registration Receipt Card with photograph (INS Form I-551 Note that Form 1-151 is no longer acceptable).

- Unexpired Temporary Resident Card (INS Form I-688).

- Unexpired Employment Authorization Card (INS Form I-688A).

- Unexpired Employment Authorization Documentation issued by the INS which contains a photograph (INS Form I-688B).

Forms for all current employees (other than those employed on or prior to November 6, 1986) must be kept on file and made available for inspection by government officials. The employer may dispose of Forms I-9 relating to terminated employees, after the longer of (1) three years from the date of hire (2) one year after employment of the individual has ended. One way of avoiding problems with this confusing rule is to keep all Forms I-9 until three years after an employee has been terminated.

Note: Employers are not required to complete a Form I-9 for independent contractors. However, employers may not knowingly use contract labor to circumvent the law against hiring unauthorized aliens.

Applicants with Disabilities

Failure to hire claims resulting from questions eliciting illegal information are common and expensive, even if the employer is the ultimate victor. For example, the Americans with Disabilities Act (ADA) specifically prohibits an employer from asking an applicant, either in writing on the application or orally during the interview process, whether the individual has any physical or mental disabilities. This prohibition applies even if the employer includes, as a follow-up question, an inquiry whether the employer can make any reasonable accommodations on the applicant's behalf.

Notwithstanding the ADA, the employer may ask an applicant whether the individual can perform, with or without accommodations, the essential physical and mental functions of the job for which the applicant has applied. The ADA requires that employers focus on the job responsibilities as opposed to underlying disabilities. However, if the employer asks a job function question on the application, a follow-up question must be included as to the nature of any accommodation which the applicant may require.

WARNING: By asking for this additional information on the application, the organization runs a risk! If an applicant who indicates the need for an accommodation is rejected, the applicant may assume, and later claim, that the rejection was because the organization did not wish to make the accommodation requested or because of the undisclosed disability giving rise to the need for the accommodation. Therefore, it is preferable to inquire orally during the interview whether an applicant can perform the essential functions of the job. It is imperative that the interviewer asks the same question of each applicant interviewed.

Diversity in the Workplace

Attaining true diversity in the workforce is not just a question of legal compliance; it is a matter of good values and good business. According to the U.S. Department of Labor, by the year 2000, 85 percent of the entering workforce were women and minorities and 15 percent are white males. At the turn of the century, as many Americans were over age 75 as under age 5, and the largest of all minority groups in America are individuals with disabilities. Finally, racial minority purchasers currently represent an annual market in excess of $600 billion in goods.

Risks

A contemporary workplace that does not reflect, respect, or encourage diversity and equal employment opportunity is at risk in a number of ways. Perhaps the most visible risk is the legal one: costly class actions, usually focusing on lack of opportunity for females and minorities in the management ranks of the organization. Successful class actions present lessons evident in their end result as follows:

- Outside task forces, subject to court and plaintiff attorneys' scrutiny.

- Difficult reporting and oversight mechanisms administered and monitored by the courts and plaintiffs' attorneys.

- Imposition of hiring, promotion, evaluation, and reporting mechanisms that are burdensome and, at times, counter to companies' business judgment or culture.

- Payment of plaintiff attorneys' fees.

- Multi-million dollar backpay awards.

- Bad publicity.

The other risks of workplaces that lack diversity include the following:

- The lack of development of human talent and potential.

- Deprivation of full exchange of ideas and viewpoints that are critical to imaginative growth.

These risks are equally damaging to the present and future prospects of each business enterprise as well as its employees, customers, shareholders, suppliers, and partners.

Commitment

The process of developing and maintaining a climate hospitable to employees of diverse backgrounds requires a systematic commitment of corporate resources and willpower emanating from the very top. Every organization must manage diversity by changing the relevant question from "why?" to "how?" Those companies that are able to create workplaces supportive of a diverse environment will most successfully prepare themselves for the business challenges of the 21st century.

Adverse Impact

Adverse impact exists when a personnel procedure has a disproportionately negative impact on a legally protected group, such as ethnic minorities, women, and employees over age 40. As an example, if 50 percent of the whites but only 25 percent of the ethnic minorities applying for employment with an organization are hired, the hiring procedure has an adverse impact on the minority group.

Warning: This impact is regardless of the organization's intended use of the procedure or of the business value of the procedure. Adverse impact simply reflects the procedure's results. When adverse impact exists, the organization may be vulnerable to charges of illegal discrimination.

Adverse impact may result from such organizational procedures as hiring, promotion, training and development, transfer, layoff, and even performance appraisals. Adverse impact may be found in an overall procedure or in any step in the overall procedure.

Adverse impact also may be shown by a disproportionate under-representation of a legally protected group in the workforce. As an example, if an organization's workforce is 5 percent Hispanic, however its qualified applicant pool is 20 percent Hispanic, its workforce composition indicates adverse impact for Hispanics. In other words, the workforce does not reflect the proportions of its available qualified applicants.

Negligent Hiring, Retention, and Training

Liability for Negligent Hiring

Employers are coming under increased scrutiny for "negligent" hiring and retention of employees whose criminal records, history of drugs and alcohol, or related problems involve unreasonable risks to others.

When an employer fails to conduct an adequate pre-employment investigation including, as circumstances warrant, reference checks, post-employment verifications, credit checks, and criminal record checks, that employer risks the potential for negligent hiring liability for injuries caused by a disruptive or violent employee to third parties such as customers, clients, suppliers, visitors, or others.

While the legal standards vary from state to state, damages may be awarded for actual injuries and for pain and suffering; punitive damages are not uncommon. In addition, under state workers' compensation laws, employers may be required to compensate victims for on-the-job violence.

The Theory

This cause of action, based on the theory that an employer is responsible for the acts of its employees, holds employers liable for improperly screening applicants who subsequently cause harm to third persons. This principle holds whether the harm caused was within the scope of the individual's employment or not.

Generally, employers are not liable for every act of their employee, only those acts that could have been avoided through a reasonable background investigation. Recent cases have found an employer liable for problems caused by employees who were knowingly hired with a background of conviction for assault and battery, sexual offenses, negligent driving records, or even current drug and alcohol dependency problems.

This emerging legal theory makes it very important for employers to hire qualified and competent employees by carefully screening all applicants for employment.

Reasonable Care

Employers have a duty to exercise reasonable care when hiring employees who, if incompetent and unreliable, might pose a risk of injury to the public or to a fellow employee.

This duty includes making reasonable investigation of the employee's background. For example, a high degree of care is mandatory when hiring employees of an apartment complex, such as security guards, who will have passkeys to the individual apartments.

It is recommended that employers conduct the following during the hiring process:

- ◆ Be alert for long gaps in an applicant's work history, which may have been for periods of incarceration.

- ◆ Attempt to obtain reference information from former employers.

- ◆ Increase the scope of the pre-employment investigation when hiring for positions where there is greater risk to the public or to fellow employees.

- ◆ Consider criminal record investigations. Although some costs are involved, they are insignificant when compared to the potential liability for negligent hiring.

- ◆ Document all pre-employment investigatory efforts, including nonproductive contacts with former employers.

Avoiding Negligent Hiring Claims

Employers have relied on references to gauge the suitability of job applicants. However, companies may restrict the amount of information they provide about a former employee as a result of their concerns about privacy and defamation claims.

To avoid reasonable investigations before they make hiring decisions, employers may have to supplement their reference checks by conducting investigations appropriate for a given position. Complete investigations may be appropriate for management positions but not for laborer positions. Criminal record checks may be appropriate for all employees in certain businesses or may depend on an employee's level of contact with the public and other employees.

Employers may require applicants to consent to the release of information during background and reference check.

Negligent Retention

Employers are exposed to claims for negligent retention if one of their employees causes harm to others and has a history of violence that the employer knew of or could have discovered through a reasonable investigation. Negligent retention differs from negligent hiring only with respect to when an employer learns, or should have learned, of a lack of suitability of an employee. It occurs when an employer continues to retain an unsuitable employee. Failing to take action against an employee known or suspected to pose a risk of harm to co-workers, customers, and others can expose an employer to liability for actual injuries, pain, suffering, and even punitive damages.

Negligent Training

Negligent training claims may arise when the employer fails to train or incorrectly trains an employee. Common negligent training claims include the following:

- ◆ The employer fails to properly train and/or educate an employee responsible for securing an employer's facility or guarding the safety of the employer's property on how to perform the job safely and effectively.

- ◆ The employer fails to provide the necessary knowledge and/or training to an employee in using instruments and equipment necessary to properly perform the job.

Elements of Negligent Hiring or Retention Claims

Plaintiffs who allege an employer is liable for their injuries under a negligent hiring or retention theory generally must establish the following:

- The existence of an employment relationship.

- The incompetence of the employer that caused the specific negligent act on which the claim is based.

- The employer's actual or constructive knowledge of the employee's incompetence that resulted in the negligent act.

- The employer's legal duty to select fit and competent employees.

- That the employee's act or omission was the cause of the plaintiff's injury.

- That the employer's negligence in hiring and/or retaining the employee resulted in harm to a third party.

Note: Punitive damages are recoverable under a negligent hiring or retention theory if it is shown that the employer recklessly or intentionally hired or allowed continued employment of the employee who caused the injury.

Use of Private Investigators

Employers that seek to minimize the likelihood of negligent hiring and negligent retention lawsuits are increasingly relying upon the services of private investigators to help them make prudent hiring decisions. Private investigators depend on computer databases or courthouse records to produce the information they seek.

The following are some of the services that private investigators can perform for employers:

- Confirm or refute a job applicant's education, professional licenses, and previous employment history.

- Determine if the applicant has been arrested, charged, or convicted of a crime.

- Find out if the applicant was sentenced to jail and if so, how long of a sentence the individual served.

- Uncover any aliases that a job applicant may have used.

- Unearth any judgments or liens that have been filed against the applicant.

- Turn up a job applicant's credit history, driving record, telephone records, and date of birth, home addresses, and addresses of relatives.

Because private investigators are expensive, most companies decide to limit the use to candidates for managerial or upper management positions. Therefore, employers should implement internal measures to reduce their legal liability in the area of negligent hiring.

Privacy in the Workplace

Laws protect employees' right to privacy in pre-employment screening situations. Privacy issues may potentially arise in a variety of pre-employment screening contexts, including the following:

- ◆ Background reference checks.

- ◆ Psychological testing.

- ◆ Access to employee records.

- ◆ Reference checks.

- ◆ AIDS and drug testing.

Employers obviously need to investigate the qualifications, job abilities, and trustworthiness of potential employees. However, the applicant is right to and expectation of privacy always competes with the employer's need for information.

Employers must remember that a right to privacy in the workplace does exist to a certain extent. The need for — and depth of — pre-employment screening procedures should be evaluated and conducted accordingly.

Additionally, it is well recognized that employees have privacy interests in their personnel files. First, the types of information that an employer may collect or keep records about may be restricted under various state laws. For example, in the absence of employee consent, employers may be prohibited from keeping records about an employee's nonemployment activities such as associations with other people, political activities, or publications. Second, the information in personnel files is often of a confidential nature and, as such, should be protected from unrestricted or unauthorized disclosure. To this end, some states' constitutions prohibit disclosure of personnel files to certain third parties (such as co-workers). Similarly, most states' public records statutes exempt from disclosure any personnel file information of public employees other than name, job description, and salary classification.

However, privacy rights in personnel files are not absolute. Exceptions to state law prohibitions against the collection of information about nonemployment activities may be made for activities occurring on work premises or during work hours, for criminal conduct, or for activities harmful to the employer's property or business. Similarly, there are circumstances in which disclosure of personnel file information is mandated by law or is otherwise justified or privileged.

Reducing Violence in the Workplace

Violence in the workplace is a serious problem. Statistics suggest that more than 1,000 homicides and one million physical assaults occur at work each year. One of the most important ways to minimize violent incidents at work is to engage in preventive steps during the hiring process. These include the following:

- ◆ Criminal record checks.

- ◆ Substance abuse testing.

- ◆ Reference checks.

- ◆ Interview techniques.

Criminal Record Checks

Conducting a criminal record check creates minimal exposure if employers only inquire about convictions, not arrests. For example, in Pennsylvania and in most other states, it is against public policy for an employer to consider any experiences an applicant has with the criminal justice system which fall short of conviction.

At a minimum, criminal record checks should be done for certain positions, such as security guards, evening supervisors who may be alone with people, and employees who must carry weapons. Whether an employer expands its criminal record checks beyond these types of positions is really a business decision based on a cost/benefit analysis.

If an employer decides to do this type of check, the employment application must provide notice that a criminal record check will be conducted. If an applicant is denied a position in whole or in part because of a criminal conviction (and only a criminal conviction that is job-related), the applicant must be notified in writing.

Note: If a criminal record report is obtained from a consumer-reporting agency, employers will be subject to additional requirements under the FCRA.

Substance Abuse Testing

Approximately 20 percent of workplace violence is committed by individuals who have substance abuse problems. Given the prevalence of substance abuse in general and the specific link to violence, pre-employment drug testing can be an effective mechanism for "weeding out" potentially violent employees.

If an employer conducts drug testing, the following procedures should be considered:

♦ Use an independent SAMHSA drug-testing lab.

♦ Perform these tests consistently, either on all employees, or those employees with a particular job description.

♦ Ensure the validity of the tests by securing the chain of custody.

♦ Request a second test to confirm the results.

♦ Use an independent medical review officer to review the results of all of the tests.

Note: For more information about drug testing compliance, please see the chapter entitled **Drug and Alcohol Testing in the Workplace.**

Reference Checks

Reference checks are a simple exercise for obtaining insight into an applicant's prior work experiences, ability to work with supervisors, and handle work-related stress. Employers should speak with prior direct supervisors, co-workers, and subordinates when possible.

Although employers may feel reference checks only provide neutral information, the failure to conduct this simple exercise may subject employers to a negligent hire claim. Therefore, even if useful information is not obtained through a reference check, an employer should keep a record of any such attempts. Additionally, at the very minimum, employers should **always** verify an applicant's educational background.

Improving Hiring and Other Personnel Practices

Employers should frequently evaluate their hiring process and seek to make improvements to ensure the most efficient procedure, while complying with federal and state laws. Ongoing evaluations or re-evaluations prior to beginning the hiring process due to a job opening or change in employment structure are ideal times to review and improve hiring and personal practices.

The following elements should be taken into consideration when attempting to enhance hiring and personal practices:

- **Do not** offer false promises to applicants or employees such as the following:
  - **Do not** oversell the position or make false statements about the nature of the job, the opportunities for advancement, or the organization's stability or financial status.
  - **Do not** limit the grounds for discharge.
  - **Do not** make promises about job security or longevity.
- Get all hiring documents in order as follows:
  - Prepare the application for employment.
  - Create articulate offer letters.
  - Defeat claims of an implied contract not to terminate except for good cause as follows:
    - Include "at-will" language in the job applications, offer letters, employment agreements, and employee handbooks or manuals.
    - Use integration clauses that will defeat an employee's future claims of misrepresentations, fraudulent inducements, and detrimental reliance on broken promises.
    - When it is necessary or desirable to offer certain employment guarantees (for example in order to recruit or retain a particular employee), consider offering the guarantees in a written employment contract with a limited duration.
    - When written employment contracts are up for renewal, include in the new agreement a provision acknowledging that all promises and representations are contained in the new contract and that any former obligations or understandings are no longer binding.
- Use extreme care not to misrepresent the nature or condition of an employment position when recruiting an employee who will be required to relocate as follows:
  - **Do not** misrepresent the financial health, merger or reorganization plans, or any other information concerning the future of the organization.
  - **Do not** misrepresent the following:
    - The autonomy or level of responsibilities the applicant's position will entail.
    - The length of probable employment, the opportunities for advancement.
    - The compensation.
    - Any other terms or conditions of employment.

♦ Review and update employee handbooks and/or manuals to ensure that they comply to all applicable federal and state laws and that they contain only true representations of company policies, practices, and procedures, actually applied to all employees as follows:

- Delete from manuals any policies or procedures that are ignored or not customarily followed.

- Immediately distribute any changes to company policies or procedures and require employees to acknowledge receipt in writing.

- Written policies and procedures must specifically include any rights or prerogatives that the employer wishes to preserve, such as the following:

  ▪ Flexibility in whether to award — as well as discretion in the amount — of bonuses or raises.
  ▪ Discretion to assign additional job duties as needed.

- Keep disciplinary procedures as general as possible to allow for immediate dismissal without triggering a breach of contract or fraud claim for failing to follow prescribed warnings or progressive discipline steps.

- If grievance procedures are provided, state that the procedure only guarantees that an employee will be heard, not that the outcome will be favorable.

- Identify who in the organization is authorized to make representations or promises, and train managers and supervisors not to make additional representations to employees about any of the following:

  ▪ Employment prospects.
  ▪ Compensation.
  ▪ Benefits.
  ▪ Transfers.
  ▪ Discipline.
  ▪ Other personnel matters.

- Eliminate any reference to a probationary period during which a new employee may be terminated "for any reason," to avoid the argument that after expiration of the probationary period, the employee may only be terminated for cause.

- Include language in the employee manual that its provisions can only be modified in writing by certain company representatives.

♦ Openly communicate all company policies in order to enjoy their protection as follows:

- Immediately provide all employee manuals and handbooks to new hires, with instructions that the information is to be studied as part of their initial training.

- Do not open discussion on an employment-related matter without being prepared to disclose all the related facts.

- Consider publishing key policies in employees' native languages.

♦ Be honest.

♦ **Do not** make affirmative representations that conceal the organization's future intent to reduce out, lay off, or terminate employees.

- ♦ Be sure any representations that are made in regard to employee health benefit plans are accurate, and are made as required by law as follows:

  - Unless absolutely certain, do not reassure the employee about waiting periods, pre-existing conditions, transferability, or other terms or conditions of insurance coverage.

  - Provide new employees with information about the company's insurance and benefit plans as soon as possible, and provide all employees with prompt notice of any changes in a plan. Obtain a written acknowledgment of receipt and include a statement requesting that employees study the material.

  - If a company ERISA plan is internally administered or if the company self-administers any such plan be aware of the greater fiduciary duty to disclose information regarding the plan, and always act "solely" in the best interest of the plan participants and beneficiaries.

  - Comply with the Health Insurance Portability and Accountability Act of 1996 (HIPAA), which provides that effective since January 1, 1998, group medical plan administrators must give notice of a reduction of medical insurance benefits within 60 days after adopting the reduction or as part of a regular summary description of the plan issued not more than every 90 days.

  - Comply with HIPAA's provisions regarding notice to COBRA beneficiaries of changes in coverage provisions.

Note: Please refer to the chapter entitled **Health Care Plans and COBRA** for further information about health care compliance.

- ♦ Use the following precautions when supplying references to a potential employer or employment agency concerning a present or former employee:

  - Appoint specific employees to respond to reference requests, and notify all other supervisors that they are not to respond in any way if contacted about a former employee.

  - Provide any job references only by request, and preferably, by written request, from a prospective employer.

  - Do not give false or misleading information to a prospective employer about a current or former employee.

  - If a job reference is provided, do not misrepresent or conceal information that obviously would make the employee unsuitable.

  - Truthful employment information must be fully disclosed to a law enforcement agency to which a present or former employee has applied for a peace officer position if any of the following apply:

    - The request is in writing.
    - It is accompanied by a notarized affidavit from the employee releasing the employer from liability.
    - A sworn officer or other authorized representative of the law enforcement agency presents the request.

  - If a settlement or release agreement with a former employee has been signed, which specifies the content of future job references to be given by the employer, notify all persons who might be contacted for job references of the terms of the agreement.

Pre-Hiring Checklist

The following should be taken into consideration prior to hiring:

- ◆ Use a good employment application that has passed a legal review and require the applicant to complete all relevant information on the application.

- ◆ State on the application how long the application is active (such as 90 days), only if unsuccessful applications are actually considered during the stated period when future openings occur.

Note: If file applications are not consulted, it is better not to make such a statement on the application, as it may extend the limitations period for filing a hiring claim.

- ◆ Do not accept applications unless there is a job position open. Return unsolicited résumés and inquiries to the applicants.

- ◆ Write and maintain interview notes separate from the application.

- ◆ Develop a job description for each position consistent with ADA requirements. When soliciting new employees, accurately define these stated skill, education, experience and physical requirements of the open position.

- ◆ Before the interview, develop a list of open-ended questions that elicit job-related information. All personnel conducting interviews should have a basic knowledge of discrimination laws and understand the characteristics protected by applicable law.

- ◆ Interviewers should avoid monopolizing the conversation and allow the applicant to talk and to fully respond to the open-ended questions; the more the applicant talks, the more information the employer will obtain about the candidate.

- ◆ Perform a background check prior to an offer of employment. Require and check references. Conduct checks of driving records or conviction history when required for the position.

- ◆ Do not tell applicants that they are hired, a "shoe-in" or "probably will get the job" during the initial interview. Applicants should not be made an offer of employment until all pre-employment checks are conducted (except medical examination, in accordance with the ADA), and final hiring approval is obtained.

- ◆ Never make any promises or assurances of permanent employment, job security, employment for a definite period of time, etc.

- ◆ Have a pre-employment drug and alcohol testing policy reviewed by an attorney prior to implementation.

Conclusion

The hiring process mandates employers to carefully balance gathering as much information as possible to determine an applicant's ability to do the job and not asking questions or engaging in pre-employment testing that runs afoul of federal and state discrimination laws. Employers should continually review whether their inquiries elicit information that is job related. Any inquiries that are not job related must be eliminated. Finally, all screening procedures should be reviewed for compliance with the ADA.

Reference Check Form (Sample)

Applicant's name: _____

Address: _____

Position being considered for: _____

Previous employer: _____

Address: _____

_____

Telephone: _____

Immediate supervisor: _____

_____ states he or she was employed from _____ to _____ as a
_____ and was paid $_____ per _____ when he or she left. Is this correct?

____ Yes.

____ No. Corrections: From _____ to _____ as a _____

at $_____ per _____.

What were his or her duties?

Was he or she a supervisor?

____ Yes. Number of employees supervised: _____

____ No.

How would you rate the quality of his or her work?

Did he or she work well with other people?

Were there any problems with excessive absences or lateness?

Was he or she otherwise dependable?

What were his or her strong points?

What about any weak points?

Why did he or she leave the job with you?

Would you re-employ him or her?

Would you recommend him or her for a position as a _____?

Note: This is a generic sample policy and does not necessarily reflect the employment laws in any or all of the 50 U.S. states. Before establishing any company policy, one should review the applicable state laws or seek guidance from legal counsel.

Waiver to Check References
(Sample)

I hereby authorize the company to thoroughly investigate my references, work record, education, and other matters related to my suitability for employment and, further, authorize the references I have listed to disclose to the company any and all letters, reports and other information related to my work records, without giving me prior notice of such disclosure. In addition, I hereby release the company, my former employers, and all other persons, corporations, partnerships and associations from any and all claims, demands, or liabilities arising out of or in any way related to such investigation or disclosure.

_____   _____

Signature of Employee   Date

Note: This is a generic sample policy and does not necessarily reflect the employment laws in any or all of the 50 U.S. states. Before establishing any company policy, one should review the applicable state laws or seek guidance from legal counsel.

Investigative Report Disclosure Statement
(Sample)

"By this document, [the employer] discloses to you that a consumer report, including an investigative consumer report containing information as to your character, general reputation, personal characteristics, and mode of living, may be obtained for employment purposes as part of the pre-employment background investigation and at any time during your employment. Should an investigative consumer report be requested, you will have the right to demand a complete and accurate disclosure of the nature and scope of the investigation requested and a written summary of your rights under the FCRA. Please sign below to signify receipt of the foregoing disclosure."

_____ Signature of Candidate

_____ HR Representative Signature

_____ Date

Note: This is a generic sample policy and does not necessarily reflect the employment laws in any or all of the 50 U.S. states. Before establishing any company policy, one should review the applicable state laws or seek guidance from legal counsel.

Certification from Company to Consumer Reporting Agency (Sample)

In compliance with the FCRA as amended by the Consumer Credit Reporting Act of 1996, Client hereby certifies to [Consumer Reporting Agency] that it will comply with the following provisions:

- ◆ Client certifies that prior to obtaining or causing a "consumer report" and/or an "investigative consumer report" to be obtained for the following employment purposes:

  - • A clear and conspicuous disclosure, in a document consisting solely of the disclosure, will be made in writing to the consumer. The disclosure will explain that a consumer report and/or investigative consumer report may be obtained for employment purposes, and will be presented to the consumer before the report is procured or caused to be procured. The disclosure will satisfy all requirements identified in Section 606(a)(1) of the act.

  - • The consumer will have authorized, in writing, the obtaining of the report by Client.

- ◆ Should the consumer make a written request within a reasonable amount of time, Client will provide the following:

  - • Information about whether an investigative consumer report has been requested.

  - • If an investigative consumer report has been requested, written disclosure of the nature and scope of the investigation requested.

  - • The name and address of the outside agency to whom requests for any of these reports have been made.

Note: The above information will be provided no later than five days after the date on which the request for such disclosure was received from the consumer or such report was first requested, whichever is later.

- ◆ Should the consumer be denied employment, or other adverse action taken, in whole or in part on the basis of the report, Client will provide the following to the applicant or employee:

  - • A copy of the report.

  - • A description, in writing, of the rights of the consumer entitled: "A Summary of Your Rights under the FCRA."

- ◆ The information from the report will not be used in violation of any applicable federal or state equal employment opportunity law or regulation.

Client hereby acknowledges receipt of the Summary of Consumer Rights.

_____Subscriber Name/Title

_____Signature/Date

Note: This is a generic sample policy and does not necessarily reflect the employment laws in any or all of the 50 U.S. states. Before establishing any company policy, one should review the applicable state laws or seek guidance from legal counsel.

Disclosure Statement
(Sample)

"By this document, [the employer] discloses to you that a consumer report may be obtained for employment purposes as part of the pre-employment background investigation and at any time during your employment. Please sign below to signify receipt of the foregoing disclosure."

_____ Candidate Signature

_____ HR Signature

_____ Date

Note: This is a generic sample policy and does not necessarily reflect the employment laws in any or all of the 50 U.S. states. Before establishing any company policy, one should review the applicable state laws or seek guidance from legal counsel.

Authorization Form
(Sample)

"This shall authorize the procurement of a consumer report by [the employer] as part of the pre-employment background investigation. If hired, this authorization shall remain on file and shall serve as an ongoing authorization for [the employer] to procure consumer reports at any time during my employment period."

_____ Candidate Signature

_____ HR Signature

_____ Date

Note: This is a generic sample policy and does not necessarily reflect the employment laws in any or all of the 50 U.S. states. Before establishing any company policy, one should review the applicable state laws or seek guidance from legal counsel.

"Before" Adverse Action Letter (Sample)

Date

Dear _____,

Recently, you authorized us to obtain a consumer report about you from a consumer-reporting agency. Enclosed please find (1) a copy of the consumer report we obtained and (2) a summary of your rights under the FCRA.

Sincerely,

Note: This is a generic sample policy and does not necessarily reflect the employment laws in any or all of the 50 U.S. states. Before establishing any company policy, one should review the applicable state laws or seek guidance from legal counsel.

"After" Adverse Action Letter (Sample)

Date

Dear _____,

We regret to inform you that [Client] is unable to offer you employment [or will terminate your employment effective (Date)], [or has decided not to offer you a promotion].

This decision was based in whole or in part on information contained in a report from [consumer credit reporting agency name, address, and telephone number, including toll-free number], a copy of which was previously given to you. The agency did not make this employment decision and is unable to supply you with specific reasons why the decision was made. Under Section 612 of the FCRA, you have the right to obtain a free copy of the report if you submit a written request to the agency identified above no later than 60 days after you receive this notice. Under Section 611 of that act, you also have the right to dispute with the consumer reporting agency the accuracy or completeness of any information in the report.

Sincerely,

Note: This is a generic sample policy and does not necessarily reflect the employment laws in any or all of the 50 U.S. states. Before establishing any company policy, one should review the applicable state laws or seek guidance from legal counsel.

Employment Interview Form
(Sample)

Applicant's Name: _____ Date: _____

Interviewer's Name: _____ Title: _____

General Interview   Promotional Interview

Applicant Applied For: _____

Please rate the candidate on the following. Use a scale where 1 = lowest and 5 = highest rating.

Creativity 1 2 3 4 5

Job Experience 1 2 3 4 5

Job Knowledge... 1 2 3 4 5

General Knowledge and Understanding of the Field............................... 1 2 3 4 5

Communication Skills... 1 2 3 4 5

Initiative 1 2 3 4 5

Motivation.. 1 2 3 4 5

Appearance 1 2 3 4 5

Attitude 1 2 3 4 5

Composure 1 2 3 4 5

Overall rating 1 2 3 4 5

Recommendation:

_____Highly recommended   _____Not Recommended

_____ Recommended   _____Other (comments)

                                            _____

Type of position for which applicant seems best suited: _____

Offer Letter
(Sample)

Dear _____:

It is a pleasure to inform you that the ABC Corporation of ____ has recommended your appointment as the director of ____, effective ____. This recommendation has been forwarded with your credentials to the Human Resources Department, and the company has authorized me to inform you of the terms of the offer.

The proposed annual salary is $____ ($____ per month) on a ____-month basis (____ percent time). For any salary increase approved by management, you will be eligible for the increase pending the result of an evaluation by your immediate supervisor.

In addition to your salary, you will receive full health benefits, including dental but excluding vision. You will also be provided with a term life insurance policy.

The general function and responsibilities of the position include _____.

If you accept our offer, you should upon arrival at the ABC Corporation examine the sections of the employee handbook that pertain to the responsibilities and expectations of all employees. Particular attention should be paid to the rules of employment and re-employment contained in Chapter 24 of the handbook.

Before your appointment recommendation can be acted upon formally, we must receive your written concurrence with the proposed terms of appointment as specified above. Please provide this as soon as possible. Enclosed are a company Biography Form, Personal Data Form, Affirmative Action Data Form, Form I-9, and Form W-4. Please complete, sign, and return them with your letter of concurrence.

A condition of this appointment is that you resign any appointment or other employment that you are holding elsewhere by the effective date of your ABC Corporation appointment.

I look forward to receiving your response.

Sincerely yours,

Note: This is a generic sample policy and does not necessarily reflect the employment laws in any or all of the 50 U.S. states. Before establishing any company policy, one should review the applicable state laws or seek guidance from legal counsel.

Rejection Letter
(Sample)

[Company Name]

Address

City, State/Province Zip/Postal

Telephone-Fax

Date

[Applicant's Name]

[Street Address]

[City, State/Province Zip/Postal]

Dear [Name]:

Thank you for your inquiry about employment at (your company's name). We appreciate your interest in our company.

Although your background is impressive, we currently have no openings that match your skills and qualifications. We will keep your résumé on file for (the period of time you will retain the résumé) for review should we have an opening for which you are qualified.

Again thank you for your interest. Best wishes for success in your career search.

Sincerely,

[Name]

Human Resources Manager

Note: This is a generic sample policy and does not necessarily reflect the employment laws in any or all of the 50 U.S. states. Before establishing any company policy, one should review the applicable state laws or seek guidance from legal counsel.

U.S. Department of Justice
Immigration and Naturalization Service

OMB No. 1115-0136
Employment Eligibility Verification

INSTRUCTIONS
PLEASE READ ALL INSTRUCTIONS CAREFULLY BEFORE COMPLETING THIS FORM.

Anti-Discrimination Notice. It is illegal to discriminate against any individual (other than an alien not authorized to work in the illegal to discriminate against work eligible individuals. Employers **CANNOT** specify which document(s) they will accept from an employee. The refusal to hire an individual because of a future expiration date may also constitute illegal discrimination.

Section 1 - Employee. All employees, citizens noncitizens, hired after November 6, 1986, must complete Section 1 of this form at the time of hire, which is the actual beginning of employment. **The employer is responsible for ensuring that Section 1 is timely and properly completed.**

Preparer/Translator Certification. The Preparer/Translator Certification must be completed if Section 1 is prepared by a person other than the employee. A preparer/translator may be used only when the employee is unable to complete Section 1 on his/her own. However, the employee must still sign Section 1 personally.

Section 2 - Employer. For the purpose of completing this form, the term "employer" includes those recruiters and referrers for a fee who are agricultural associations, agricultural employers, or farm labor contractors.

Employers must complete Section 2 by examining evidence of identity and employment eligibility within three (3) business days of the date employment begins. If employees are authorized to work, but are unable to present the required document(s) within three business days, they must present a receipt for the application of the document(s) within three business days and the actual document(s) within ninety (90) days. However, if employers hire individuals for a duration of less than three business days, Section 2 must be completed at the time employment begins. **Employers must record:** **1)** document title; **2)** issuing authority; **3)** document number, **4)** expiration date, if any; and **5)** the date employment begins. Employers must sign and date the certification. Employees must present original documents. Employers may, but are not required to, photocopy the document(s) presented. These photocopies may only be used for the verification process and must be retained with the I-9. **However, employers are still responsible for completing the I-9.**

Section 3 - Updating and Reverification. Employers must complete Section 3 when updating and/or reverifying the I-9. Employers must reverify employment eligibility of their employees on or before the expiration date recorded in Section 1. Employers **CANNOT** specify which document(s) they will accept from an employee.

- If an employee's name has changed at the time this form is being updated/ reverified, complete Block A.

- If an employee is rehired within three (3) years of the date this form was originally completed and the employee is still eligible to be employed on the same basis as previously indicated on this form (updating), complete Block B and the signature block.

and • If an employee is rehired within three (3) years of the date this form was originally completed and the employee's work authorization has expired **or** if a current employee's work authorization is about to expire (reverification), complete Block B and:
- examine any document that reflects that the employee is authorized to work in the U.S. (see List A **or** C),
- record the document title, document number and expiration date (if any) in Block C, and
- complete the signature block.

Photocopying and Retaining Form I-9. A blank I-9 may be reproduced provided both sides are copied. The Instructions must be available to all employees completing this form. Employers must retain completed I-9s for three (3) years after the date of hire **or** one (1) year after the date employment ends, whichever is later.

For more detailed information, you may refer to the INS Handbook for Employers, (Form M-274). You may obtain the handbook at your local INS office.

Privacy Act Notice. The authority for collecting this information is the Immigration Reform and Control Act of 1986, Pub. L. 99-603 (8 U.S.C. 1324a).

This information is for employers to verify the eligibility of individuals for employment to preclude the unlawful hiring, or recruiting or referring for a fee, of aliens who are not authorized to work in the United States.

This information will be used by employers as a record of their basis for determining eligibility of an employee to work in the United States. The form will be kept by the employer and made available for inspection by officials of the U.S. Immigration and Naturalization Service, the Department of Labor, and the Office of Special Counsel for Immigration Related Unfair Employment Practices.

Submission of the information required in this form is voluntary. However, an individual may not begin employment unless this form is completed since employers are subject to civil or criminal penalties if they do not comply with the Immigration Reform and Control Act of 1986.

Reporting Burden. We try to create forms and instructions that are accurate, can be easily understood, and which impose the least possible burden on you to provide us with information. Often this is difficult because some immigration laws are very complex. Accordingly, the reporting burden for this collection of information is computed as follows: **1)** learning about this form, 5 minutes; **2)** completing the form, 5 minutes; and **3)** assembling and filing (recordkeeping) the form, 5 minutes, for an average of 15 minutes per response. If you have comments regarding the accuracy of this burden estimate, or suggestions for making this form simpler, you can write to both the Immigration and Naturalization Service, 425 I Street, N.W., Room 5304, Washington, D. C. 20536; and the Office of Management and Budget, Paperwork Reduction Project, OMB No. 1115-0136, Washington, D.C. 20503.

Form I-9 (Rev. 11-21-91) N

EMPLOYERS MUST RETAIN COMPLETED I-9
PLEASE DO NOT MAIL COMPLETED I-9 TO INS

U.S. Department of Justice
Immigration and Naturalization Service

OMB No. 1115-0136
Employment Eligibility Verification

Please read instructions carefully before completing this form. The instructions must be available during completion of this form. ANTI-DISCRIMINATION NOTICE. It is illegal to discriminate against work eligible individuals. Employers CANNOT specify which document(s) they will accept from an employee. The refusal to hire an individual because of a future expiration date may also constitute illegal discrimination.

Section 1. Employee Information and Verification. To be completed and signed by employee at the time employment begins

Print Name: Last   First   Middle Initial   Maiden Name

Address *(Street Name and Number)*   Apt. #   Date of Birth *(month/day/year)*

City   State   Zip Code   Social Security #

I am aware that federal law provides for imprisonment and/or fines for false statements or use of false documents in connection with the completion of this form.

I attest, under penalty of perjury, that I am (check one of the following):
A citizen or national of the United States
A Lawful Permanent Resident (Alien # A_____
An alien authorized to work until___/___/___
(Alien # or Admission #_____

Employee's Signature   Date *(month/day/year)*

Preparer and/or Translator Certification. *(To be completed and signed if Section 1 is prepared by a person other than the employee.) I attest, under penalty of perjury, that I have assisted in the completion of this form and that to the best of my knowledge the information is true and correct.*

Preparer's/Translator's Signature   Print Name

Address *(Street Name and Number, City, State, Zip Code)*   Date *(month/day/year)*

Section 2. Employer Review and Verification. To be completed and signed by employer. **Examine one document from List A OR examine one document from List B and one from List C** as listed on the reverse of this form and record the title, number and expiration date, if any, of the document(s)

	List A	OR	List B	AND	List C
Document title:					
Issuing authority:					
Document #:					
Expiration Date *(if any)*:	__/__/__		__/__/__		__/__/__
Document #:					
Expiration Date *(if any)*:	__/__/__				

CERTIFICATION - I attest, under penalty of perjury, that I have examined the document(s) presented by the above-named employee, that the above-listed document(s) appear to be genuine and to relate to the employee named, that the employee began employment on *(month/day/year)* ___/___/___**and that to the best of my knowledge the employee is eligible to work in the United States. (State employment agencies may omit the date the employee began employment).**

Signature of Employer or Authorized Representative   Print Name   Title

Business or Organization Name   Address *(Street Name and Number, City, State, Zip Code)*   Date *(month/day/year)*

Section 3. Updating and Reverification. To be completed and signed by employer

A. New Name *(if applicable)*   B. Date of rehire *(month/day/year) (if applicable)*

C. If employee's previous grant of work authorization has expired, provide the information below for the document that establishes current employment eligibility.
Document Title:_____Document #:_____Expiration Date (if any):__/__/__

I attest, under penalty of perjury, that to the best of my knowledge, this employee is eligible to work in the United States, and if the employee presented document(s), the document(s) I have examined appear to be genuine and to relate to the individual.

Signature of Employer or Authorized Representative   Date *(month/day/year)*

Form I-9 (Rev. 11-21-91) N

LISTS OF ACCEPTABLE DOCUMENTS

LIST A		LIST B		LIST C
Documents that Establish Both Identity and Employment Eligibility	**OR**	**Documents that Establish Identity**	**AND**	**Documents that Establish Employment Eligibility**

LIST A	LIST B	LIST C
1. U.S. Passport (unexpired or expired)	1. Driver's license or ID card issued by a state or outlying possession of the United States provided it contains a photograph or information such as name, date of birth, sex, height, eye color and address	1. U.S. social security card issued by the Social Security Administration *(other than a card stating it is not valid for employment)*
2. Certificate of U.S. Citizenship *(INS Form N-560 or N-561)*	2. ID card issued by federal, state or local government agencies or entities, provided it contains a photograph or information such as name, date of birth, sex, height, eye color and address	2. Certification of Birth Abroad issued by the Department of State *(Form FS-545 or Form DS-1350)*
3. Certificate of Naturalization *(INS Form N-550 or N-570)*	3. School ID card with a photograph	3. Original or certified copy of a birth certificate issued by a state, county, municipal authority or outlying possession of the United States bearing an official seal
4. Unexpired foreign passport, with *I-551 stamp or* attached *INS Form I-94* indicating unexpired employment authorization	4. Voter's registration card	
5. Alien Registration Receipt Card with photograph *(INS Form I-151 or I-551)*	5. U.S. Military card or draft record	4. Native American tribal document
6. Unexpired Temporary Card *(INS Form I-688)*	6. Military dependent's ID card	5. U.S. Citizen ID Card *(INS Form I-197)*
7. Unexpired Employment Authorization Card *(INS Form I-688A)*	7. U.S. Coast Guard Merchant Mariner Card	
8. Unexpired Reentry Permit *(INS Form I-327)*	8. Native American tribal document	6. ID Card for use of Resident Citizen in the United States *(INS Form I-179)*
9. Unexpired Refugee Travel Document *(INS Form I-571)*	9. Driver's license issued by a Canadian government authority	
10. Unexpired Employment Authorization Document issued by the INS which contains a photograph *(INS Form I-688B)*	**For persons under age 18 who are unable to present a document listed above:**	7. Unexpired employment authorization document issued by the INS *(other then those listed under List A)*
	10. School record or report card	
	11. Clinic, doctor or hospital record	
	12. Day-care or nursery school record	

Illustrations of many of these documents appear in Part 8 of the Handbook for Employers (M-274)

Form I-9 (Rev. 11-21-91)N Page 3

Chapter 4

Immigration

Introduction

Formerly known as the Immigration and Naturalization Service (INS), the bureau transitioned into the U.S. Citizenship and Immigration Services (USCIS) under the Department of Homeland Security (DHS). Under immigration laws and regulations, employers may legally hire workers only if they are U.S. citizens or aliens authorized to work in the United States. This chapter addresses the federal rules that govern documentation of eligible employees, antidiscrimination enforcement and temporary and permanent employment of foreign nationals. Per Secs. 274A – 274C of the Immigration and Naturalization Act (INA), all U.S. employers are required to verify that their employees are authorized to work in the United States. Verification is completed upon the submission of Form I-9 by all new hires, accompanied by documentation confirming identity and authorization to work in the United States.

While the purpose of Form I-9 requirements is to eliminate the employment of unauthorized aliens the laws also include provisions, which prohibit discrimination on the basis of citizenship and national origin. As a result, employers may be penalized if they engage in activities, such as demanding specific documents or more documents than required by Form I-9, which could have a disparate impact upon one of the protected classes of job applicants. An employer who demands more documents than the law requires or rejects documents that appear to be genuine may be subject to civil penalties ranging for each individual discriminated against. Employers found to have engaged in unfair immigration-related employment practices (UIREP) may also be subject to penalties for each individual discriminated against. UIREPs include refusing to hire or discharging a protected individual because of national origin or citizenship, requesting specific documents, or rejecting apparently valid documents during employment eligibility verification for the purpose or with the intent of discriminating on the basis of citizenship or national origin.

Form I-9

Form I-9 is required for any-individual hired on or after November 7, 1986 to perform labor or services in return for wages or remuneration. An individual is deemed as hired upon the commencement of employment. Job applicants need not complete Form I-9. Employers who request more or different documentation than the minimum necessary to meet Form I-9 requirements may constitute an UIREP as previously mentioned.

Completing the Form

A Form I-9 should be completed for every employee hired on or after November 7, 1986. Individuals retained to provide services as independent contractors or as employees of contractors (such as temporary employment agencies) are not employees and so not required to complete I-9s.

Employee's Responsibility

New employees must complete Section 1 of a Form I-9 no later than the close of business on the first day of work. The employee is held responsible for the accuracy of the information provided via signature. Any translator or person preparing Section 1 for the employee must also sign the form.

The employee should be given Form I-9 by the employer and asked to provide either one document on List A or one document on each of Lists B and C.

Employer's Responsibility

Employers are responsible for ensuring the completion of the entire Form I-9, including ensuring that the employee completes Section 1 in full. The employer should immediately review Section 1 to ensure proper completion and require the employee to make any necessary corrections. Employers need not receive any documentation to substantiate the employee-provided information in Section 1. However, the employer should supply the employee with the official list of acceptable documents for establishing identity and work eligibility.

The employer must complete Section 2 of the form no later than the close of business on the new employee's third day of employment. To ensure consistency and accuracy, employers should review the information provided in Section 1 against the documents produced by the employee for Section 2. If there is a discrepancy between the two sections, the employee should be given an opportunity to make necessary corrections.

Employers should have a sufficient understanding of the immigration system to know whether a proffered document is consistent with an employee's claimed status, although, the employer is not required to be a document expert. The employer can consult the USCIS handbook, however be advised that it does not contain all variations of every document that can be submitted. If a document is approved and does not appear to have been tampered with or to be forged, the employer should accept it. In fact, employers should accept any document specified on Form I-9, provided that it appears genuine and relates to the employee. Employers should neither ask for an USCIS document to confirm the expiration date of work authorization nor consider the expiration date of work authorization in making the hiring decision.

Employers are not required to make copies of the documents that are produced for Section 2. However, employers may attach photocopies of documentation submitted to satisfy Form I-9 requirements to the employee's Form I-9. This must be consistently applied to every employee, without regard to citizenship or national origin, should employers choose to make and attach photocopies.

Employers should be particularly careful when an employee offers a filing receipt instead of an actual document. There are four situations in which a filing receipt is acceptable as follows:

♦ The filing receipt indicates that the employee has applied for a replacement List A, B, or C document because the original was lost, stolen, or damaged (the actual document must be submitted within 90 days after the date of hire).

♦ The filing receipt is a temporary I-551 stamp (green card) in the employee's passport or on a Form I-94 until the indicated expiration date or, if there is no expiration date, one year from the date of issuance.

♦ The filing receipt takes the form of a refugee admission stamp on a Form I-94 (an employment authorization card, Form I-766, or a Social Security card must be submitted within 90 days after the date of hire).

♦ The filing receipt is for an application to renew an H, L, E, O, or P visa with the same employer (the USCIS approval notice or new visa and Form I-94 must be submitted within 240 days after expiration of the present period of authorized stay).

Employers must retain Form I-9 for the longer of three years from the date of hire or one year after termination of the employment relationship. A safer way of implementing this requirement is to keep Form I-9 for at least three years after the termination of employment. The employer must have an I-9 on file for all current employees other than employees hired after November 6, 1986.

Documents Establishing Identity and Eligibility

List A

The following documents are included in List A:

♦ U.S. passport (unexpired or expired).

♦ Unexpired foreign passport, with I-551 stamp; or with attached Form I-94 indicating unexpired employment authorization for specific employer.

♦ Permanent Resident Card or Alien Registration Receipt Card with photograph (Form I-551).

♦ Unexpired Temporary Resident Card (Form I-688).

♦ Unexpired Employment Authorization Card (Form I-688A).

♦ Unexpired Employment Authorization Document issued by the USCIS that contains a photograph (Form I-688B or I-766).

List B

The following documents may also be used to establish identity:

♦ Driver's license or ID card issued by a state or outlying possession provided it contains a photograph or information such as name, date of birth, gender, height, eye color, and address.

♦ ID card issued by federal, state, or local government agencies or entities, provided it contains a photograph or information such as name, date of birth, gender, height, eye color, and address.

♦ School identification card with a photograph.

♦ Voter's Registration Card.

♦ U.S. Military card or draft record.

♦ Military dependent's ID card.

♦ U.S. Coast Guard Merchant Mariner Card.

♦ Native American tribal document.

♦ Driver's license issued by a Canadian government authority.

♦ School record or report card, child care or nursery school record, or clinic doctor or hospital record (for individuals under age 18 who are unable to produce an identity document).

List C

The following documents may be used to establish employment eligibility:

- U.S. Social Security card issued by the Social Security Administration (other than a card stating it is not valid for employment).

- Certification of Birth Abroad issued by the Department of State, Form FS-545, or Form DS-1350.

- Original birth certificate issued by a state, county, municipal authority, or outlying possession of the United States bearing an official seal.

- Native American tribal document.

- U.S. Citizen ID Card (Form I-197).

- Identification card for use of a resident citizen in the United States (Form I-179).

- Unexpired employment authorization document issued by the USCIS (other than those listed under List A).

Employee's Failure to Produce Documents

Employers should terminate an employee who fails to produce the required documents for employment within three business days of the date employment begins. An employee may present a receipt for a replacement document (in the case of lost, stolen, or destroyed documents) as a temporary solution. However, if an employee has presented a receipt for a replacement document, the employee must produce the actual document within 90 days of when employment began. Employers must apply these practices uniformly to all employees because without uniformity a termination may be grounds for a discrimination lawsuit.

Penalties

The USCIS is authorized to enforce the requirements on employment eligibility verification. Employers who fail to properly complete, retain, and/or make available for inspections Forms I-9 may incur civil penalties between $110 and $1,100 for each employee for which the form was incorrect.

Employers who knowingly hired unauthorized aliens or knowingly continue to employ aliens who have become unauthorized to work in the United States may be ordered to cease and desist from such activity and pay the following for each unauthorized alien:

- **First Offense:** Between $275 and $2,200.

- **Second Offense:** Between $2,200 and $5,500.

- **Subsequent Offenses:** Between $3,300 and $11,000.

Liability is also imposed when an employer uses a contract or subcontract — renegotiated or extended — to obtain the labor of an alien and knew the alien was not authorized to work in the United States.

Employers who require a bond or indemnity from an employee against liability may be incur a penalty of $1,000 for each violation and ordered to make restitution, either to the person who was required to pay the indemnity or to the U.S. Treasury.

Criminal penalties of up to $3,000 in fines and imprisonment for up to six months are possible when a pattern or practice of knowingly employing unauthorized workers is demonstrated. People who use fraudulent identification or employment eligibility documents, documents that were lawfully issued to another person, or who make a false statement or attestation for purposes of satisfying the employment eligibility verification requirements, may be fined, imprisoned for up to five years, or both.

Good Faith Defense

If an employer can show compliance with the Form I-9 requirements, then the employer has established a good faith defense with respect to a charge of knowingly hiring an unauthorized alien unless the government can show that the employer had actual knowledge of the unauthorized status of the employee.

Antidiscrimination Enforcement

The Department of Justice's Office of Special Counsel and the USCIS are authorized to enforce the antidiscrimination provisions of the law. Employers are prohibited from discriminating when hiring or promoting on the basis of national origin citizenship status. The responsibility for investigating and prosecuting claims of discrimination resides with the Department of Justice. An employer may be required to hire, promote, reinstate, and pay back salary, and/or attorneys' fees to a successful discrimination complainant. In addition, the employer may be assessed a large civil penalty for each offense. These enforcement efforts are generally paired with Office of Federal Contract Compliance Program or Wage-and-Hour-Division inspections.

Employment of Non-U.S. Citizens

Temporary Employment

H-1B Classification

The H-1B is a nonimmigrant classification used by an alien and provides temporary admission to the United States for professionals in specialty occupations. A *specialty occupation* is an occupation that requires theoretical and practical application of a body of highly specialized knowledge. The individual must posses at the minimum a bachelor's degree in the specific specialty prior to consideration for entry into the occupation. For example, mathematics, physical sciences, medicine and health, and the arts are recognized specialty occupations. With exceptions, an alien can hold H1-B status for a maximum of six consecutive years. H1-B status will be initially granted for a term of three years and can be renewed for an additional three years. After six years, an alien must remain outside the United States for one year before another H1-B petition can be approved. Certain aliens working on Department of Defense projects may remain in H1-B status for 10 years.

H1-B status requires a sponsoring U.S. employer. Before filing the H-1B *Nonimmigrant Visa Petition*, employers will need to file a *Labor Condition Application* with the U.S. Department of Labor that certifies the following:

- ◆ The employer is offering the position at the higher of the actual wage or the prevailing wage and with working conditions that will not adversely affect similarly employed U.S. workers.

- ◆ The employer will offer benefits to H1-B employees on the same basis as similarly employed U.S. workers.

- ◆ There is not a strike or lockout involving the position at the place of employment.

- ◆ The employer has provided notice of the petition to any bargaining representative or has posted notice of the petition in conspicuous locations at the place of employment if there is no bargaining representative.

- ◆ The employer will provide a copy of the completed, required application to the H-1B workers.

The U.S. Department of Labor established procedures for receipt, investigation, and disposition of complaints filed by any party. If the department finds the complaints to be justified, it may sanction the employer in the following ways:

 ♦ Impose a civil monetary fine from $1,000 to $35,000 per violation, depending upon the type and severity of the violation.

 ♦ Bar the employer from having H-1B petitions approved for at least one year.

 ♦ Impose possible reinstatement and backpay awards.

Note: Only 65,000 aliens may be issued a visa or otherwise provided H1-B status for fiscal years 2004 and beyond.

H-2B Certification

The H-2B certification allows employers to hire foreign workers to come to the United States and perform temporary nonagricultural work. This temporary employment may be one-time, seasonal, peak load, or intermittent, and the job must be for less than one year. Importantly, the H-2B certification is issued to the employer, not the worker, and is not transferable from one employer to another or from one worker to another. The total number of employees who may be issued H-2B visas per fiscal year may not exceed 66,000.

H-2B status is available when the following criteria are met:

 ♦ An employee has a residence in a foreign country with no intention of abandoning that country.

 ♦ An employee is coming to the United States to perform temporary services or labor in a temporary position.

 ♦ Qualified persons willing to perform such service or labor at the prevailing wage cannot be found in the United States.

Employers submitting H-2B petitions must consider available U.S. workers for the temporary services or labor to be performed. Employers must also offer U.S. workers terms and conditions of employment that are consistent with the nature of the occupation, the activity, and the industry in the United States. H-2B workers may not displace U.S. workers capable of performing such services or labor or adversely affect the wages and working conditions of U.S. workers.

An *Application for Alien Labor Certification* must be filed with the local State Workforce Agency (SWA) serving the area of proposed employment. The SWA then forwards the application to the appropriate regional office within the U.S. Department of Labor. This certification, which is issued by the Department of Labor, demonstrates that qualified workers in the United States are not available and that the terms of employment will not adversely affect wages and working conditions of similarly employed U.S. workers. The department's decision to grant or deny certification is only offered as an advisory opinion to the USCIS. For example, if the Department of Labor denies certification, the employer may still file with the USCIS and the USCIS may grant the certification, regardless of the previous denial.

The purpose of the certification is for employers to offer the certification as support for a visa petition that is filed with the district director of the USCIS. To obtain the H-2B work visa, the employer uses Form I-129, *Petition for Nonimmigrant Worker*. The labor certification determination and the Form I-129 are submitted to the USCIS along with filing fees.

An approved H-2B petition is valid for a maximum of 364 days. Employers can apply for recertification for an additional two years, as long as on each new application the employer justifies the reason for the renewal request.

E-1 (Trader) and E-2 (Investor)

E-1 and E-2 visas allow foreign nationals to come to the United States to conduct trade or to manage substantial investments. Treaty traders or investors are individuals from a country with a treaty of commerce and navigation or equivalent agreement with the United States. The requirements for traders or investors to conduct business in the United States are as follows:

♦ Nationals of the foreign country must have majority ownership and control of the business.

♦ Each employee or principal of the organization who seeks entry into the United States under the treaty must hold citizenship of the same country as the majority owners of the organization.

♦ Such person must be considered an E-1 Trader or an E-2 Investor as follows:

  • An *E-1 (Trader)* is one who enters solely to carry on substantial-trade, including trade in services or in technology, principally between the United States and the foreign state of which the trader is a national.

  • An *E-2 (Investor)* is one who enters solely to develop and direct the operations of an enterprise in which they have invested or is in the process of actively investing a substantial amount of capital. The amount of investment needed to qualify as "substantial" will vary, depending on the nature of the business, but in general, the investment will need to be in excess of $100,000 at risk. New businesses must show the investment is an amount normally considered necessary to establish a viable enterprise of the nature contemplated. Ongoing businesses must show the investment is an amount sufficient to cover operating expenses.

♦ A foreign employee of treaty investors must be employed in a responsible capacity. The employee must assume a managerial position or be a highly trained or specially qualified person.

L-1 Intra-Company Transferee

The L-1 visa category is for intra-company transferee.

L-1A Managerial or Executive Transferee

An L-1A is an alien coming temporarily to perform services in a managerial or executive capacity. This intra-company transferee is a person who worked for an organization abroad in an executive-managerial, or specialized knowledge capacity for at least one year within the three years prior to coming to the United States and is coming to work for a related (parent, subsidiary, affiliate, or branch) company in a managerial or executive position. The initial L visa petition for managers or executives is granted for a period of up to three years and may be renewed in increments of up to two years, with a maximum stay of seven years. A petition filed by a *new office* (an office, subsidiary, or affiliate which has been established in the U.S. for less than one year) will be approved for only a one-year period. The employer may thereafter file extensions in increments of two years, with evidence that the employer has successfully commenced business operations.

L-1B Specialized Knowledge

An L-1B is an alien coming temporarily to perform services that entail specialized knowledge. An L-1B alien must meet the same time and prior employment requirements as an L-1A (employed for at least one year, etc.). An individual with specialized knowledge is thoroughly learned in regard to the employer's product or its application in international markets and the employer's processes and procedures.

L-1B workers hold positions that require the theoretical and practical application of a body of highly specialized knowledge to fully perform the occupation. Such a classification requires the completion of a specific course of education culminating in a baccalaureate degree in a specific occupational specialty. The total period of time an L-1B recipient may stay within the United States is five years.

Individual L Petitions

Requirements for an individual L petition are as follows:

♦ The employer abroad and the petitioning U.S. organization must be properly related. For example, enjoy parent-subsidiary, sibling, joint venture, or affiliate relationships.

♦ The transferee must have worked in a managerial, executive, or specialized knowledge capacity for the employer abroad for at least one continuous year within the three years immediately preceding entry into the United States.

♦ The transferee must be coming to work for the U.S. employer in a managerial, executive, or specialized knowledge capacity for a temporary period.

♦ In addition, to obtain an L-1B visa for specialized personnel continuing employment with an international firm or corporation, the employer must justify its need for the transferee's specialized knowledge in the United States.

Blanket L Petitions

A blanket L petition simplifies the process of later filing for individual L-1A and L-1B workers. A U.S. employer, who will be the single representative between the USCIS and the qualifying organizations, must file the blanket L petition.

Requirements for a blanket L petition are as follows:

♦ The organization and each of the entities must be engaged in commercial trade or services.

♦ The organization has an office in the United States conducting business for at least one year.

♦ The organization has three or more domestic and foreign branches, subsidiaries, or affiliates.

♦ The organization has obtained petitions for at least 10 "L" managers or executives during the previous 12 months.

♦ The organization has U.S. subsidiaries or affiliates with combined annual sales of at least $25 million or a U.S. workforce of at least 1,000 employees.

O-1 Extraordinary Ability Nationals

A An O-1 visa is for aliens with extraordinary ability in the sciences, arts, education, business, or athletics and may be granted only after consultation by the USCIS with peer groups in the area of the alien's ability. Thus in the case of a person seeking entry for a motion picture or television production, consultation shall occur with the appropriate union representing the occupational peers and with the management organization in the area of the ability of the applicant. An individual seeking an O visa is mostly likely at the top of the profession or endeavor for which admittance into the United States is being sought. An employer must petition for the alien and the statutory requirements of O-1 visa.

To be eligible for this type of O visa, an alien must posses the following:

♦ Extraordinary ability in the sciences, arts, education, business, or athletics as demonstrated by sustained national or international acclaim or a record of extraordinary achievement.

♦ Achievements recognized in the field through extensive documentation.

♦ Intent to enter the United States to continue work in the area of extraordinary ability.

The O visa may be issued for three years; thereafter one-year increments may be sought to complete the activity, event, or project in which the alien is participating.

Permanent Employment

The INA provides a yearly minimum of 140,000 employment-based immigrant visas divided into five preference classifications. The first, second, and third priority workers receive 28.6 percent of the yearly worldwide limit of visas.

- ♦ **First Preference: Priority Workers**. The subcategories of priority workers are as follows:

  - Persons of extraordinary ability.

  - Outstanding professors and researchers.

  - Certain multinational executives and managers.

- ♦ **Second Preference: Advanced Degree or Exceptional Ability Aliens.** Qualified employee immigrants must be members of the professions holding advanced degrees (or the equivalent) or have exceptional ability in sciences, arts, professions, or business that will substantially benefit the national economy of the United States. The requirements of a job offer and labor certification may be waived if a determination is made that it would be in the national interest to admit an applicant for lawful permanent residence.

- ♦ **Third Preference: Skilled Workers, Professionals, and Other Workers.** This category includes the following:

  - *Skilled workers* are defined as aliens capable of performing a job requiring at least two years of experience or training.

  - *Professionals* are defined as immigrants who hold baccalaureate degrees (for example, bachelors' degrees in engineering, computer science, or economics) and are members of a profession.

  - *Other workers* are defined as immigrants petitioning for classification as unskilled labor that requires less than two years of training or experience.

- ♦ **Fourth Preference: Special Immigrants**. Special immigrants receive 7.1 percent of the yearly worldwide limit. This category includes the following subgroups:

  - Religious workers coming to carry on the vocation of a minister of religion, to work in a professional capacity in a religious vocation, or to work for a tax-exempt organization affiliated with a religious denomination.

  - Overseas employees of the U.S. government, consulate, and embassy offices.

  - Former employees of the Panama Canal Company and their families.

  - Foreign medical graduates.

  - Retired employees of international organizations and their family members.

  - Certain members of the U.S. Armed Forces.

- ♦ **Fifth Preference: Employment Creation Investors**. Employment Creation Investors receive 7.1 percent of the yearly worldwide limit. To qualify for this employment-based preference category, a foreign investor must establish a new commercial enterprise and invest $500,000 (in areas of high unemployment) or $1 million (in areas of normal unemployment) in the new enterprise. The new investment must create at least 10 full-time jobs for U.S. workers, excluding the investor and immediate family members.

Note: The second and third preferences for advanced degree or exceptional ability aliens and for skilled workers, professionals, and other workers require labor certification before a permanent visa can be issued. An employer must file a labor certification application with the State Workforce Agency (SWA) in the state where the alien is to be employed. Additionally, supporting documentation of the alien's qualifications and the employer's recruiting efforts must be provided with the application.

Wages

Wages offered to the alien must meet or exceed the prevailing wage for that occupation. All job requirements must be reasonable and minimum, as provided by federal and applicable state laws.

Recruiting

The employer must demonstrate to the U.S. Department of Labor their attempts to recruit U.S. workers and must also adhere to the following requirements:

♦ In an attempt to recruit U.S. workers a job order must run for a minimum of 30 days through the National Employment Service recruitment system.

♦ The employer must conspicuously post the job opening on the premises for at least 10 days.

♦ The employer must place an advertisement for the job in a newspaper of general circulation or in a professional, trade, or ethnic publication — whichever will elicit responses from U.S. workers.

  • If published in a newspaper of general circulation, the advertisement must be published for at least three consecutive days.

  • If published in a professional, trade, or ethnic publication, the advertisement must be published in the next published edition.

An employer may request a reduction in recruitment efforts upon the demonstration of the employer's adequate testing of the labor market with no success at recruiting a U.S. worker. An employer's request for a reduction in recruitment (RIR) must contain the following:

♦ Evidence that the employer conducted substantial recruitment during the six months immediately prior to the filing of the labor certification.

♦ The employer has made good faith efforts to recruit U.S. workers for the job.

If a union represents the organization's employees in the occupational classification and geographical areas for which aliens are sought, the law requires employers to notify a union representative or bargaining agent that such alien labor certification application has been filed. If no such bargaining agent or representative exists, the employer must post a notice conspicuously on its premises informing its employees that an alien labor certification application has been filed.

Additional Information

Contact Information

U.S. Citizenship and Immigration Services

U.S. Citizenship and Immigration Services (USCIS) is located within the Department of Homeland Security (DHS). The USCIS was once in the former Immigration and Naturalization Service (INS).

U.S. Citizenship and Immigration Services (USCIS)
Telephone (Toll-Free): 800-375-5283
Forms Line (Toll-Free): 800-870-3676
Internet: *www.uscis.gov*

Office of Business Liaison

The primary function of the Office of Business Liaison (OBL) is to educate the United States public on immigration-related employment, investment, and school issues. The OBL provides information on the employment eligibility verification process, as well as the opportunities available to employers to hire and/or "sponsor" foreign workers in accordance with U.S. government regulations administered by a variety of federal agencies

Office of Business Liaison
 20 Massachusetts Avenue, NW
Room 2000
Washington, DC 20529

Telephone (Toll-Free): 800-357-2099
TDD (Toll-Free): 800-767-1833
Fax: 202-272-1864
Internet: *http://uscis.gov/graphics/services/employerinfo/oblhome.htm*

Chapter 5
Employee Handbooks

Introduction

A properly drafted employee handbook relays valuable information about the organization and its policies. It helps management promote nonarbitrary, consistent application of its policies and practices. However, lawsuits based on language contained in employee handbooks and other written employment policies are common. Because improperly drafted employee handbooks and policy and procedure manuals can appear to be contractual, potential problems arise for unsuspecting employers. Employers should continuously review their handbooks and policy and procedure manuals to determine whether they contain language that can lead to a wrongful discharge suit or other employment claim. Furthermore, when an employer distributes a handbook or policy and procedure manual to employees, it should always follow the specific terms and conditions of employment described in the document.

Drafting Employee Handbooks

Each employer must decide whether it needs or wants to develop an employee handbook or policy manual. When the employer decides to do so, the provisions of the handbook or manual must be tailored to the employer's specific characteristics, such as the following:

- Size.
- Public vs. private.
- Unionized vs. nonunionized.
- Industrial, professional, or service orientated.
- Other relevant characteristics.

The law may provide certain rights and privileges to public employees that are not applicable to employees in the private sector. Examples of these laws include the following:

- Disability.
- Pension funds.
- Civil service laws.

The handbook or policy manual should always be reviewed to make sure that the written language actually means what it says. It should not say or imply something about the employment relationship that the organization does not intend.

Every word of an employee handbook should be read carefully to see if it can be interpreted to mean something different from what the organization intended it to mean. In other words, the handbook should "say what it means and mean what it says." Furthermore, any promises or guarantees in a handbook or policy manual should be removed unless an employer is prepared carry them out.

Contract Disclaimers and Employment-at-Will Policies

Many states allow employees to bring breach of contract lawsuits because of statements made in their employee handbooks. Consequently, every handbook in a prominent place should contain disclaimer and employment-at-will language similar to the following:

"The employee is aware that this Employee Handbook is not intended to create a contract of employment. Rather, it is simply intended to describe the ABC Company and its present policies and procedures. These policies and procedures, which supersede all prior policies and procedures, may, and likely will be, changed from time to time, as the ABC Company deems appropriate. Further, your employment and compensation can be terminated, with or without cause, and with or without notice, at any time at the option of ABC Company. No one other than the President of the ABC Company has the authority to enter into any agreement — oral or written — with any individual for employment for any specified period of time. Any such agreement with the President must be an individual agreement in writing and signed by you and the President. No one has the authority to make verbal statements of any kind that are legally binding on the ABC Company."

Promises of Job Security, Promotions, Vested Benefits, Education, Etc.

An employer should review handbooks regularly to ensure that promises or representations are not being made with respect to "job security" or promotional opportunities. Employees often file a lawsuit based on such promises. These statements are often found in the introductory portions of a handbook or policy manual. An employer might state that its goal is to provide employees with "job security" and a long, rewarding career, or make assurances that "employees can look forward to promising careers as long as their work is satisfactory."

Use Clear and Concise Language

The provisions should clearly and accurately describe the employer's practices and policies and avoid interpretations the employer does not intend. In this regard, individual provisions that do not apply to certain employees otherwise covered by the handbook should clearly indicate which employees are covered. For example, many employers do not grant vacation or other benefits to part-time employees, or only grant such benefits on a prorated basis. Therefore, these provisions should clearly identify which employees are eligible for the described benefits.

Specifically Allow for Flexibility and Modification

It is neither possible nor practical to address in a handbook every policy or employment situation that may arise. Therefore, an employer should specifically state that the handbook is not all-inclusive and contains only general statements of company policies. It should also be stated that provisions may be modified at the employer's discretion. Moreover, certain individual provisions, such as discipline rules, should also specifically retain management flexibility and clearly state that the terms are not all inclusive.

Permanent Employment

All references to "permanent employment" in the handbook should be eliminated and replaced with the term "regular full-time employment." In defining "regular full-time employment," an employer should also state that an employee is hired for no definite period of time. This type of language makes it more difficult to conclude that an employment contract for a specified period of time exists or that an employee has been hired permanently.

Who the Handbook Applies To

Every handbook must specify which employees the handbook covers. In most cases, the handbook will apply to all employees. For certain other employers, it may be necessary to distinguish certain types of employees, such as the following examples:

- ◆ A collective-bargaining agreement.
- ◆ Salaried and hourly employees.
- ◆ Employees in various locations.
- ◆ Senior executives.

When the handbook applies to all employees, a simple statement to this effect will suffice: "Unless otherwise stated, the provisions of this handbook apply to all company employees."

When some employees are covered by a labor union, include a statement like the following: "For those employees covered by a labor contract between the organization and the union, the terms of the labor contract are intended to control where a direct conflict exists."

Policies to Include

Acknowledgment and Receipt

Employers must distribute an acknowledgment and receipt form signed by employees and returned for placement in their records. This form evidences receipt, understanding, and agreement to abide by the provisions of the handbook. This form establishes that employees had notice of employer policies, expectations, and prohibitions and is critical when defending a wrongful termination claim.

Arbitration

Employers should not include agreements to arbitrate employment termination or other disputes. Arbitration agreements should be a separately executed document.

Discipline of Employees

Employers should make performance standards, personal conduct required in the workplace, and any other conduct that could result in discipline clear to all employees. These should be conditions of employment. Such conditions include arriving to work on time, not drinking during working hours, and not using illegal narcotics. This policy must specifically indicate the potential discipline for violation and must be applied uniformly to all employees.

Hours of Work

Employers should include an "hours of work" section for the following:

 ♦ Work schedules.

 ♦ Breaks and meal periods.

 ♦ Workweek.

 ♦ Overtime provisions.

 ♦ A method for recording work time.

 ♦ Additional work requirements.

Note: These must be applied uniformly to all employees based upon status as exempt or nonexempt.

Job Abandonment

Neither federal nor state law regulates the amount of time an employer must hold a job for an employee who neither appears for work nor calls in to explain reasons for the absence. Company policy is the sole means of the employers' control in these situations. Most companies use the "no-call, no-show" policy which means employees will be considered as having quit employment if "no-call, no-show" occurs for two or more scheduled workdays.

Employers may indicate that exceptions may be made for emergencies but must specifically identify what is or is not an emergency. This policy must be applied uniformly to all employees to help prevent discrimination claims.

Job Requirements

Employers have complete control over the work requirements for jobs offered by the organization. Employers should continuously review job descriptions and requirements to fulfill changing needs.

Safety

Employers should inform all employees of work safety and/or conduct rules required to meet the employers' expectations regarding workplace behavior. Employers should not include references to disciplinary consequences for particular acts or omissions in order to avoid claims that termination actions may only be taken for "just cause."

EEO Policy

Various laws that prohibit discrimination on the basis of certain protected characteristics cover most employers. An employee handbook should include a provision such as the following indicating the employer's intent to comply with all applicable federal, state, and local antidiscrimination laws:

> "The ABC Company affords equal opportunity to all qualified persons and does not without regard to race, color, creed, religion, age, sex, national origin, ancestry, disability, or any other legally protected status in accordance with applicable local, state, and federal law. This policy is applicable to all aspects of the employment experience, including recruitment, hiring, compensation, layoff, discharge, training, and all other terms, conditions, or privileges of employment."

When the employer is a federal government contractor, veteran status should be included in this provision. When the facilities are located in only one state, employers may want to include the protected classes covered by the state's law.

Harassment Policy

Employers should establish a specific written policy prohibiting harassment — particularly sexual harassment. The harassment policy should set forth a procedure by which all complaints will be investigated, and give assurances that no employee will be retaliated against for reporting any harassment. A sample **Harassment Policy** is located at the end of this chapter.

Note: A sexual harassment policy may be encompassed within a general harassment policy that prohibits harassment based upon other protected characteristics, such as race, age, sex, or disability.

No Solicitation/No Distribution Policy

Employers may want to establish a no solicitation/no distribution policy. Such rules must be carefully drafted to comply with legal restrictions developed under the National Labor Relations Act (NLRA). Additionally, employers should be aware that a valid no solicitation/no distribution rule may nevertheless be unlawful if it is enforced in an inconsistent, discriminatory manner. Finally, somewhat different rules apply to health care facilities and to retail stores than to other employers.

The policy should be worded in the following manner:

♦ Solicitations will not be permitted during working time or during nonworking time in areas where it will disturb other employees who are working. Distribution or circulation of printed material by employees will not be permitted during working time or during nonworking times in areas where it will disturb other employees who are working, nor will distribution be permitted at any time, including working and nonworking time, in working areas.

♦ Working time refers to that portion of any workday during which an employee is supposed to be performing actual job duties; it does not include other duty-free periods of time.

♦ Solicitation and distribution by nonemployees on company property or within the confines of company premises is strictly prohibited. The sole exception to this rule's restrictions is the allowance of an annual campaign for the local government.

Job Classifications

Employers may choose to adopt job classification systems. For purposes of salary administration and eligibility for overtime payments and employee benefits, an organization may classify its employees as follows:

♦ **Regular Full-Time Employees.** Employees hired to work the organization's normal, full-time 40-hour workweek on a regular basis. Such employees may be exempt or nonexempt as defined by applicable wage and hour laws.

♦ **Regular Part-Time Employees.** Employees hired to work fewer than 40 hours per week on a regular basis. Such employees may be exempt or nonexempt as defined by applicable wage and hour laws.

♦ **Temporary Employees.** Employees engaged to work full-time or part-time by the organization for a specified period of time or for a specific assignment. (Note that a temporary employee may be offered and may accept a new temporary assignment with the organization and still retain temporary status. Employees hired from temporary employment agencies for specific assignments are employees of the respective agency and not of the organization.)

Wage Payment Policies

Most states require an employer to notify employees of its pay period and procedures. Handbooks or policy manuals are a good way to ensure that employees are notified of pay procedures. They can also be used to explain overtime compensation procedures.

Regular Pay Procedures Statement

A handbook may include a statement covering regular pay procedures. For example:

All employees are normally paid by check on a weekly or biweekly basis. If a scheduled payday falls on a Saturday, Sunday, or company-observed holiday, employees will be paid on the preceding weekday. All required deductions, such as federal, state, and local taxes, and all authorized voluntary deductions, will be withheld automatically from employee paychecks.

Employees should review their paycheck for errors. If an employee finds a mistake, it should be reported to the supervisor immediately. The supervisor will help employee take the steps necessary to correct the error.

Overtime Statement

Additionally, a handbook may incorporate an overtime policy statement, such as the following:

Nonexempt employees will receive overtime pay, at a rate of one and one-half times the employee's regular straight-time rate, for all hours worked in excess of 40 hours in any given workweek. Overtime provisions must be in accordance with the requirements of federal and/or state law. Any hours worked in excess of 40 hours per week must be authorized in advance by the employee's supervisor or the supervisor must be aware that an employee is working overtime. Employees who work overtime without obtaining proper authorization may be subject to discipline by the employer. However, the employee will be paid. For purposes of overtime calculations, hours paid for time off for any reason whatsoever will not be deemed hours worked in accordance with applicable state and federal law. Examples of these types of hours include lunch, vacation holiday, illness, or other causes.

Time Sheets

Employers should maintain specific records of hours worked by nonexempt employees. It is helpful to explain general time-keeping requirements in the employee handbook as follows:

- ♦ It is necessary to maintain accurate and complete records of time worked. Therefore, the following should apply to all nonexempt employees:
  - Time sheets or time cards are to be turned in daily.
  - Employees are to record their starting time, time in and out for lunch or other unpaid breaks, quitting time, and total hours worked for each workday.
  - Overtime must be pre-approved by a supervisor or department head, one of whom must also indicate that approval by signing a time sheet where the approved overtime hours are recorded.
- ♦ Employees will not be required or permitted to work any period of time before or after scheduled starting or quitting times for the purpose of making up time lost due to tardiness, unauthorized absence, authorized absence or any other reason, except with the prior approval of their supervisor or department head.

Attendance

Employee absenteeism is one of the most frequent problems faced by employers and is also the most frequent cause of discipline. Specific procedures for reporting absences should be included in the employee handbook.

Employees are expected to report to work whenever scheduled and be at their workstation at their starting time and again after their lunch break at the prescribed time. Failure to observe working hours reduces productivity and places an unfair burden on fellow employees.

Whenever an employee is unable to report to work because of illness or emergency, the employee must call a supervisor as far in advance as possible before a scheduled shift time, or in the event of an emergency, as soon as practicable. If the supervisor is unavailable, employees should notify a department head. Such notification should include a reason for the absence or tardiness and an indication of when the employee can be expected to report to work. The absent employee is responsible for ensuring that proper advance notice of absence or late arrival is given to the employee's supervisor or department head.

Messages left with co-workers or other employees are not acceptable.

Failure to provide proper notification of an absence or lateness, unexcused absences, late arrivals or early departures from work may result in disciplinary action, up to and including discharge.

Any employee who fails to report to work for up to three consecutive workdays, and fails to notify the supervisor in advance of the reason for the failure to report to work, will be considered to have resigned a position with the organization.

Vacations and Holidays

Most states have laws that address issues regarding the accrual of and payment for holidays and vacation time, particularly upon termination. Such state laws and regulations will determine the appropriate language.

Samples of vacation and holiday polices are locate at the end of this chapter.

Employee Assistance Programs

When an employer decides to provide its employees with an employee assistance program (EAP), the employee handbook is a good place to notify employees of its availability.

Please see the end of this chapter for a sample **EAP Statement**.

Salary and Performance Reviews

Salary review and performance reviews can lead to legal problems and affect employee morale unless they are done objectively and consistently.

A sample **Salary and Performance Review Policy** is included at the end of this chapter.

Probationary Periods

Many employers have policies that establish probationary periods so that they can evaluate an employee's work performance and presumably terminate the employee without following any progressive procedures. However, employers must carefully word any probationary policy because the establishment of a probationary period implies that once employees complete the period they may be terminated only for just cause. In that regard, the concept of "probationary employee" is inconsistent with the concept of an "at-will employee."

Employers who choose to implement probationary periods should initially consider changing the title from "probationary period" to "introductory period" or use some other language that does not implicitly promise additional rights upon completion of the period. In addition, it should be stated that when an employee completes probation, the relationship with the employer is still one of employment-at-will. To set the introductory period apart from an implied promise of continued employment, an employer might link the completion of the period with the commencement of a benefit, such as eligibility for holiday pay.

Group Health Insurance Benefits

The employee handbook should only provide a general description of available benefit programs. Employees should be referred to summary plan descriptions or master plan documents for a detailed outline of their benefits. An employer should review the benefit plan documents with legal counsel regularly to insure compliance with the federal Employee Retirement Income Security Act (ERISA).

The following language can be used as an introduction for group employment benefits:

♦ The organization's group insurance benefit program includes a medical plan, life insurance, and disability insurance. Full-time employees and part-time employees normally scheduled to work at least 30 hours per week may be eligible for these group insurance benefits. Additional information, including summary plan descriptions, which explain coverage of employee benefits in greater detail, is available in the human resources department.

♦ The actual plan documents or the summary plan descriptions are the final authorities in all matters relative to the benefits described in this handbook and will govern in the event of any conflict. The organization reserves the rights to change or eliminate benefits at any time in accordance with applicable law.

Family and Medical Leave Act Policy

When an employer distributes handbooks to employees concerning leaves, wages, attendance and similar matters, and the employer is covered by the Family and Medical Leave Act (FMLA), the employer should include information concerning FMLA rights and the employer's policies regarding FMLA leave in the handbook. Some states have family leave laws which provide additional benefits and should be also explained in this section as well.

Unless greater rights are provided under applicable state law, employees who work in a facility where there are 50 or more employees employed within a 75-mile radius may be eligible for unpaid Family and Medical Leave in accordance with the FMLA. A sample **FMLA Policy** is included at the end of this chapter.

Time Off

Federal and state laws also require employers to grant other types of leaves of absence, such as military leave, jury/witness duty leave, and voting leave. In addition to the federal law, several states also have parental and disability leave requirements. Employers need to review their leave policies with legal counsel regularly to insure compliance with applicable state or federal laws. A sample **Leave of Absence Policy** is included at the end of this chapter.

Searches

An employee will usually be deemed to have a higher expectation of privacy concerning his or her own person, as compared to places where personal effects are kept. Accordingly, body searches create a more serious threat to an employee's privacy, but fewer restrictions exist on the right of a private sector employer to search articles on its premises.

Searches of the Person

Body searches may consist of pat-down or strip searches. In determining whether or not a body search invades a person's privacy, courts consider whether there was a compelling need for the search and whether it was conducted in the least intrusive manner possible. It is difficult to demonstrate a compelling and reasonable need for an intrusive body search in most employment contexts.

Searches of Personal Items

In contrast to the strong restrictions against body searches, private sector employers can generally search employees' desks, lockers, cars, and other areas of personal space, as long as the search is done for legitimate work-related reasons and the search itself is reasonable in scope. In other words, employees may still prevail in privacy claims arising from a search if they can show they had a reasonable expectation of privacy in the area searched or that the search was conducted in a manner that is highly offensive to a reasonable person.

Electronic Communications

Employers have always found it necessary to monitor an employee's job performance for quality, efficiency, and productivity. Traditionally, they have relied on supervisors for that purpose. Increasingly, however, employers are using workplace technology to monitor employees. Typically monitored might be telephone calls, computer files, electronic mail, and voice mail. In some industries, listening to employees' telephone conversations or viewing employees' computer files gives employers an accurate picture of the employee's contact with clients and the public, and helps monitor nonbusiness related uses.

While technological advances have assisted employers in their monitoring efforts, those advances also have enabled employers to obtain virtually unlimited amounts of information about their employees and have created privacy issues that no one could have anticipated. Despite the growing practice of monitoring, employees often feel that their interpersonal communications, whether transmitted by telephone, computer, or other electronic device, are private. Further, studies link electronic monitoring with increased stress and feelings of social isolation.

Federal and State Law Protections

Employee privacy rights affected by the use of new technologies are protected under the Federal Omnibus Crime Control and Safe Streets Act of 1968. The act was amended in 1986 by the Electronic Communications Privacy Act (ECPA), which updated the protection in light of new, widespread telecommunications technologies.

Known as the Federal Wiretapping Act, this law prohibits the interception of any public or private wire, oral, or electronic communication without the consent of the parties to the communication. Consent can be express or may be implied where at least one party knows that a communication will be intercepted.

In addition, interceptions by an employer in the ordinary course of its business **are not prohibited**. This practice is referred to as the "business extension exception."

For example, the business extension exception gives an employer the right to access communications such as an employee's email and voice mail messages maintained on a system provided by the employer. Communications maintained on a system provided by an outside entity such as a provider of telephone services may not be accessed without the authorization of either the employee who communicated the message or the intended receiver of the message.

Many states have wiretapping laws that prohibit the intentional overhearing or recording of wire communications through the use of any electronic, mechanical, or other device. The state wiretapping acts vary from state to state and may differ substantially from the Federal Wiretapping Act. For example, unlike the Federal Wiretapping Act, some state laws define "wire communication" to include the radio wave portion of a cordless telephone conversation. Also unlike the federal law, some states prohibit the recording of a conversation without consent from all parties to the conversation. Finally, some states prohibit employers and employees from using monitored communications in legal proceedings involving employment decisions.

Federal legislation has been proposed in the past that would substantially restrict an employer's ability to monitor its employees through telephones, computers, or other electronic means. To date, such initiatives have not been successful.

Monitoring of Email

The belief of many employees that their email is private is enhanced by the security aspects of email systems, such as private passwords. The reality is that increasing numbers of employers are monitoring email. To such employers, the permanency of email makes it similar to file drawers and desks, and the transmission capabilities of email make it similar to posting a message on a bulletin board. Employees may, therefore, have reduced expectations of privacy in email, in contrast to their greater expectations of privacy in such matters as phone calls, which are transitory and personal.

In addition, email and other computer files have been held to be discoverable in certain cases. Accordingly, employees' email communications may be accessed not only by employers, but also by adverse parties in litigation.

Relatively few employers, however, have implemented email policies or taken other steps to reduce employees' expectations of privacy in their email. A 1996 study by SHRM reported that 80 percent of 3,000 surveyed employers used email, but only 36 percent of such employers had email policies and only 32 percent had written email policies (*Privacy and American Business* 1996). Because so much of employee communication is delivered by email, it can be expected that litigation of privacy issues related to email will also increase.

Applicable Law Regarding Email

Email monitoring must first be analyzed in light of the Federal Wiretapping Act, which provides for criminal and civil penalties against any person who intentionally intercepts an electronic communication including email.

The act makes an exception for situations where one of the parties to a communication gives consent to the interception of the communication. Next, where an employer is the provider of a communications system and adopts a policy that fraudulent, unlawful, or abusive use of the service is prohibited, monitoring of an employee's email will be allowed as "in the ordinary course of its business." Finally, the disclosure of stored electronic communications is permitted with the consent of one party to the communication or as is incident to the rendition of the service or the protection of the rights or property of the provider of the service.

Court decisions considering the monitoring of email, to date, have balanced the employer's legitimate business needs against the employee's privacy expectation.

For example, where an employee had signed a computer-user registration card stating that email should be used only for business purposes and had known that the employer would read email from time to time; a California court rejected the employee's claim for invasion of privacy. The court reasoned that the employee's privacy expectation was lessened by the registration card and ultimately outweighed by the employer's legitimate purposes for monitoring.

In another case an employee claimed that a supervisor violated her privacy by systematically printing out all her incoming and outgoing email messages, and that she was wrongfully terminated after she complained about the supervisor's practice. A California court disagreed, holding that the employee did not have an expectation of privacy in her email and that lawmakers never intended the law to protect an employee's electronic messages.

Similarly, a Pennsylvania court recently ruled that when an employer intercepted an employee's email and later terminated the employee on the basis of the inappropriate and unprofessional content of the message, the employer did not violate the employee's privacy rights. The employee had exchanged email messages with his supervisor from his home computer using the employer's email system. In the messages the employee made derogatory remarks about the employer's sales management, with threats to "kill the backstabbing bastards" and referred to a holiday party as the "Jim Jones Kool-Aid Affair."

Despite the fact that it was stipulated factually by the court for the purposes of its ruling that the employer had made assurances that email messages were confidential and private, the court ruled that the employee had no reasonable expectation of privacy in the email system nor was management's interception of the message a substantial or highly offensive invasion of privacy.

Nonetheless, the court rejected the employee's attempt to compare his case with one where an individual was held to have been wrongfully discharged for refusing to submit to urinalysis screening and a personal property search under an employer's drug and alcohol policy. The court distinguished between an individual's refusal to disclose personal information through involuntary searches and an individual's voluntary use of an email system.

The court also found it significant that the plaintiff had voluntarily communicated the alleged unprofessional comments over the company's email system. Further, the court said that the company's interest in preventing inappropriate conduct over its email system outweighed any privacy interest that an employee may have.

Preserving Employers' Access to Email

To protect an employer's right to control and access email communications and to avoid potential liability for invasion privacy, employers that plan to monitor their employees' email should formulate a policy to establish a legitimate business purpose for monitoring and to diminish any expectations of privacy an employee may have in email. The policy should be contained in employee handbooks and/or on a user registration and consent form signed by employees when receiving email capabilities. A disclaimer can be added to email sign-on screens and can reiterate the fundamentals of the policy and indicate that use of the system is deemed to be consent to monitoring. The policy should notify employees of the following:

♦ Email systems are company property.

♦ Email can be used only for business purposes.

♦ Email may be monitored without further notice to protect confidential information, to prevent theft or abuse of the system, to examine workflow and productivity, and for other legitimate business purposes.

♦ Employees do not have a personal privacy right in any email they create, receive, or send.

The policy should address the permissible uses of information that may be intercepted during monitoring. As noted above, there may be restrictions on how such information is used and on the extent of the legitimate business purpose. For example, searches should be based on reasonable suspicion or legitimate business needs and should be limited in scope to what is reasonably necessary to achieve that purpose.

Discovery Aspects and Issues

In addition to addressing privacy issues, email policies should contain information and guidelines about appropriate subject matter for email. For example, company policy should make it clear that harassment policies apply to all email communications. More and more litigants are seeking email files as part of the legal discovery process. To the extent such files contain inappropriate or unlawful content, they have the potential to be damaging to an employer's case or defense. Employers and employees need to understand that deleting an email message does not always make it irretrievable. Software is available that can actually destroy email files and make them irretrievable, and employers may want to consider making routine use of such software.

Monitoring of Voice Mail

No reported cases have considered the nature and extent of employee privacy rights in voice mail. A lawsuit filed against a major food chain was settled without resolving the privacy issues. In that case, an employee's voice mail messages had been intercepted by management. The messages were romantic and left for another employee on her voice mail at work. When the employer discovered the "steamy" voice mail messages, a supervisor allegedly shared the transmissions with the sender's wife. The romance ended, and the marriage stayed intact; however, the sender and his wife sued the retail chain for $1 million for invasion of privacy. Although a federal judge in Rochester required public notice the case had been resolved, none of the details of the settlement were disclosed.

Since voice mail combines attributes of email, regular mail, and live phone calls, the privacy rights analysis used in connection with those forms of communication may apply. Thus, in situations where an employee has not consented to monitoring of voice mail, or where the business extension exception does not apply, a court will have to balance the employer's legitimate business needs to monitor against the employee's privacy expectation. An employer's best defense against liability for invasion of privacy stemming from monitoring voice mail is a policy that reduces employees' expectations of privacy and obtains employee consent of monitoring.

Monitoring of Phone Calls

In some industries, listening to an employee's telephone conversation gives an employer an accurate picture of the employee's contact with clients and the public and helps monitor use of company equipment for nonbusiness related use. While employers are increasingly using workplace technology to monitor their employees' telephone calls, one national workplace privacy poll has, indicated that 81 percent of Americans believe that employers do not have the right to do so.

Who is right? As previously noted, the Federal Wiretapping Act allows an employer to monitor phone calls if the parties to the call have consented to monitoring or if monitoring is in the "ordinary course of its business." Various state laws and court decisions also address when employers can monitor or record the phone conversations of their employees.

In light of these laws, employers should consider having all new hires sign a written consent to monitoring and recording of their phone conversations. In the customer service context, an additional safeguard would be to have a recording inform customers before being connected to a service representative-that their calls may be monitored or recorded for quality assurance purposes. In any event, employers must make it clear by way of policy that the right to monitor phone calls is reserved by management should the organization wish to do so.

Ordinary Course of Business Monitoring

A general monitoring policy will not in and of itself qualify a particular monitoring activity as being "in the ordinary course of business" under the Federal Wiretapping Act. Rather, each particular monitoring activity must be considered separately to determine whether it occurred in the ordinary course of business.

For example, one court found that monitoring was in the ordinary course of business when a supervisor listened to a business call between an employee and a competitor because the supervisor had warned the employee that he suspected the employee was disclosing confidential information to the competitor and the supervisor's suspicions were reasonable.

Another court found that monitoring was in the ordinary course of business when an employer began to record a phone conversation between two employees after overhearing the employees berate their supervisors. The court explained that "[c]ertainly the potential contamination of a working environment is a matter in which the employer has a legal interest."

Conversely, monitoring was found not to be in the ordinary course of business where an owner of a liquor store who suspected that an employee was involved in a recent burglary of the store installed a device to surreptitiously record all calls made to or from the store. The employer was not able to implicate the employee in the burglary, but did learn that she was having an extramarital affair and that she sold some beer at cost to the individual with whom she was having the affair. The employee was terminated and sued for invasion of privacy. The employer argued that the monitoring was in the ordinary course of business, but the court disagreed and held that the employer violated the Federal Wiretapping Act by using the recording device.

Another court found that an organization's installation of a voice logger, which recorded all phone calls to certain phone numbers, was not in the ordinary course of business. A security guard employed by a subcontractor of the organization claimed that the taping violated the Federal Wiretapping Act. The court held that there was no business justification for the drastic measure of 24 hour-a-day, seven-day-a-week recording of telephone calls.

Monitoring of Station Message Details

Computerized accounting of phone calls made from employees' telephones can be used by employers to track personal, unauthorized long-distance and other calls placed by employees. While such devices do not intercept or record the content of calls (and therefore are not prohibited under the Federal Wiretapping Act), employees engaged in union or whistleblowing activities may be able to state a claim for invasion of privacy or violation of law if they face reprisals stemming from their calls to unions or reporters, unless the employer had a clear and consistent practice of not allowing either personal calls or long-distance personal calls, no matter what the purpose.

Access to Computer Files and Systems

Employers may monitor other computer activity by employees to ensure that only authorized users are accessing restricted areas and to track the amount and type of work being done.

In many respects, computer files are no different from paper files maintained in a file cabinet. For that reason, many employers take the position that employees have no greater privacy interest in their computer files than they have in traditional paper files.

In a recent Nevada case that involved the search by a city police department of messages stored on a computer network, it was held that two police officers did not have any privacy rights in the stored messages. The officers generated messages on a computer and transmitted them to visual display pagers through a system installed by the police department to free up regular phone lines. The officers argued that the messages were as private as the telephone calls for which they were substituted, but this argument was rejected by the court on a number of grounds. First, as the provider of the system the department was free to access any messages on it. Second, the officers had no reasonable expectation of privacy because the police chief had informed his department that all messages were logged and that discriminatory messages or messages that were critical of the department were barred. Third, functional attributes of the system diminished any expectation of privacy that system users might otherwise have had, such as free access to the entire system by all users and lack of password protections. The court likened the system to email systems, rather than phone systems, and found that the electronic storage of messages is not an interception of communications in violation of the Federal Wiretapping Act.

Companies wishing to reduce the risks that accessing computer files will lead to privacy claims should consider implementing policies that, among other things, inform employees that their computer files used for company business can be accessed, regardless of who owns the particular equipment on which the files reside (that is, company-owned or employee-owned equipment).

Closed Circuit Television and Surveillance Cameras

The Federal Wiretapping Act does not apply to video surveillance of employees. A proposed federal bill that would have required employers to notify employees of monitoring and explain how the monitoring is done and used was generally opposed by industry and not enacted into law. A few states, however, have laws that prohibit the use of video surveillance of employees in areas such as restrooms and locker rooms.

The critical inquiry in cases involving video surveillance will be whether the employee has a reasonable expectation of privacy in the areas under video surveillance.

Generally, informing employees that they are being monitored will effectively reduce employees' expectations of privacy and help companies avoid lawsuits and liability. However, in most cases employers are not required by law to inform employees about monitoring immediately before it occurs, and employers may have valid reasons for not wanting to inform employees.

Monitoring by Video

Permissible

Employers may openly film or photograph employees at work as part of work efficiency studies, for investigations, or for other reasonable business purposes.

Some courts have held that the presence of video cameras in the workplace for security purposes is permissible. Consider, for example, a California case in which a retail employee sued for invasion of privacy on the grounds that the retailer had a video camera in a storeroom that employees used for personal conversations and to change clothes. The storeroom was adjacent to the store's jewelry department, had no lock, and was primarily used to store jewelry. For those reasons the court accepted the retailer's claim that the video camera was not used to videotape employees, and it held that the employees did not have a reasonable expectation of privacy in the storeroom.

The use of cameras to monitor hallways, lunchrooms, and other public areas is also permissible. For example, an Illinois court upheld the use of a hidden video camera, which was installed in a university police station and which detected an officer's unlawful gambling habit.

Impermissible

Generally, an employee's reasonable expectation of privacy will extend to areas reserved for employee use only. For example, a court held that where hidden cameras were installed in a break room at the post office (a government employer) to investigate suspected gambling, the tapes could not be used as evidence because the taping violated the employee's reasonable expectation of privacy.

Similarly, the use of hidden cameras in areas where employees dress or in restrooms may be deemed to invade employees' privacy. Thus, when a security service placed video cameras in a dressing room used by models at a fashion show, a court held that the models had a claim for invasion of privacy. In contrast, an employer's placement of a video camera in a women's locker room to investigate claims that a male and female employee were going into the locker room was held not to be an invasion of the female employee's privacy. The employer pointed the camera only at the door to the locker room, and there was no allegation or evidence that anyone had been seen undressed.

Use of Videotapes or Photographs of Employees

It should be noted that issues of privacy may arise in connection with the advertising, promotional, or other commercial use of videotapes or photographs of employees performing on the job or engaging in activities at the employer's facilities, such as union organizing. As noted earlier in this book, the common law causes of action for invasion of privacy include appropriation of a person's name or likeness to another person's advantage. Some states have enacted statutes that give individuals statutory legal rights if their images or other personal attributes are used or appropriated without consent by a third party.

In the employment context, consent cannot be implied from the mere fact of employment. Accordingly, whenever an employer wishes to use videotapes or photographs of employees for commercial purposes, the employer must obtain the consent of the employees, preferably in writing.

However, the mere asking for consent from employees engaged in union activities may be inherently coercive or may create other problems under the National Labor Relations Act. The question is whether an employer exercises such economic clout over its employees that the mere asking of employees to participate in a pro-management video to talk about their views on unionization might be a per se violation of federal labor law. The National Labor Relations Board's (NLRB) general counsel issued a complaint in a case involving an organizing drive where employees were asked by their employer to sign forms to appear in a video and to talk about their views on unionization or about the hotel. The video included testimonials, as well as "close-panning shots." Employees included in the film were asked to sign "consent to be photographed" forms. In issuing the complaint, the NLRB's general counsel reasoned that solicitation to sign consents and participate in the video constrained employees to reveal their pro-union sympathies. The employer in the case conversely argued that the procuring of voluntary signatures on the forms and lack of any retaliation against those who refused to appear in the video is not coercion. An administrative law judge for the NLRB ruled in favor of the employer, concluding that the videotaping of employees and requesting their consent to be featured in the video did not violate the act.

Internet Issues

Employee Usage

More and more businesses are giving their employees access to the Internet. Among businesses, 40 percent give employees access to the Internet, and within two years that figure will be 80 percent according to market researcher Simba Information (*ACLU*, 1996).

Giving employees Internet access is akin to allowing them to make long distance phone calls. They may need to make such calls to fulfill their responsibilities, but they also may make personal or 900-number calls. Such use can lead to loss of productivity and extra expense for unauthorized accesses by employees. According to Surf Watch, a computer software company that develops programs to block access to specific sites, loss of productivity from employees' surfing the Web and liability in the event of a harassment claim are two common worries of corporate clients (*Rosenthal*, 1996).

Employers can be exposed to liability for unlawful employee activities on the Internet. For example, openly viewing sexually explicit Web sites or posting lewd jokes on on-line company bulletin boards may constitute behavior that creates a "hostile work environment" sexual harassment claim. Also problematic is the posting of defamatory or libelous material that may create a claim for defamation or libel. Downloading of materials may create a claim for infringement of copyright or other proprietary rights.

Generally, employees will be found to have little or no expectation of privacy in Internet usage through their employer's computer systems and service providers. Thus, companies are generally free to monitor Internet usage through software that blocks access to certain Internet sites, monitors what is being viewed, and identifies potentially pornographic materials and/or that creates activity logs.

However, companies wishing to reduce the risks that monitoring Internet usage will lead to privacy claims should consider implementing policies that address this and other issues of concern. Among other things, such a policy should inform employees that their Internet usage is being monitored and should prohibit access to and downloading of offensive material, material unrelated to their work, or material to which third parties have proprietary rights. Some employers may consider prohibiting any personal use of Internet email. Companies may want to instruct employees about the types of Internet activities that pose legal risks. Employees can be required to consent to monitoring. For those employers who feel they should not regulate personal use for business reasons or otherwise, employees can be required to include on all their personal Internet email messages that the messages are their own and not the company's.

Finally, employers may want to inform employees about the general lack of privacy in Internet email. The Internet is a public medium and underlying security concerns associated with its use may apply, irrespective of a particular employer's internal privacy and monitoring policies. Some employers, such as law firms, may want to limit Internet email to routine and nonconfidential communications', unless clients expressly instruct otherwise.

Employer Usage

An employer's use of the Internet to access databases of personal information may affect employees' privacy rights. The ease of access to information over the Internet may make it possible or practical for the first time for employers to routinely obtain certain types of information concerning their employees.

This access raises numerous privacy issues. First, there may not be adequate controls over the types of information that are available. Second, employees may have no awareness of the information or ability to review and contest it. Third, employers may be able to access, in relative secrecy, information on an employee that they are not otherwise legally entitled to obtain.

As we go to print, we are not aware of any cases involving an employer's use of the Internet to access information about its employees. However, it can be expected that such a case will eventually be brought as both Internet usage and the availability of information grow.

Consumers have already demonstrated concern about Internet privacy issues. For example, a database of personal information made available by Lexis-Nexis caused enormous privacy concerns among consumers. A computer file called P-TRAK was designed for use by lawyers who need to find individuals; the file contains names, addresses, phone numbers, and some information on maiden names. Social security numbers can be used to identify their "owners." Consumers who (mistakenly) believed that social security numbers were being made directly available and that mothers' maiden names were being provided complained that revealing this information invaded their privacy and invited fraud. Lexis-Nexis' response was that the P-TRAK information was all publicly available and that consumers could request that their names be deleted by filling out a form on the Internet's World Wide Web. In any event, this recent incident clearly demonstrates the greatly heightened sensitivity concerning privacy in our electronic age.

Internet Code of Conduct

If access to the Internet has been provided to staff members, it has been done for the benefit of the organization and its customers. It allows employees to connect to information resources around the world.

Every staff member has a responsibility to maintain and enhance the organization's public image and to use the Internet in a productive manner. To ensure that all employees are responsible, productive Internet users and are protecting the organization's public image, an organization may establish guidelines for using the Internet.

Acceptable Uses of the Internet

Employees accessing the Internet are representing their organization. All communications should be for professional reasons. Employees are responsible for seeing that the Internet is used in an effective, ethical, and lawful manner. Internet relay chat channels may be used to conduct official company business or to gain technical or analytical advice. Databases may be accessed for information as needed. Employees may use email for business contacts.

Unacceptable Uses of the Internet

The Internet should not be used for personal gain or advancement of individual views. Solicitation of noncompany business or any use of the Internet for personal gain should be strictly prohibited. Use of the Internet must not disrupt the operation of the company's network or the networks of other users. It must not interfere with productivity.

Communications

Each employee is responsible for the content of all text, audio, or images that they place or send over the Internet. Fraudulent, harassing, or obscene messages are prohibited. All messages communicated on the Internet should have the employees name attached. No messages should be transmitted under an assumed name and users may not attempt to obscure the origin of any message. Information published on the Internet should not violate or infringe upon the rights of others. No abusive, profane, or offensive language should be transmitted through the system. Employees who wish to express personal opinions on the Internet should be encouraged to obtain their own user names on other Internet systems. A sample **Email Policy Acknowledgment Form** is located at the end of this chapter.

Employee Handbook Policy Changes

Employers generally have the right to unilaterally terminate or change policies contained in their employee handbooks without having to be concerned about violating an implied contract of employment. A policy may be changed or eliminated as long as the employer does the following:

   ♦ Makes the change after the policy has been in place for a reasonable amount of time.

   ♦ Gives employees reasonable notice.

   ♦ Does not interfere with any vested employee benefits.

Questionable Handbook Policies

The following policies are questionable regarding their inclusion in employment handbooks and policy manuals. Employers choosing to include these policies should do so carefully and under constant review to protect against violations or possible suit.

No Nepotism/No Spouse Rules

Disparate enforcement of an otherwise valid anti-nepotism policy will constitute unlawful discrimination. Thus, in a case where an employer inconsistently applied anti-nepotism rules, and the uneven application resulted in discrimination against women, the activity was found to be unlawful.

To be found lawful, anti-nepotism policies should focus on legitimate business concerns such as the risk of a conflict of interest. Such a risk exists, for example, when married individuals will have control over money or property transfer (negating normal "checks and balances"), or when there is a potential for favoritism or bias because an individual supervises a spouse. In all cases, the policy should be applied so that it does not always have an adverse effect on one gender to the exclusion of another.

Note: Such policies may also violate laws prohibiting marital status discrimination.

Dress Codes

An employee's dress and grooming may be viewed as personal expression. The fact that dress and grooming is a mandatory subject of bargaining in the union context serves to underscore the importance to employees of this means of expression.

An employer's imposition of a dress and grooming code may impose unlawful restrictions on an employee under federal and state fair employment laws if the code is not rationally related to a legitimate business necessity, is applied under different standards for men and women, or results in religious discrimination if an accommodation to an employee can be made without undue hardship to the employer. In contrast, a dress code may be lawful if the code is imposed for health and safety reasons, to maintain an employer's professional image with its clients, or because an employer requires employees to wear uniforms.

Employers should also be cautious not to discriminate against employees based on their dress or appearance if it has religious or cultural significance. For example, a Hindu woman with a red dot on her forehead or a Jewish man wearing a yarmulke should be accommodated under a dress code policy.

Note: If a dress code is implemented, it is very important that the code be enforced uniformly and without exception. Inconsistent enforcement could provide grounds for employee discrimination.

Off-Duty Activities and Lifestyles

A recent trend among the states is to enact laws to protect employees' off-duty activities and lifestyles from employer scrutiny. While religious beliefs and practices have long been protected by Title VII of the Civil Rights Act of 1964, state laws often safeguard against discrimination that is based on characteristics not covered by federal law, such as dating and marital status, sexual orientation, and off-duty use of lawful products.

At the same time these new protections are being created, employers are becoming increasingly concerned about employees' off-duty conduct for a variety of reasons. First, employers may be concerned with how employees' off-duty activities will reflect upon the organization's credibility and reputation in the community at large. Second, employers may want to know if their employees will be available to take work home or to work extended hours.

Trends in telecommuting suggest that more employees will be performing their jobs away from the office, further blurring the distinction between personal and work time.

As the workforce becomes more diverse and moves out of the traditional workplace, and as laws are enacted that create new protections, employers will have to contend with the friction that occurs when an employee's protected lifestyle conflicts with an employer's needs or becomes an issue in the workplace. Employers' efforts to regulate off-duty conduct of employees generally fall into two areas: personal relationships and inappropriate conduct.

Discipline and Termination

Discipline of employees often gives rise to employment litigation. Employers should always reserve flexibility to determine what discipline to apply in each situation and the right to discipline employees as appropriate for offenses not necessarily listed. Termination policies specifying causes for discharge should also contain a disclaimer stating that such causes are illustrative only and the employer reserves the right to terminate with or without cause at any time. A sample **Employee Conduct/Discipline Policy** is included at the end of this chapter.

Resignation

Requiring employees to follow specific procedures to resign their employment can raise contractual issues. Some state laws may impose a requirement upon employers who require resigning employees to provide notice to pay the employee for the same period. The following language merely requests that an employee give two weeks notice, rather than requiring such notice:

"An employee who intends to resign employment with the Company is requested to provide at least two week's advance written notice to a supervisor. Failure to provide advance notice may affect subsequent re-employment consideration."

Acknowledgement

When distributing handbooks (whether new or revised) to employees, it is highly recommended that the employer include a separate acknowledgment form to be signed by the employee and returned for retention in the employee's personnel file.

The form should include the following:

- ♦ Acknowledge receipt of the handbook.

- ♦ Indicate that the employee has agreed to read and become familiar with the provisions contained in the handbook.

- ♦ Acknowledge the at-will relationship.

A form that contains this above information and is signed by the employee will provide the employer with a better defense against breach of contract claims. A sample **Acknowledgement Form** is included at the end of this chapter.

Parts of the Handbook

A variety of other policies and procedures reflect the business practices of a particular employer. Whatever form the handbook takes, it should try to ensure consistency, objectivity, and uniformity. An employer should give employees the opportunity to understand the rules and regulations that govern their working environment.

In addition to the suggestions provided in this chapter, an employer may want to consider including in a handbook some of the following sections and/or policies and procedures.

Introduction

In this section the employer should welcome employees to the organization. The president of the organization may wish to draft the first page of the employee handbook.

Other Employment Issues

Many issues arise in the day-to-day running of any business.

Employers may also want to consider writing rules relating to any of the following:

- Employment of relatives.
- Employee medical exams.
- Immigration law compliance.
- Conflict of interest issues.
- Outside employment.
- Noncompete statement.
- Nondisclosure statement.
- Access to personnel files.
- Drug testing policy.
- AIDS policy.
- Personnel (personal status changes) data changes.
- Introductory period.
- Safety.
- Work schedules.
- Use of phone and mail systems.
- Smoking.
- Rest and/or meal periods.
- Use of company equipment and vehicles.
- Emergency closing.
- Business travel expenses.

Grievance or Complaint Procedures

If an organization is not covered under a collective-bargaining agreement, employers should consider inclusion of a grievance or complaint procedure. An employer may even institute a binding dispute resolution procedure such as arbitration. However, employers must recognize that such a grievance procedure, depending upon how it is written, may be a binding, contractual term of employment.

Right to Revise/Update

The handbook should clearly state that the employer has the right to revise any policies at any time and that the handbook does not alter the employment-at-will policy.

Additional Considerations

Binder

A three-ring binder may be the best format for maintaining employee handbooks. Revisions can be made without reprinting the entire document. This also allows multi-state employers to customize handbooks by a particular state, since laws governing employment may vary on a state-by-state basis.

Pages

Each page in the manual should be dated to reflect its timeliness.

Employee's Understanding

Employers may want to add a statement to the employee acknowledgment form or in the introduction section recommending that employees consult their supervisor or human resources manager if they do not understand any statements or policies or procedures in the handbook.

Permanent Employee

The use of the term "permanent employee" can lead to contractual liability problems. This may mean an employee is hired for life. To avoid liability issues, the term "regular employee" should be used instead.

Shall/Will/Must

Handbooks should avoid the use of "will," "shall," or "must" when discussing employer's obligations toward employees. These words tend to connote a contractual guarantee.

Job Security

Employee handbooks should eliminate promises or representation made of "job security" or promotional opportunities. If statements are in the handbook, the employer may have a legal obligation to fulfill the promises.

Review

It is a good idea to have the employee handbook annually reviewed to see whether any revisions are required. Although the cost of regularly updating the handbook is a consideration, the ramifications of not doing so could be much more substantial. Failing to maintain the handbook increases the likelihood of legal action by a disgruntled employee.

Probationary Employee

Handbooks should avoid the use of the term "probationary period." Probationary period implies that the employee will be terminated only for just cause after the probationary period is completed. This is inconsistent with the employment-at-will doctrine.

Management Discretion

No employer is required to develop and disseminate an employee handbook or policy manual. Remember, however, that anything committed to writing can become a contract between the organization and its employees. With this thought in mind some employers may still want to create an employee handbook or policy manual. One option may be to create a very brief handbook or policy manual.

A flexible organization should be able to change directions when business requires a change. Any time an employer creates a written policy, the employer limits the flexibility of the organization. Once policy is created it usually proves difficult to change it.

The right to direct the organization through changes should not be encumbered. Therefore, give careful consideration and long thought to creating any form or policy that is not mandated by law, whether in a handbook or otherwise, that could give rise to contractual claims by employees.

Harassment Policy
(Sample)

The organization is committed to maintaining a work environment that is free of discrimination. In keeping with this commitment, we will not tolerate harassment of employees by anyone, including any supervisor, manager, co-worker, vendor, client, contractor, customer, or other visitor.

Harassment consists of unwelcome conduct, whether verbal, physical, or visual, that is based upon a person's protected status, such as sex, color, race, ancestry, national origin, age, disability, or other legally protected group status. The organization will not tolerate harassing conduct that affects tangible job benefits; that interferes unreasonably with an individual's work performance; or that creates intimidating, hostile, or offensive working environment. Such harassment may include, for example, jokes about another person's protected status, kidding, teasing or practical jokes directed at a person based on a protected status. The prohibited conduct also includes the following:

- ♦ Epithets, slurs, negative stereotyping, or intimidating acts that are based on a person's protected status.

- ♦ Written or graphic material circulated within or posted within the workplace that shows hostility toward a person or persons because of their protected status.

- ♦ Sexual harassment deserves special attention. Unwelcome sexual advances, requests for sexual favors, and other physical, verbal, or visual conduct based on sex constitutes sexual harassment when:

  - Submission to the conduct is an explicit or implicit term or condition of employment.

  - Submission to or rejection of the conduct is used as the basis for an employment decision.

  - The conduct has the purpose or effect of unreasonably interfering with an individual's work performance or creating an intimidating, hostile, or offensive working environment.

Sexual harassment is conduct based on sex, whether directed towards a person of the opposite or same sex and may include explicit sexual positions, sexual innuendo, suggestive comments, sexually oriented "kidding," or "teasing," "practical jokes," jokes about obscene printed or visual material, and physical contact such as patting, pinching' or brushing against another person's body.

All employees are responsible for ensuring that we avoid harassment. If you feel that you have experienced or witnessed harassment, you are to immediately notify your supervisor, the human resources manager, or any other member of company management. The organization forbids retaliation against anyone for reporting harassment, assisting in making a harassment complaint, or cooperating in a harassment investigation. If you feel you have been retaliated against, you are to notify the human resources manager, your department head, or your supervisor.

The organization will investigate all complaints of harassment thoroughly and promptly. To the fullest extent practicable, the organization will keep complaints and the terms of their resolution confidential. If an investigation confirms that a violation of this policy has occurred, the organization will take appropriate, corrective action including discipline up to and including immediate termination of employment.

Note: This is a generic sample policy and does not necessarily reflect the employment laws in any or all of the 50 U.S. states. Before establishing any company policy, one should review the applicable state laws or seek guidance from legal counsel.

Policy for Vacation Time
(Sample)

The organization recognizes the importance of vacation time in providing employees the opportunity for rest, recreation and personal activities. The organization grants, therefore, annual, paid vacations to its full-time and part-time employees.

The amount of vacation for which an employee may be eligible depends upon the length of service as determined by the hire date:

Completed Years of Service	Annual Vacation
1 year	1 week
2 to 5 years	2 weeks
5 to 10 years	3 weeks
10 and more years	4 weeks

Part-time employees are entitled to vacation time proportionate to the above schedule based upon the hours they normally work.

A supervisor should approve an employee's vacation schedule at least 30 days in advance. The number of employees permitted to take vacation at the same time will be determined by the organization in order to maintain efficient and safe operations. Vacations will be scheduled according to individual employee choice on a first-request, first-serve basis and in accordance with staffing needs. In case of conflict, the employee with the longest company service will usually be given preference.

You must inform Payroll two weeks before your vacation if you want to receive your vacation pay before your vacation.

Employees are required to take their earned vacation in order to receive vacation pay. No payments will be made in lieu of taking vacation, except for earned, unused vacation time at the time of termination. Once vacation is earned, an employee must take it before the next vacation anniversary date or the employee will forfeit any unused vacation days.

Employees may not carry over any unused earned vacation time beyond the next anniversary date, unless expressly authorized in writing by (title).

Note: This is a generic sample policy and does not necessarily reflect the employment laws in any or all of the 50 U.S. states. Before establishing any company policy, one should review the applicable state laws or seek guidance from legal counsel.

Policy for Holiday Pay
(Sample)

The organization observes the following paid holidays for its full-time employees:

- ♦ New Year's Day (January 1).

- ♦ Memorial Day.

- ♦ Independence Day (July 4).

- ♦ Labor Day.

- ♦ Thanksgiving Day (and the day after Thanksgiving).

- ♦ Christmas Eve and Christmas Day (December 24 and 25).

Holidays falling on Saturdays will be observed on the preceding Friday. Those falling on Sunday will be observed on the following Monday. To be eligible for holiday pay, an employee must have worked both the last scheduled workday before the holiday and the first scheduled workday after the holiday. If an employee misses work on any of these days because of an illness or injury, and provides acceptable written documentation from a doctor, holiday pay may be granted.

Note: This is a generic sample policy and does not necessarily reflect the employment laws in any or all of the 50 U.S. states. Before establishing any company policy, one should review the applicable state laws or seek guidance from legal counsel.

EAP Statement
(Sample)

The organization recognizes that a wide range of problems, such as marital or family distress, alcoholism, and drug abuse, not directly associated with an individual's job function, can nonetheless be detrimental to an employee's performance on the job. The organization believes it is in the interest of employees and the organization to provide an effective program to help employees and their families resolve problems such as these as the need arises.

Our EAP provides consultation services for referrals to local community treatment sources. All employees are free to use this program and are encouraged to do so. Employee visits to the EAP are held in confidence to the maximum extent possible.

Participation in our EAP does not excuse employees from complying with normal company policies or from meeting normal job requirements during or after receiving assistance, nor will participation in our EAP prevent the organization from taking disciplinary action against any employee for performance problems that occur before or after the employee's seeking assistance through the program.

Note: This is a generic sample policy and does not necessarily reflect the employment laws in any or all of the 50 U.S. states. Before establishing any company policy, one should review the applicable state laws or seek guidance from legal counsel.

Salary and Performance Review Policy (Sample)

To attract and retain the best employees, the organization attempts to pay salaries competitive with those paid by other employers in our industry and in applicable labor markets in which we maintain facilities. Each position at the organization has been studied and assigned a salary grade. Each grade has been assigned a corresponding salary range. The organization may revise its job descriptions and evaluate individual jobs to ensure that they are rated and paid appropriately, and review job specifications at any time to ensure that they are directly job related.

Employee salaries generally will be reviewed on an annual basis. When you are granted a salary increase, it will normally be effective on your anniversary date. Salary increases are not automatic and may be granted at the organization's discretion.

The employees' total compensation at the organization consists not only of the salary paid but also of the various benefits received, such as group health insurance and life insurance and employee retirement plans.

Performance Reviews

To help employees perform their jobs to the best of their abilities, it is important that they receive feedback regarding good performance and that they receive appropriate suggestions for improvement when necessary. Consistent with this goal, the organization will attempt, subject to business demands, to evaluate employee performance on an ongoing basis and provide employees with periodic written evaluations of performance.

Evaluations will normally occur on the first anniversary date and annually thereafter. In addition, when an employee is promoted or transferred to a new position, performance will normally be evaluated in writing after six months on the new job.

All written performance reviews will be based on overall performance in relation to the job responsibilities and will also take into account conduct, demeanor, and record of attendance and tardiness.

In addition to the regular performance evaluations described above, supervisors may conduct special written performance evaluations at any time to advise employees of performance or disciplinary problems.

Note: This is a generic sample policy and does not necessarily reflect the employment laws in any or all of the 50 U.S. states. Before establishing any company policy, one should review the applicable state laws or seek guidance from legal counsel.

FMLA Policy
(Sample)

An employee is eligible for up to 12 workweeks of unpaid leave during a 12-month period under this policy if the employee has been employed for at least 12 months and has worked at least 1,250 hours during the previous 12-month period. The 12-month period for an employee is measured backward from the date the employee requests any leave.

Reasons for Leave

A leave may be requested for any of the following reasons:

- ♦ To care for a child born to or placed with you for adoption or foster care.
- ♦ To care for a spouse, child, or parent (covered family member) with a serious health condition.
- ♦ Because of your own serious health condition.

Leave Because of Reason

Leave must be completed within the 12-month period beginning on the date of birth or placement. In addition, spouses employed by the organization who request leave because to care for an ill parent may only take a combined aggregate total of 12 weeks leave during any 12-month period. Employees will not be granted an FMLA leave to gain employment or work elsewhere, including self-employment. Employees who misrepresent facts in order to be granted an FMLA leave are subject to immediate termination.

Leave is Unpaid

Family medical leave is generally unpaid leave. However, employees requesting leave because of a birth, adoption or foster care placement of a child, must have any accrued vacation and personal leave substituted first and used for unpaid family/medical leave. When employees request leave because of their own serious health condition, or to care for a covered family member with a serious health condition, any accrued paid vacation, personal leave, and sick leave must first be substituted and used for any unpaid family/medical leave. In addition, the organization's short-term and/or long-term disability may apply as part of the 12-week leave period when the leave is requested due to a serious health condition or the birth of a child. The substitution of paid leave time for unpaid leave time does not extend the 12-week leave period.

Notice of Leave

When the need for family/medical leave is foreseeable, an employee must give the organization at least 30 days prior written notice. Failure to provide such notice may be grounds for delay of leave. Where the need for leave is not foreseeable, the employee is expected to notify the organization as soon as practicable, generally within one or two business days of learning of your need for leave. The organization has request for family/medical leave forms available in the human resources department. Employees should use these forms when requesting leave.

Medical Certification

When employees are requesting leave because of a personal or covered family member's serious health condition, the employee and the relevant health care provider must supply appropriate medical certification. Employees may obtain Medical Certification Forms from the director of human resources. The medical certification must be given within 15 days after it is requested, or as soon as reasonably possible under the circumstances. Failure to provide requested medical certification in a timely manner may result in denial of leave until it is provided. In its discretion and at its own expense, the organization may require a second medical opinion, and if the first and second opinions differ, a third medical opinion. The third opinion will be provided by a health care provider approved jointly by the employee and the organization and will be binding. The organization may also require recertification periodically during a leave, and the employee is required to present a fitness-for-duty certificate upon return to work following a leave for personal illness.

Medical and Other Benefits

During the leave the organization will maintain employee health benefits the same as if the individual had continued working. When paid leave is substituted for unpaid family/medical leave, the organization will deduct the employee portion of the health plan premium as a regular payroll deduction. When the leave is unpaid, the employee must make arrangements with the human resources to pay a portion of the monthly premium. Group health care coverage may be terminated if premium payments are more than 30 days late. Additionally, if employees fail to return from leave, the organization may require repayment of any premium that was paid for maintaining health coverage, unless the employee does not return because of a continuing or recurring serious health condition, or because of other circumstances beyond the employee's control. Employees are not entitled to other benefits or seniority accrual during the leave.

Returning from Leave

Any employee taking a leave under this policy is generally entitled to return to the same position or to an equivalent position with equal benefits, pay or other terms and conditions of employment.

Reporting While on Leave

The organization may require employees to report periodically during FMLA leave on their status and intent to return to work.

Intermittent and Reduced-Schedule Leave

Leave because of a serious health condition may be taken intermittently or on a reduced leave schedule if medically necessary. If leave is unpaid, the organization will reduce your salary based on the amount of time actually worked. In addition, while you are on an intermittent or reduced-schedule leave, the organization may temporarily transfer you to an available alternative position that better accommodates an employee's recurring leave and which has equivalent pay and benefits.

The application of this policy, and the procedures and definitions set forth herein, will be determined and may be modified in accordance with changes in applicable Department of Labor regulations and legal precedent.

Note: This is a generic sample policy and does not necessarily reflect the employment laws in any or all of the 50 U.S. states. Before establishing any company policy, one should review the applicable state laws or seek guidance from legal counsel.

Leave of Absence Policy
(Sample)

Under the following circumstances, employees may be granted a leave of absence if approved by the department manager and the human resources department.

Medical Disability Leave (Non-FMLA)

If an employee is medically disabled for any reason, including pregnancy or pregnancy-related disability, the organization will grant the employee up to a maximum of *[_____ months/weeks]* of unpaid medical disability leave of absence. Employees requesting a disability leave must submit a request for leave in writing, stating the reason for the leave, at least 30 days in advance to a supervisor. In emergencies, written notice must be provided as soon as possible under the circumstances. The employee must also submit a statement from a physician stating that the employee is disabled, why the disability will preclude the employee from working, and the estimated length of time that the employee will be out of work because of the disability. This medical certification generally must be provided at the time of the request of the leave, but no later than 15 days after the request for leave is made.

An employee who goes on disability leave must use sick days and/or vacation at the start of a disability leave. An employee on unpaid disability leave does not accrue vacation time or sick leave and is not eligible for holiday pay. Group insurance benefits will continue in force for 90 days provided the employee makes timely payment of the employee's regular monthly premium contributions during the absence. Employees may also be eligible for short-term disability benefits under the organization's short-term disability insurance. Employees who have not used the maximum of *[_____days/months]* of disability may be granted extensions of their original leave up to this maximum. Employees requesting an extension must do so in writing before the expiration of their original approved leave and provide a statement from their physician indicating the reason why the employee cannot report back to work and the estimated additional time required for recovery.

The organization will return an employee who is on disability leave to the former position or to a similar position when the employee returns from a disability leave of absence within 30 days. If the employee's disability continues beyond 30 days, the organization will attempt to return the employee to the former position or to a similar position if open when an employee returns from extended disability leave. However, the organization's need to fill a position may override its ability to hold a position open until an employee returns from extended disability leave. The organization, therefore, cannot assure that it will be able to return an employee to any position after the extended disability leave is over. The organization retains the discretion to determine the similarity of available positions and the employee's qualifications. Failure to return from a disability leave or extended disability leave upon the expiration of the leave period will be considered a voluntary quit.

When an employee returns from a disability leave or an extended disability leave, the employee must provide a release from a physician stating that the employee is medically fit to return to work and setting forth medical restrictions, if any, that may be imposed by the physician on the employee's ability to work. The organization, at its discretion, may require an employee to be examined by a physician designated by the organization before the employee is permitted to return to work from a disability leave or an extended leave. The final decision on whether you are ready to return to work rests with the organization.

Long-Term Disability

If you anticipate that your disability will exceed *[_____ months]* in length, you may apply for long-term disability benefits if you have previously enrolled for this insurance under the Basic Insurance plan. If approved, you may receive up to *[___ percent]* of regular pay up to the age of *[_____]*.

Personal Leave

Under special circumstances, the organization may grant an unpaid personal leave of absence of up to *[_____ days]*. Employees requesting a personal leave of absence must submit the request in writing, stating the reason for the leave, at least *[_____ days]* in advance to a supervisor. In emergency situations, written notice must be provided as soon as possible. The organization has sole discretion in determining whether the leave will be granted. An employee on personal leave does not accrue vacation time or sick hours and is not eligible for holiday pay. The organization will attempt to return an employee to the former position or to a similar position when the employee returns from a leave of absence. However, the organization's need to fill a position may override its ability to hold a position open until an employee returns from leave. The organization, therefore, cannot assure that it will be able to return the employee to any position after the leave of absence is over. The organization retains the discretion to determine the similarity of any available positions and the employee's qualifications. Failure to return from a personal leave of absence upon the expiration of the leave will be considered a voluntary quit.

Military Leave

Military leave will be granted for military or reserve duty in accordance with applicable law. Employees called to or volunteering for active/training duty or to reserve or National Guard training should submit copies of military orders to their supervisor as soon as possible so that production schedules and vacation schedules may be arranged consistent with operating needs. Eligible employees called for annual or special reserve or National Guard duty training during regularly scheduled workdays may receive the difference between regular pay and military service pay, up to a maximum of three weeks per year. To be eligible for military leave pay, an employee must be a full-time regular employee who has completed *[____ months]* of employment, who is actively employed and on the payroll up to the time the employee reports for duty, and return to employment after completion of duty. In accordance with applicable law, employees on military leave will be reinstated upon satisfactory completion of military service and timely notice of intent to return to work, provided the employee is qualified and the organization's circumstances have not changed to the extent that it would be impossible or unreasonable to provide re-employment.

Bereavement Leave

In the event of the death of an immediate family member (spouse, mother, father, brother, daughter, son, step-children, step-parents, grandchildren, grandparents, mother- and father-in-law, sister- and brother-in-law, and daughter- and son-in-law), you must notify your supervisor of the situation as soon as possible. The supervisor will then notify the Human Resources Department in writing of the death and the relationship of the deceased to you. The organization will provide you leave, with pay, for an appropriate period up to *[____ regularly scheduled workdays]*. You may be required to provide evidence of a death and your relationship to the deceased before any leave time is paid.

Jury/Witness Leave

The organization recognizes the responsibility of each individual to perform civic duties as called upon. If you are called upon to serve on a jury or to appear as a witness in a criminal prosecution, the organization will grant you the necessary time off from work for the period of service. A copy of the summons or subpoena must be shown to your supervisor the next working day after receipt thereof. For each day of jury duty or court service up to a maximum of *[____ weeks]*, you will receive your regular straight time compensation less any amount received for service by the court.

Note: This is a generic sample policy and does not necessarily reflect the employment laws in any or all of the 50 U.S. states. Before establishing any company policy, one should review the applicable state laws or seek guidance from legal counsel.

Email Policy Acknowledgment Form
(Sample)

As an employee, I recognize and understand that the company's email systems are to be used for conducting the organization's business only. I understand that use of this equipment for private purposes is strictly prohibited. Further, I agree not to use a password that has not been disclosed to the company. I agree not to access a file or retrieve any stored communication other than where authorized unless there has been prior clearance by an authorized organization representative.

I am aware that the company reserves and will exercise the right to review, audit, intercept, access, and disclose all matters on the company's email systems at any time, with or without employee notice, and that such access may occur during or after working hours. I am aware that use of a company provided password or code does not restrict the company's right to access electronic communications. I am aware that violations of this policy may subject me to disciplinary action, up to and including discharge from employment. I authorize that I have read and that I understand the company's policy regarding email located at [refer to applicable manual]. I authorize that I have read and that I understand this notice.

Date: _____ **Employee's Signature:** _____

Note: This is a generic sample policy and does not necessarily reflect the employment laws in any or all of the 50 U.S. states. Before establishing any company policy, one should review the applicable state laws or seek guidance from legal counsel.

Acknowledgement Form
(Sample)

"I acknowledge having received a copy of the Company's Employee Handbook and I agree to become familiar with its contents. I understand that neither this handbook, nor any other Company policy, practice, or procedure, is intended to provide any contractual obligations relating to continued employment, compensation or employment in a particular position, and should in no way be construed as creating any sort of employment contract. I further understand that my employment relationship may be terminated by the Company or by me at any time, with or without notice, and for any or no reason.

I also understand that all of the policies, rules, and regulations in the handbook may be changed at any time at the sole discretion of the Company with or without prior notice to employees."

Date: _____ **Employee's Signature:** _____

Note: This is a generic sample policy and does not necessarily reflect the employment laws in any or all of the 50 U.S. states. Before establishing any company policy, one should review the applicable state laws or seek guidance from legal counsel.

Employee Conduct/Discipline Policy (Sample)

As an employee of the organization, you are required to adhere to certain rules of conduct necessary for the organization's operations. As in any organization, a code of conduct is necessary to establish and maintain a productive and respectful working atmosphere. Any employee conduct that interferes with the effective operation of the organization's business is prohibited. The performance standards listed below, and others that may be established from time to time, are not all-inclusive. Rather, they are published to provide a general understanding of what the organization considers to be unacceptable conduct. These performance standards are merely examples of the types of misconduct for which employees may be disciplined or dismissed. The organization may impose disciplinary action in those instances where management decides it is appropriate. Disciplinary actions include, but are not limited to, oral warnings, written warnings, suspension, and discharge. The organization retains the right to determine what discipline will be imposed in each individual situation. Violations of any of the following performance standards may result in disciplinary action and/or immediate discharge:

- Failure or refusal to follow the written or oral instructions of a supervisor or manager.
- Insubordination.
- Neglecting job duties and responsibilities.
- Engaging in unauthorized personal business during work hours.
- Falsifying or misrepresenting company or employment records.
- Discourtesy or rudeness in dealing with employees of the organization and/or representatives of our clients or prospects.
- Failure to give proper notice when unable to report for or continue work as scheduled.
- Unexcused or excessive absenteeism.
- Abuse of sick leave privileges.
- Theft, abuse, or misuse of company property, materials, or supplies.
- Unauthorized use of company property and equipment including telephones, copy machines, and mail service.
- Threatening, harassing, or inflicting bodily harm to fellow employees.
- Making false and malicious statements concerning employees or the organization.
- Intentionally discriminating against employees in violation of applicable laws and/or engaging in harassment of any employee.
- Possession, use, purchase, consumption, transfer, or sale of alcoholic beverages, controlled substances or illegal drugs at any time during working hours, on company premises, or while representing the organization, or reporting to work under the influence of alcohol, controlled substances, or illegal drugs.
- Violating any company policies, rules, regulations, or practices.

Note: This is a generic sample policy and does not necessarily reflect the employment laws in any or all of the 50 U.S. states. Before establishing any company policy, one should review the applicable state laws or seek guidance from legal counsel.

Chapter 6

New-Hire Reporting

Introduction

All employers, exclusive of the federal government, must report the hiring, rehiring, and return to work of all paid employees. A few of the many procedural goals of reporting are to detect fraud, help locate individuals for establishing paternity, and/or establishing, notifying, and enforcing child support orders. New-hire reports are matched against child support records at the state and national levels to locate parents that owe child support.

Reporting Process

Information to Be Reported

Federal law requires employers to collect and transmit several data elements to fulfill their new-hire reporting responsibilities. However, if the returning employee had not been formally terminated or removed from payroll records, there is no need to report that individual as a new hire.

Required information to be reported includes the following:

- ◆ **Employee Information.** The following employee information must be reported upon the hiring, rehiring, or return to work for all employees:
  - • Name.
  - • Address.
  - • Social Security number.
  - • Date of hire, rehire, or return to work.
- ◆ **Employer Information.** The following employer information must be reported upon the hiring, rehiring, or return to work for all employees:
  - • Name.
  - • Address.
  - • Employer Identification Number (EIN).

Employers are not required to report an individual if the work performed is based on a contract rather than an employer/employee relationship. However, some states have laws requiring new-hire reporting of independent contractors. In either case, the contractor is responsible for the reporting of their employees.

Means of Reporting

Submitting any of the following items may fulfill an employer's reporting requirements:

◆ A copy of the employee's Form W-4 or an equivalent form.

◆ Any other hiring document, data storage device, or mechanism authorized by state law.

Employers Operating in Two or More States

An employer with employees in more than one state has two options in fulfilling new-hire reporting requirements. Multi-state employers may choose either of the following:

◆ Abide by the new-hire reporting program of each state and report newly hired employees to the various states in which employees are working.

◆ Select one state where employees are working and report all new hires to that state's designated new-hire reporting office.

Multi-state employers who opt to report to only one state must submit new-hire reports electronically or magnetically. Such employers must also notify the Federal Department of Health and Human Services as to which state they have designated to receive all their new-hire information. *The National Directory of New Hires* then maintains a list of multi-state employers who have elected to use single-state notification.

When notifying the department, the multi-state employer must include all generally required reporting information along with the following:

◆ The specific state selected for reporting purposes.

◆ Other states in which the company has employees.

◆ A corporate contact person.

◆ List the names, EIN's, and the states where the employees are located if the company is reporting new hires on behalf of subsidiaries operating under different names and EIN's.

Deadlines

Unless the submission is made electronically or magnetically, employers must submit information concerning every new hire within 20 days of the date of hire. However, states have the option of establishing reporting time frames shorter than 20 days. An employer reporting electronically or by magnetic medium is required to submit two transmissions each month (if necessary, based on the volume of hiring) at least 12 to 16 days apart. Employers must abide by new-hire reporting requirements for employees who quit before the reporting deadline because an employer/employee relationship existed and wages were earned. Employers need to report all new hires regardless of the short duration of employment

Penalties

An employer who fails to make a report as indicated by law may be liable for up to $25 for each newly hired employee. Additionally, if the failure to make a report is the result of a conspiracy between the employer and the employee not to supply the report or to supply a false or incomplete report, the employer will be required to pay a fine of up to $500 for each such failure. Under state law, civil penalties for noncompliance with new-hire reporting may be either monetary or nonmonetary.

Chapter 7

Performance Evaluations

Introduction

Employers use performance evaluations to assess work performance. The evaluations also acquaint employees with deficiencies in work performance and the organization's expectations for the future. Written performance evaluations are best.

The evaluation process generally involves a series of steps as follows:

♦ Developing guidelines and standards against which an employee's performance may be compared.

♦ Gathering appraisal information reflecting the employee's performance compared to those standards.

♦ Discussing the appraisal information with the employee.

♦ Documenting the evaluation process in the employee's personnel file.

Employers use performance evaluations for all of the following:

♦ In the disciplinary process where an employee's job performance is unacceptable and could lead to discipline or termination.

♦ As positive communication tools to help employees improve job performance.

♦ In salary administration for determining merit increases.

♦ As regular workforce monitoring tools.

Employer Objectives

An effective performance evaluation system helps an employer meet the following objectives:

Assess Employee Potential

An effective performance management system helps employers make decisions about employee promotions and transfers. It also identifies employees with special abilities and skills.

Identify Training Needs

Performance ratings help evaluate the effectiveness of an established training effort. The employer can design and target its training program to better address the performance problems caused by a lack of training.

For example:

♦ Widespread common problems may indicate a work group needs general or specialized training.

♦ Isolated performance problems might identify an individual's need for training in a specific area.

Assist in Compensation Planning

An increasing number of employers link pay to performance and use performance evaluations to validate their compensation practices among their different operating units. A reliable and consistent performance evaluation process enables an employer to predict future payroll costs more accurately and reward employees who perform well.

Identify and Correct Poor Work Performance

Performance evaluations generate discussions between employees and supervisors that identify poor work habits. The discussions often yield mutually agreeable ways to correct deficiencies. In addition, the evaluation helps identify personal problems that can hamper an employee's performance.

Validate Employment Tests

A sound evaluation system exposes weaknesses in the criteria that an employer uses in making hiring, placement, and other personnel decisions. For instance, the evaluation may reveal that testing a particular employee for a given skill is inappropriate because that skill is irrelevant to satisfactory job performance.

Defend Against Lawsuits

The performance evaluation process allows employers to document poor job performance. Employers depend on such documentation to defend themselves successfully against employee claims of unfair termination or disciplinary action.

Motivate Employees

Performance evaluations motivate employees to meet the employer's performance standards. A positive evaluation assures the employee that the employer recognizes the employee's work performance and that the employer will reward the employee for excellence.

Supervisor Training

Employers should teach supervisors or managers to conduct performance reviews that evaluate employees carefully and accurately.

The training should take several hours and include a number of practice exercises, which result in the following:

♦ Increase the overall reliability of the evaluation.

♦ Establish the typical types of errors made in performance evaluations.

Well-trained supervisors conduct performance evaluations that enhance employee efficiency and provide documentation that can be used for defense in case of litigation. However, supervisors often make the following errors when evaluating employees:

- Being excessively lenient.

- Avoiding the ends of a rating scale (like "superior" or "poor").

- Applying an overall impression to specific areas, rather than focusing on the employee's performance in each specific area.

Supervisor Review

Supervisors should review employee performance regularly. The supervisor or manager should discuss any problems with the employee as soon as possible and suggest ways of correcting the problem. All discussions should be documented and placed in the employee's personnel file.

All supervisors and human resource professionals who are responsible for performance evaluations should be trained and aware that the evaluations must meet the following criteria:

- Be honest, accurate, and candid, evaluating both the strengths and weaknesses of the employees.

- Be reviewed by another member in management who has no direct personal interest or bias regarding the evaluated employee.

- Be discussed with the evaluated employee, who should be given a chance to respond or comment on the evaluation.

Implementing Performance Evaluations

An employer who wants to implement an effective employee performance evaluation process should consider providing the following:

- Clear written instructions to all supervisors and managers involved in the evaluation process.

- Relevant training for supervisors and human resource professionals involved in the evaluation process to ensure that they understand employee job duties.

- A performance appraisal system that is job related.

- Reasonable precautions to guard against improper bias by the supervisor or manager who is evaluating the employee.

- A procedure that includes multiple levels of review and approval of the evaluation.

- Central monitoring by human resources to ensure uniform performance rating standards among all supervisors and managers conducting the evaluations.

- A procedure that allows the employee to comment or respond to the evaluation.

- A procedure providing an appeal process of a poor evaluation within a reasonable time after the evaluation.

- A procedure that requires the supervisor to identify specific performance goals as part of the evaluation process.

Performance Dimensions — What Should Be Evaluated

All written performance reviews must be based on the employee's overall performance in relation to job responsibilities and should also take the following into account.

Achievements

Employees with high levels of achievement are interested in improving their skills and abilities. They take advantage of opportunities to learn new capabilities and show interest in advancing to positions with greater levels of responsibility.

Attendance

Employees with good attendance show a strong concern for adhering to work schedules. The employer can always count on them to show up to work or let the employer know in advance that they will be late or absent.

Courteousness

Courteous employees are easy to get along with. They are never rude, insensitive, or mean.

Work Ethics

Employees with high levels of work ethic are always looking for ways to contribute to the job. They are concerned with getting every detail right. They carefully follow rules and procedures. They are willing to work late or come in on off-days when they are needed and do not spend time at work doing things that are unrelated to the job.

Job-Related Appraisals

Use job-related evaluation forms. The rating choices on the form should be as specific as possible and related to the area of performance being evaluated. Ratings of "unsatisfactory," "satisfactory," "good," and "excellent" are too general and meaningless to properly evaluate particular jobs.

Note: In some instances, the choice of "not observed" or "not applicable" should be available.

When an employer designs the performance evaluation forms, categories that call for the evaluation of specific job behavior, not personality traits, should be used. Similarly, supervisors should be trained to evaluate and comment upon job performance, not personality. This will yield evaluations that focus on the employee's job performance, rather than evaluations that may seem to be a personal attack upon the employee.

Criteria

Make evaluation criteria as objective as possible. Supervisors and managers get into trouble with performance evaluations when they rely on subjective statements, opinions, impressions, or assumptions that are unsupported by hard facts, concrete explanations, specific examples, or first-hand observation.

Note: Occasionally, subjective indicators of performance must be used; in these cases, the evaluator should illustrate the subjective criteria with specific examples.

Take steps to ensure that the specific performance criteria to evaluate the employee include all relevant aspects of job performance. Compare the job tasks for which to evaluate an employee with the job description. Problems can sometimes arise if these key job aspects are not included in evaluation system.

Document Fully

If an employee is terminated due to job performance problems that were not covered by the evaluation, the employer may face a major obstacle in litigation if the reasons for termination are not documented. If an employer terminates an employee for a job performance problem, the decision to terminate is hard to justify in court if that problem is not included in the system of evaluation.

Types of Performance Evaluations

Employee performance reviews are based on a list of factors, including employees' ability to respect and work effectively with diverse people. To ensure the accuracy and usefulness of performance reviews, companies tinker with timing, rating scales, weights, and formats. Employers should choose the performance evaluation system that best fits their need based on the number of employees.

This section discusses some standard examples of performance evaluations.

Rating Scales

The rating scale method provides a high degree of structure for evaluations. The scale rates employee traits or characteristics on a bipolar scale that usually has several points ranging from "poor" to "excellent." The characteristics evaluated on these scales include employee attributes such as the following:

- ♦ Cooperation.
- ♦ Communication ability.
- ♦ Initiative.
- ♦ Punctuality.
- ♦ Work skills competence.

An employer can select which traits to rate based on imagination and need to know, selecting traits that are relevant to the employee's job. Proper selection of traits can protect against legal action based on a claim of discrimination.

Advantages

Rating scales are structured and standardized. This allows for easy comparison and contrast of the entire workforce. The scale subjects all employees to the same evaluation process and rating criteria, with the same range of responses. This fosters equality in treatment for all employees and imposes standard measures of performance throughout the company. In addition, rating scale methods are easy to use and understand. Both employers and employees understand and appreciate the simple and efficient logic of the bipolar system. Thus rating scales have gained widespread acceptance and popularity.

Disadvantages

Although rating scales are convenient and easy to use, they have several of the following weaknesses:

- **Trait Significance.** Unfortunately, with a standardized and fixed system of evaluation, certain traits will have a greater relevance in some jobs than others. For example, the trait "initiative" might not be very important in a job that is tightly defined and rigidly structured. In this case, a low evaluation for initiative may not mean that an employee lacks initiative. It may reflect that fact that an employee has limited opportunities to use and display that particular trait. These obvious discrepancies of rating scales make this system context-sensitive. An employer must consider job and workplace circumstances.

- **Inherent Inequalities.** Many employers assume that rating scales measure all the relevant indicators of employee performance and that all irrelevant indicators are excluded. However, employees may end up with ratings that do not accurately or fairly reflect their effort or value to the employer because certain traits are missing. Employees in this situation are systemically disadvantaged by the inherent inequalities in rating scale method.

- **Errors in Perception.** Being human, supervisors often employ selective perception. This occurs when individuals make private and highly subjective assessments of what a person is "really like," and then gather evidence to support that view. At the same time they downplay or even ignore evidence that might contradict their assumptions. Essentially, we see in others what we want to see in them.

The supervisor who believes that an employee is inherently good and ignores evidence that might suggest otherwise commits an error in perception in evaluating the employee. Instead of correcting the employee, the supervisor covers for the employee and may even offer excuses for declining performance. Conversely, the supervisor may have formed a negative opinion of an employee. This leads the supervisor to give unreasonably harsh evaluations. The supervisor is always ready to criticize and undermine the employee even though the employee may actually be performing the job duties at or above the employer's expectations. Unfortunately this type of conduct can damage the significance, effectiveness, and credibility of performance evaluations.

- **Differing Interpretations.** Problems arise when supervisors and managers interpret the meaning of the selected traits and the language of the rating scales differently. For example, suppose one employee reports work problems to a supervisor, while another handles the problem personally. One supervisor may regard the first employee's actions as initiative, while another may interpret the employee's actions as excessive dependence on supervisory assistance and thus a lack of initiative.

Similarly, the language and terms used for evaluation in a scale — such as "Performs above expectations" or "Skills below average" — may mean different things to different supervisors or managers.

- **Rating Errors.** Unlike errors in perception, rating errors can be deliberate. The most common rating error is the tendency to evaluate all employees the same. Busy supervisors or managers — or those afraid of confrontations and repercussions — may give out too many middle-of-the-road ratings, regardless of an employee's actual performance. Therefore, the ratings range tends to cluster excessively around the middle of the rating scale.

This problem worsens in companies where the performance evaluation system does not enjoy strong management or human resources support or where the supervisors and managers do not feel confident with the responsibility of evaluation.

Example/Explanation of Rating Scale Questions

Technical Competence: How well does the employee know the job?

Technical competence is the amount of relevant knowledge and skill that an employee has about the job performing. This may include familiarity with and possession of special facts, techniques, procedures, manual skills, decision strategies, interpretative skills, supervisory skills, etc. that allow an employee to perform duties. Employees with high levels of technical knowledge are capable of independently performing the normal tasks in their job. Employees with low levels of technical knowledge usually require regular guidance and support from others in order to complete their normal work tasks.

Work Quality: How good is the work this employee produces?

Good quality work is effective and productive work. This means that the work produced tends to achieve its desired or expected outcome. It also means the employee completed the work with a minimum of avoidable errors and problems. Conversely, ineffective work fails to accomplish its desired or expected outcomes and is comprised of avoidable errors and problems.

Work Speed: How fast does this employee work?

Every job has a target work speed at which the assigned tasks of the job are completed within an acceptable time period. Employees with acceptable work speeds complete their assigned tasks on time. They also demonstrate that they can monitor and self-regulate their own work speed in order to fully complete job tasks on time. Employees with poor work speed are usually late in completing the assigned tasks for the job. They may also be unable to monitor and self-regulate the work rate necessary to fully complete job tasks on time.

Note: This area of evaluation may be modified if the job has a fixed rate.

Communication Competence: How well does the employee communicate with peers, supervisors, customers, and others?

Communication competence means the ability to communicate effectively and with clarity in person and in writing. It also includes the ability to understand clearly and quickly when instructions, orders, and complaints are received. Furthermore, it means that the employee knows what information to communicate, to whom, and when. Employees with low levels of competence will be slow to communicate and/or understand information or may fail to fully communicate and/or understand information.

Interpersonal Competence: How well does the employee get along with peers, supervisors, customers, and others?

Interpersonal competence means the ability to work well with others, establish and maintain good working relationships, and be a member of the team. Often, employees involved in conflicts and misunderstandings with other employees, customers, and supervisors possess low levels of interpersonal competence. Many avoidable problems are caused by their "personal style." Others may describe them as rude, indifferent, insensitive, overbearing, impatient, untrustworthy, and so on. Employees inspiring trust and cooperation among work mates, customers, and others possess high levels of interpersonal skills.

Policy Compliance: How well does the employee understand and comply with policies and practices?

Every company develops its own policies and practices that relate to issues such as record-keeping, private use of organizational property, sexual harassment, and safety. Employees with high compliance know and understand the accepted policies and practices. These employees also willingly comply with all reasonable requirements. Employees with low compliance tend to show that they either do not know or do not understand accepted policies. Low policy compliance employees often tend to "bend or break the rules" at every opportunity.

Attendance: What is the employee's attendance record?

Attendance is the consistency that an employee shows in arriving for work and completing expected work hours. Employees have attendance problems when there are any of the following:

♦ Unexplained and/or unjustified lateness in starting work.

♦ Unexplained and/or unjustified absences for part or whole workdays.

♦ Unexplained and/or unjustified early departures.

Example/Explanation of Rating Scale Answers

Each area reviewed should be given one of the following ratings and comments should be provided in the appropriate section.

[A] Exceptional
Employees at this level regularly exceed the given qualifications for their job duties. Their work and related duties nearly always reach the intended outcome and often exceed such outcomes. Their work attitude with respect to the given category is consistently high and reliable.

[B] Good
Employees at this level almost always meet the expectations for their job. Although they often exceed required expectations, higher levels are not consistent. Nevertheless, work is generally above average. Employees in this classification show that they can individually correct their errors and problems.

[C] Acceptable
Employees at this level regularly meet the expectations for their job. They usually provide a prompt notification and reasonable explanation for any problems with performance. They usually do not exceed their normal expectations and may even fall below expectations.

[D] Some Improvement Needed
Employees at this level may be showing inconsistency in ability to meet the requirements of their job. Their errors and problems, and failure to achieve expected outcomes, is cause for concern. Employees at this level do not often demonstrate the ability to individually correct their errors and problems.

[E] Major Improvement Needed
Employees at this level regularly fail to meet expectations for their job requirements. Their work does not reach the level of acceptability for the desired or expected outcomes. Others must regularly correct their work, and they show no ability to individually correct their errors and problems.

Supporting Comments by Supervisor

This area allows the supervisor or manager conducting the performance evaluation to give specific examples of the employee conduct that led to the given evaluation.

Performance Blocks

This area should be filled in after the supervisor and employee discuss the possibility of any blocks contributing to the employee's deficient performance. These blocks may be organizational inefficiencies, skill limitations, or any other kind of problems, internal and external, that appear to be blocking or undermining the ability of the employee to perform better.

Action

After the supervisor and employee discuss the employee's evaluation, this area should describe what will be done to remove or lessen the block or problem.

Employee Comments and Appropriate Signatures

Often, a first evaluation is followed up by a progress report (normally every six months). Both the main evaluation and progress review should provide space for comments by the employee. They employee may wish to disagree with the evaluation or suggest how the employee may improve performance. The employee, the evaluating supervisor, and the supervisor's manager should sign and date the evaluation.

Essay Method

In the essay method approach, the supervisor or manager prepares a written statement about the employee being evaluated. The essay describes specific strengths and weaknesses of the evaluated employee in job performance. It also includes suggestions for courses of action to correct the problem(s) identified in the evaluation. The statement may be written and edited by the supervisor or manager alone. It may also be composed in collaboration with the employee who is evaluated.

Advantages

The essay method is not as structured and confined as the rating scale method. It allows the person conducting the evaluation to examine almost any relevant issue or condition of performance by the employee. This differs greatly from methods where the evaluation criteria are rigidly defined and the supervisor must make a selection based on the available choices.

Supervisors can place emphasis on appropriate issues or attributes that apply to individual employees. This permits great flexibility in the evaluation process. The supervisor is not confined by an evaluation system that limits expression or assumes that employee traits can be uniformly applied and scaled.

Disadvantages

Essay methods are time-consuming and usually difficult to administer. Supervisors often find the essay technique more demanding than methods such as rating scales. The greatest advantage of the essay technique — freedom of expression — is also its greatest handicap. In addition, the difference in writing skills of supervisors and managers can upset the results and lead to distortion of the entire process. Because the process is subjective, it is also difficult to compare and contrast or to draw any broad conclusions about company needs.

Results Method

Management by objectives (MBO) performance evaluation is results-oriented. It attempts to measure employee performance by examining the extent to which employees meet predetermined work objectives. The objectives are usually established jointly by the supervisors and employees. An example of an objective for a customer service manager might be the following: "Increase the gross monthly volume of contacts to 100,000 by September 30, 2002."

Once an objective is established, the **employee** is usually expected to identify the skills needed to achieve the objective. Employees do not rely on others, such as supervisors or managers, to locate and specify their strengths and weaknesses. They are expected to monitor their own development and progress toward achieving the objective.

Advantages

The MBO approach helps overcome some of the problems that arise when employers assume that they can reliably identify and measure the traits needed for job success. Instead of assuming traits, the MBO method concentrates on the actual outcome of the employee objectives.

When the employee meets or exceeds the set objectives, then the employee has demonstrated an acceptable level of job performance. Employees are judged according to actual outcomes — not on their potential for success or on someone's subjective opinion of their abilities.

The guiding principle of the MBO approach is that supervisors can observe direct results. In other performance evaluations, the traits and attributes of employees — which do not always contribute to performance — must be guessed at or inferred.

The MBO method recognizes that it is difficult to evaluate all the complex and varied elements that make up employee performance. It operates on the principle that employee performance cannot be broken up into parts and then evaluated on the basis of these parts as one might take apart a machine. However, when all the parts are working together, the performance may be directly observed and measured.

Disadvantages

MBO methods of performance evaluations can give employees a satisfying sense of self-worth and achievement. Unfortunately, they can also lead to unrealistic expectations about what can and cannot be reasonably accomplished by the employees. Supervisors and employees must be extremely careful not to lose their perception of reality when using MBO evaluation methods. This is especially true when implementing the method and for the purposes of self-auditing and self-monitoring. Unfortunately, the ability to be objective about oneself is not easily conveyed by training. Reality itself tends to be mostly an intensely personal experience, subject to all forms of individual perceptual bias.

The strength of the MBO method is the clarity of purpose that follows from a set of well-described and understood objectives, but this can be a source of weakness also. Objectives, by their very nature, have a tendency to impose a certain rigidity. On the other hand, variable objectives can result in employee confusion. Furthermore, fluid objectives may become distorted and disguise or even justify failures in performance by the employee.

Common Mistakes

Most often, performance evaluations fail to work as well as they should because top-level management fails to support them. For instance, management may subvert or ignore performance evaluations due to the following:

- ♦ Political motives.
- ♦ Ignorance.
- ♦ Lack of confidence in the concept of evaluations.

Top management must embrace the value of evaluations and express their support of them. Top managers are powerful role models for other managers and employees, and their approval of performance evaluations will lead to support from these managers and employees. Those attempting to introduce performance evaluations — or even to revise an existing system — must be aware of the importance of top managerial support and the problems that occur without it.

Fear of Failure

Many supervisors who conduct the evaluations believe that a poor evaluation tends to reflect badly upon them also, since they most likely supervise the employee. Many supervisors have a vested interest in making their subordinates "look good" on paper. When this problem exists, it may point to a problem in the company's attitude regarding its employees.

The cause may be an organization that is intolerant of failure. Supervisors may fear the possibility of repercussions — for both themselves and the employee— if the evaluation is not positive.

Most supervisors protect their own interests first, and this leads to inaccurate performance evaluations. Supervisors are not willing to use the performance evaluations properly if the results adversely affect them. This results in a deliberate distortion in the performance evaluations of employees that is almost impossible to safeguard against.

Surveys have shown that not only do many managers admit to a little "fudging," they actually defend it as a tactic necessary for effective management. The fudging motives of supervisors have, at times, a certain plausibility. A supervisor who has given an overly generous evaluation to a mediocre performer might claim that the legitimate motive was encouragement for better performance. Unfortunately, this is not always the case. For example, the supervisor who fudges for the following reasons may regret it later:

♦ To avoid an unpleasant confrontation.

♦ To protect and hide employee difficulties from senior managers.

♦ To punish or reward employees.

Avoiding Judgment

Many people are reluctant to "play judge" and create a permanent record that may affect an employee's future career opportunities, especially where negative performance evaluations are necessary. When this occurs, training in the techniques of constructive evaluation may help. Supervisors need to recognize that problems left unchecked could potentially cause more harm to an employee's career than early detection and correction. Companies might also consider the confidential archiving of performance evaluations more than three years old.

Seeking Positive Feedback

This occurs where a poor performing employee regularly seeks informal praise from a supervisor at inappropriate times. Often the employees will get the praise they want, since they control the time and place to ask for it. They effectively surprise the supervisor by seeking positive feedback at moments when the supervisor is unable or unprepared to give them a full and proper answer, or in settings that are inappropriate for an honest assessment. The supervisor feels "put on the spot," and will often provide a few encouraging words of support. This seems harmless enough until performance evaluation time comes around. At this time the supervisor will find that the employee recalls, without hesitation, every casual word of praise ever said by the supervisor.

This places the supervisor in a difficult position for making an accurate evaluation. If the evaluation is negative, employees may remind the supervisor of past praise. Employees may even say that the supervisor lied when giving past praise or misled them into thinking that their performance was acceptable. In fact, this may be an attempt to deflect responsibility for poor performance. Employees may be trying to improve their performance evaluation by bringing in all the evidence of the supervisor's casual praise. The employees are usually successful in making the supervisor feel partly responsible. As a result, the flustered supervisor may upgrade their performance evaluation, making it inaccurate.

In fact, the poor performing employee has effectively blackmailed the supervisor. Companies need to make supervisors aware of this employee tactic so it may be prevented. The supervisors need to explain to the employee when asked for casual praise that the time is inappropriate and offer to speak to the employee later. This puts the supervisor back in control of the performance evaluation process and allows for an honest assessment of the employee's performance.

Supervisor Preparation

Supervisors need to be conscious of the importance of the performance evaluation and should be discouraged from performing evaluations "off the cuff." Top levels of management should stress the importance and technical challenge of a good performance evaluation system. Supervisors should receive regular training to help them see the critical issues that must be considered.

Employee Participation

It is vital that employees participate with their supervisors in the creation of their own performance goals and development plans. Mutual agreement is a key to the success of performance evaluations. A plan that involves the employee — providing some degree of ownership — is more likely to be accepted than one that is imposed.

Note: This does not mean that employees do not require guidance from their supervisors, and the supervisors should not neglect this responsibility.

Performance Management

Supervisors should consider performance evaluations as an ongoing process rather than an isolated event. Employees require more frequent feedback than can be provided by an annual performance evaluation. It may not be necessary to conduct full performance evaluations more than once or twice a year; however, performance management should be regarded as an ongoing process.

Bimonthly shortened performance evaluations and feedback sessions will help ensure that employees receive the ongoing guidance, support, and encouragement they need. Although supervisors may complain that time restrictions do not allow this type of ongoing feedback, this is not likely the case, and the company should do its best to enforce these policies.

Stress Priorities

When supervisors say they "do not have time," they actually mean that the supervision and development of employees is not as high a priority as certain other tasks. It does not make sense for an organization to allow supervisors to neglect their responsibilities to monitor and facilitate the performance of their employees. If performance evaluations are viewed as an isolated event, supervisors will come to view their responsibilities in the same way. More importantly, this may result in the employees neglecting their own responsibilities until a month or two preceding the performance evaluations.

Special Performance Evaluation

Often, supervisors use special performance evaluations to address specific problems or even to dispense praise. The special performance evaluation can be used in both positive and negative employee conduct or behavior situations. A sample of special performance evaluation is at the end of this chapter.

Conflict and Confrontation

Sometimes the need arises during a performance evaluation to provide an employee with less than flattering or outright negative feedback. The skill and sensitivity used to handle these difficult situations are critical. There is no problem when the employee accepts the negative feedback and agrees to improve performance. However, the process of correction has failed when the result is an angry or hurt employee. It is in these situations that the performance of an employee is unlikely to improve and may even deteriorate further.

Employee Self-Auditing

Supervisors should not immediately criticize the employees. Instead, try to let the evidence of poor performance evolve "naturally" during the course of the performance evaluation discussion. This can be accomplished by using questioning techniques that encourage the employees to identify their own performance weaknesses or problems. The supervisors should encourage employees to openly talk about their own impressions of their performance.

Example: An Employee Who Has Had Too Many Absent Days

Accusatory Mode:

"Your attendance record is not acceptable to the company. You will have to improve it."

Better Approach:

"Your attendance record indicates that you had five days off work in four months. What can you tell me about this?"

Using this technique, the employer calmly and accurately present the evidence without labeling it as good or bad and then asks the employee to comment. In many situations, with just a gentle nudge from the supervisor an employee with problems often admits that weaknesses do in fact exist. When employees do not feel accused of anything or forced to make admissions that they do not wish to make, the result is usually favorable.

If an employer gets an employee to the stage of voluntary admission, the employer has accomplished the goal. This technique is a type of self-auditing because it encourages employees to address their own work and performance issues.

The technique is useful because it is more likely to promote discussion and agreement on the need for change or improvement. Conversely, techniques that are primarily accusatory tend to promote conflict leading to denial and resentment by the employee.

Responsibility for Problems

If an employer uses the self-auditing process, employees are generally more willing to accept personal responsibility for problems that have been self-identified. This responsibility provides an excellent starting point for implementing change and development.

Denial

Invariably, some employees will not admit to anything that appears to reflect poorly or negatively on them. They will most likely resist the process of self-auditing very strongly. In these cases supervisors must confront the employee directly and firmly with the evidence they have of poor performance. Sometimes this direct confrontation will lead employees to admit that they need to make improvements. However, in some cases the confrontation will only increase the employee's denial.

Provide Evidence

When an employer provides feedback, especially negative, the employer should support opinions with specific and clear examples.

The employer should try to follow these guidelines:

♦ Avoid any vague generalizations about employee conduct.

♦ Focus on job-related behaviors and attitudes.

♦ Exclude observations that cannot be supported by clear evidence or touch nonjob related issues.

♦ Carefully and accurately scrutinize perceptions, motives, and prejudices prior to performing any employee performance evaluations.

Meaningful Performance Evaluations

Honesty

The performance review must be honest. Although supervisors can be unduly harsh on employees during an evaluation, excessive leniency is ordinarily the rule rather than the exception. It is certainly appropriate to note and praise good work done by the employee in the past. However, the evaluation must also point out any deficiencies in employee performance.

Defending a wrongful termination suit is extremely difficult if the reason for termination is a problem that had been developing for time and was not noted on employee performance evaluations. The employer's case is even further damaged when the employee received favorable performance evaluations, including favorable remarks on the categories of performance that are later involved in the reasons for termination.

Forget Quota Approach

Some employers require supervisors to place a specified number of employees in each evaluation category. This is not advisable because some supervisors may have an imbalance of strong or weak performing employees within a particular department. However, supervisors should be given general guidelines regarding the expected distribution of rankings, and the employer should require supervisors to justify deviations from that expected distribution.

Uniformity Among Supervisors

Always monitor supervisors as they conduct performance evaluations, making sure the process is uniform throughout the company. Otherwise supervisors in one department may give more favorable (or harsh) evaluations than those in another. When these imbalances occur, it is difficult for an employer to defend against wrongful termination because it would have to attack the credibility of its own evaluation system.

Strengths and Weaknesses

Require that each evaluation include some discussion of both the strengths and weaknesses of the employee. The evaluation will appear as much fairer and objective if it includes deserved compliments.

Constructive Criticism

Constructive criticism in the performance evaluations also has advantages. Some constructive criticism of good employees may help lay the groundwork for negative evaluations of those employees in the future if their overall performance deteriorates. This is particularly true when an employee brings a wrongful termination suit after an unfavorable performance evaluation.

It can be helpful for the employer to show that the employee was criticized for some of those same faults on evaluations years earlier, even though the problem was in its infancy at that time and did not warrant an overall negative evaluation.

Communicating Results to Employees

An employer loses the value of a performance evaluation program if the employer does not communicate the results to employees. The employer should communicate in a way that will encourage the employees to take positive steps to improve their effectiveness and job performance. As a result, before the meeting supervisors may want to provide employees with a method for self-evaluation. These forms allow the employees to review the prior year before meeting with the supervisor.

Meeting with an Employee

Perhaps the most crucial part of the entire evaluation process is the meeting where the supervisor and employee discuss the evaluation. When handled well, the discussion can lead to better understanding between the employee and supervisor. Ideally, any problem(s) will be identified and the employee will become aware of what is required to improve performance. When the meeting is not conducted properly, the employee will feel resentment rather than a desire to improve.

Employee Acknowledgment and Input

Employees should have the right to review the evaluation and comment on it. Give the employee an opportunity to agree or disagree with the ratings of the job duties. This part of the process can alert an employer to actual or potential problems with an employee. It also provides proof of employer fairness.

The employee should sign an acknowledgment on the evaluation form to the effect that the employee has read the evaluation. This prevents the employee from claiming later to have been unaware of how the employee was being evaluated. The employee should also be permitted to write on the evaluation form that the employee disagrees with the evaluation if this is the case. The performance evaluation can also give an employee the opportunity to set goals to accomplish before the next review. These goals can help eliminate problems that the employee has had in the past or can set forth additional accomplishments that the employer would like the employee to make. The evaluation should include a note stating that the employer and employee agree on the new goals.

Note: All performance evaluations should be carefully documented. Consistently apply the documentation procedure to all employees. An undocumented evaluation is virtually useless in litigation.

When Not to Evaluate

Although performance reviews, when used properly, help employers, sometimes they should not be performed. All of the following are reasons **not** to use performance evaluations:

- ♦ Inconsistency of performance reviews for all employees.
- ♦ Evaluations that are not documented.
- ♦ Employee deficiencies are not clearly set forth by supervisors and managers.
- ♦ Employee improvement is required in the evaluation but not enforced.
- ♦ Employers do not take the general evaluation rules specified above seriously.

Warning: Employers should remember that periodic and continued salary increases, even though the employee may not be performing well, may allow the employee some basis for a discrimination claim later on.

Avoiding Legal Problems

Federal civil rights and state fair employment practice laws are in place to prohibit employers from using performance evaluation systems that discriminate against employees based on race, color, religion, gender, national origin, or disability. To avoid liability, an employer must ensure that its supervisors and managers base their performance evaluation judgments solely on job-related factors.

Validity and Reliability

In determining whether performance evaluation systems are discriminatory, courts generally apply the same standards used to determine whether employee selection procedures and tests are discriminatory. Under such standards, a performance evaluation system is nondiscriminatory if it is both valid and reliable. When the system does not satisfy both requirements, the discriminatory impact of the improper factors might cause the system to violate one or more federal or state laws.

Valid and reliable performance evaluation programs normally share the following characteristics:

- The performance evaluation program is formal and in writing.

- Ratings are reviewed to ensure that high and low ratings are documented with information showing what the employee did or did not do to earn the rating. Reviews also look for statistical patterns of adverse ratings and evidence that a supervisor needs more training rating employees.

- The evaluation relates to the particular job in question. This means that employees are not rated on items that are irrelevant to job performance. A rater who must use a preprinted form that is not specific to the job should have the option of checking "not applicable."

- The rater is familiar with the employee's job duties and actual performance. Raters should be allowed to state or check "not observed" when necessary.

- Employees read their evaluations, sign them to acknowledge having read them, and have the opportunity to comment on them in writing.

- Evaluations are not final until employees have had the opportunity to comment on them.

- Higher-level management reviews all evaluations.

- Supervisors receive training in evaluating employees.

- Raters receive clear written instructions.

- Evaluation forms are as clear and simple as possible.

- Definitions and examples are included to clarify the scope and meaning of various rating categories.

- Standards or expectations are identified clearly for each aspect of performance and are communicated to the employee.

- Employees have input in setting performance expectations.

- The relative importance of each aspect of performance is communicated.

- The primary goal of the evaluation is to enable employees to improve. Raters help an employee recognize strengths and weaknesses and help employees develop plans for improvement.

Note: Employees have the opportunity to appeal ratings to higher-level management.

How to Evaluate an Employee Checklist
(Sample Policy)

Management should continuously review the following list to ensure that the company's performance evaluation program is conducted properly.

❑ **Set clear, measurable standards for performance.** Employers should spell out what behavior would merit each of the ratings before assessing employees.

❑ **Base the evaluation on the typical performance of the employee during the entire period.** Employers should not overemphasize recent occurrences or isolated dramatic incidents that are not typical of the employee's normal behavior.

❑ **Base evaluations on accurate data obtained from records (whenever possible) or from careful observation (when records are not available).** Compare the performance of the employee being evaluated with the performance of all individuals who have performed the same job, keeping in mind the requirements of the job.

❑ **Do not let the evaluation on one factor influence the evaluation on other factors.** Many raters have a tendency to give an employee who rates very high on one factor a higher rating on other factors than may be merited. In like manner, when an employee is weak in one respect, the person doing the evaluation sometimes assumes the employee is weak in other respects, which may not be the case. Employers should consider each factor independently.

❑ **Do not permit grade of job, length of service, or previous experience to affect the rating.** Raters must consider only the performance of the employee in relationship to the specific requirements of the job. Do not rate an employee too highly simply because the employee has a number of years of service or a wealth of experience.

❑ **Do not let personal feelings bias the evaluation — whether positive or negative.** The supervisor or manager conducting the evaluation must be constantly on guard against the normal inclination to attribute greater proficiency to employees whom are liked personally or for whom the evaluator has sympathy. When special extenuating circumstances exist, evaluate only on performance, and explain the circumstances in the space provided.

❑ **Do not be influenced by a previous evaluation.** Past evaluations should not influence present ones. Substantial differences do not necessarily mean that an evaluation is incorrect.

❑ **Guard against letting the evaluation of factors fall into a consistent or routine pattern.** There are usually wide differences in individuals with respect to the factors evaluated.

❑ **Do not make an evaluation on vague impressions.** To rate accurately, the evaluator must have a very good knowledge of the employee's performance. When facts or records are available, the raters should use them

❑ **Do not evaluate too quickly.** Take enough time to evaluate accurately.

❑ **Do not hesitate to go on record with an honest opinion.** A good rater should be able to differentiate between the performances of the employees.

Note: The categories are guidelines. Companies should create and define their own standards for review.

Employee's Form for
Self-Auditing Performance
(Sample Policy)

Employee: _____

Title: _____

Department: _____

Supervisor: _____

Date: _____

The following questions are intended to help prepare for a performance evaluation review meeting with the supervisor. (Please be as specific as possible when giving your answers. Feel free to use more paper when necessary.)

- What do you consider to be your major on-the-job accomplishments since your last review?

- List your areas of strengths and areas needing improvement.

- How well do you know what you need to know in order to do your work? What additional information would be helpful?

- Are there any changes that could be made to improve your effectiveness?

- What skills or new knowledge would you like to develop to improve your performance?

- What can you, your supervisor, or the company do to improve your performance and increase your overall job satisfaction?

- How would you assess communication within your department? How well informed are you of the information necessary to perform your duties efficiently? What additional information do you need?

- What are your long-range career objectives and what are your plans to accomplish these objectives? Objectives include potential job rotations, promotions, additional job responsibilities, education, and training.

- What goals would you be interested in working toward between now and the next performance evaluation?

- How will you measure progress toward these goals?

Note: This is a generic sample policy and does not necessarily reflect the employment laws in any or all of the 50 U.S. states. Before establishing any company policy, one should review the applicable state laws or seek guidance from legal counsel.

Special Performance Evaluation
(Sample)

Name of Employee: _____

Job Title: _____

Department: _____

It has come to my attention that you have displayed the behavior or conduct listed below on the job recently (include dates and times where possible):

As your supervisor, I want you to know that this type of conduct or behavior on the job could or will have one of the following effects on your overall work performance:

Strongly Positive   **Negative**   **Strongly Negative**

Additional Comments by Supervisor:

Supervisor's Signature/Date: _____

Comments by Employee:

I have read and understood the content of this Special Performance Evaluation:

Employee's Signature/Date: _____

Note: This is a generic sample policy and does not necessarily reflect the employment laws in any or all of the 50 U.S. states. Before establishing any company policy, one should review the applicable state laws or seek guidance from legal counsel.

Chapter 8

Drug and Alcohol Testing in the Workplace

Introduction

Drug use on the job and the job-related effects of drug and alcohol use off the job are important concerns for employers. As a result, drug- and alcohol-testing programs are widely implemented in both the private and public sectors.

A significant number of states provide for the mandatory regulation of substance abuse policies in the workplace. However, such workplace policies are subject to scrutiny on several levels. For example, both testing and searches of employees may give rise to common-law invasion-of-privacy claims. Additionally, adoption of a workplace policy is subject to an employer's duty to bargain with a union. Further, discipline and discharge for substance abuse may be attacked through nondiscrimination laws and in court or arbitration under wrongful discharge theories.

The federal government has drafted employers to help in its war on drugs. For example, federal contractors and grantees have mandatory drug-free workplace obligations. Moreover, transportation employers such as railroads, merchant mariners, airlines, motor carriers, and pipeline operators must develop and implement applicant and employee drug- and alcohol-testing programs.

This chapter reviews federal regulations concerning drug and alcohol testing, discusses the federal Drug-Free Workplace Act and related regulations, and details procedures for employers that are planning to implement a drug- and alcohol-testing program. Where appropriate, any state laws are reviewed.

Testing Limits

Within reason, all employees **may** be tested. However, certain classes of employees sustain established limits as to how far employers may go. Those limits depend upon the nature of the employment relationship, as well as federal, state, and local laws.

Private At-Will Employees

At-will employees have brought invasion-of-privacy claims when employers have engaged in random testing, and defamation claims when reports of false positive results have been circulated to others. At-will employees also have sued for breach of contract based upon information about drug testing in an employee handbook.

Union Employees

Courts, interpreting the National Labor Relations Act (NLRA), mandate that employers bargain collectively with unions about substance abuse testing programs. This prevents an employer from unilaterally implementing drug testing for union employees unless there has been a clear and unmistakable waiver by the union of its right to bargain over these issues. The National Labor Relations Board (NLRB) generally disfavors such a waiver. The NLRB does not require employers to bargain over pre-employment testing programs, except in situations such as hiring halls where the union has become a participant in the hiring process.

Nonunion Contract Employees

A drug-testing program need not necessarily be contained within an employment contract in order for it to be valid. However, to avoid breach-of-contract lawsuits, employees should agree, in writing, to comply with all personnel policies implemented by management before or during employment and should argue specifically to abide by the employer's substance abuse testing program.

Public Sector Employees

Federal, state, and local government employees have Fourth Amendment constitutional protection generally not enjoyed by their private sector counterparts. Drug tests initiated by public employers are subject to prohibitions against unreasonable search and seizure. Random testing should be limited to employees who work in safety-sensitive positions.

Job Applicants

Applicants have fewer privacy rights than employees. Employers often make offers of permanent employment conditioned upon successful completion of a drug test. The Americans with Disabilities Act (ADA) regulations do not hold such a pre-employment test for illegal drugs to be an unlawful pre-employment medical examination. However, no such exclusion is provided for pre-employment alcohol tests. In fact, pre-employment alcohol tests are often regarded as being of questionable value, since applicants may easily abstain from drinking for the short period of time needed to obtain a negative test result.

Administering drug tests before an offer of employment is extended may prove problematical because information gathered from a drug test about a person's medical condition or history **may not** be considered before a job offer proposal. Consequently, employers should delay drug tests until they have extended a conditional offer of employment. Thus, the employer does not have pre-offer knowledge of real or apparent disabilities revealed by test results and cannot be accused of basing a decision not to hire on the applicant's actual or perceived disability.

Discipline and Discharge for Substance Abuse in a Union Setting

Employer attempts to enforce a drug and alcohol policy within a union workforce will most likely result in challenges through the grievance and arbitration process. Arbitrators have varying attitudes about the circumstances under which alcoholism or drunkenness is cause for discharge. Some arbitrators will sustain discipline based solely upon employee performance without regard to any explanations for shortcomings. Others consider alcoholic employees to be victims of a disorder who should be offered an opportunity to recover, complete with leaves of absence and appropriate treatment.

While arbitrators tend to view alcoholism as a treatable disorder, there is considerable resistance to the concept of rehabilitating an employee with a drug-related problem. Most drug offenses carry a taint of criminality. Therefore, arbitrators are more inclined to look with disfavor on drug users.

Generally, arbitrators regard an employee's activity during personal time and off the employer's premises as being of no concern to the employer **unless** the employer can demonstrate that the off-duty activity caused any of the following:

♦ Damaged the organization's reputation or product.

♦ Interfered with the employee's work attendance or performance.

♦ Resulted in a peer's reasonable refusal, reluctance, or inability to work with the employee.

Arbitrators tend to uphold the discharge and discipline of employees who test positive for drugs or alcohol when the employer has performed the following:

♦ Defined a drug-testing policy that clarifies possible consequences.

♦ Applied its policy reasonably and consistently.

Americans with Disabilities Act

According to 42 U.S.C.A. § 12114, the Americans with Disabilities Act (ADA) does not prohibit discrimination against an individual based on that individual's current use of illegal drugs. According to the ADA, the term "qualified individual with a disability" does not include any employee or applicant who is currently engaging in the illegal use of drugs, when the covered entity acts on the basis of such use. *Current use of illegal drugs* means the illegal use of drugs that occurred recently enough to justify a reasonable belief that a person's drug use is current or that continuing use is a real and ongoing problem. Current users need not be accommodated and may be discharged (or not hired) for testing positive.

A covered entity is not prohibited from adopting or administering reasonable policies or procedures including, but not limited to, drug testing — designed to ensure that an individual who formerly engaged in illegal drug use is not engaging in current illegal use of drugs.

The ADA does, however, protect former drug users who have successfully completed treatment or who are participating in treatment and persons erroneously regarded as illegal drug users. According to 42 U.S.C.A. § 12114, a covered entity **may not** discriminate on the basis of illegal drug use against an individual who is not engaging in current illegal use and who fulfills one of the following:

♦ Successfully completed a supervised drug rehabilitation program or has otherwise been rehabilitated successfully.

♦ Is participating in a supervised rehabilitation program.

♦ Is erroneously regarded as engaging in such use, but is not engaging in such use.

Additionally, individuals who are using a drug taken under supervision by a licensed health care professional or other legal uses are protected against discrimination. Given the distinction between legal and illegal drug use under the ADA, employers should use a physician as a medical review officer (MRO) to verify test results and separate illegal drug users from persons lawfully taking prescribed medications.

Under the ADA, alcoholism is treated differently in comparison to illegal drug use. According to the EEOC Enforcement Guidance on Disability-Related Inquiries and Medical Examinations of Employees, tests for alcohol use are classified as "medical examinations." Whereas, tests to determine the current illegal use of drugs are generally not considered to be medical examinations. Accordingly, employers may neither require a medical examination nor make inquiries of an employee as to whether the employee is an individual with a disability or as to the nature and severity of the disability. Alcohol tests must be job-related and consistent with business necessity and, if given to applicants, may be administered only after conditional offers of employment are extended. As a practical matter such pre-employment alcohol tests are of questionable value. Importantly, the ADA does specifically allow employers to prohibit the on-the-job use of alcohol and to prohibit employees from being under the influence of alcohol while in the workplace.

Please note, according to 42 U.S.C.A. § 12114, an employer may also hold an employee who engages in illegal drug use or who is an alcoholic to the same qualification standards for employment or job performance and behavior that such entity holds other employees, even if any unsatisfactory performance or behavior is related to the drug use or alcoholism of the employee.

Individuals who are using a drug taken under supervision by a licensed health care professional or other legal uses are also protected against discrimination. Tests to determine whether employees or applicants are using prescribed drugs must be job-related and consistent with business necessity. Under the ADA, employees who receive positive results on fitness for duty tests may be entitled to reasonable accommodation. Since the ADA increases the legal risks involved in testing for such drugs as pain relievers and tranquilizers, the risks of testing for legal drugs probably outweigh the benefits except in safety-critical jobs or cases where a substance abuse professional has authorized follow-up testing after an employee has returned to work from treatment for drug abuse. Given the distinction between legal and illegal drug use under the ADA, employers should use a physician as a medical review officer to verify test results and separate illegal drug users from persons lawfully taking prescribed medications.

The ADA permits employers to perform any testing required by Department of Transportation (DOT), Department of Defense (DOD), or Department of Energy regulations. It also allows employers to prohibit employees from using or being under the influence of illegal drugs in the workplace and from violating the Drug-Free Workplace Act.

Transportation Employee Drug and Alcohol Testing

Federal law regulated by the Department of Transportation (DOT) requires various forms of drug and alcohol testing by employers in the following transportation industries:

- ◆ Motor carrier.
- ◆ Railroad.
- ◆ Aviation.
- ◆ Maritime.
- ◆ Mass transit.
- ◆ Pipeline.

Employers in these industries are required by the DOT to implement highly specific drug-testing programs conforming to detailed regulations. Under the DOT regulations, all employees who need a commercial driver's license (CDL) to perform their work are subject to drug testing. The regulations apply to any employer with a single CDL employee. Additionally, all employers should regard the DOT rules as a benchmark for their testing programs.

DOT Drug Testing

The following is a general summary of the existing DOT drug testing regulations for transportation employees. As the regulations vary between each transportation agency, guidelines should be obtained from each agency with jurisdiction over an employer and legal counsel should be consulted.

DOT-Required Drug Tests

Pre-Employment Testing

Applicants for employment in covered positions must successfully complete a drug test before performing a safety-sensitive function.

Random Testing

According to 49 C.F.R. § 655.45, DOT employers in the motor carrier and mass transit industries must conduct a number of random drug tests each year equal to 50 percent of covered employees. (Different random testing rates may apply to employers in the DOT-covered industries.) Such tests must be spread throughout the year. Employees **may not** receive any advance warning of the random tests and must have an equal chance of being tested during each period of selection time. Employers may wish to join consortiums or to contract with third-party administrators to reduce some of the administrative problems involved in scheduling random tests.

Post-Accident Testing

Testing is required within a specific number of hours after serious accidents or rule violations. Employees who may have contributed to the accident must be drug tested after receiving any necessary medical attention. According to 49 C.F.R. § 382.303, commercial motor vehicle drivers must be tested after reportable accidents if they receive a citation for a moving violation arising out of the accident or if someone dies as a result of the accident.

Reasonable Suspicion Testing

An employer **may** conduct drug and alcohol testing when the employer has reasonable suspicion to believe that the employee has used a prohibited drug or engaged in alcohol misuse. Tests for reasonable suspicion must be based on specific, contemporaneous, articulable observations by a trained supervisor(s) concerning the employee's appearance, behavior, body odors, or speech.

Return-to-Duty Testing

Employees who violate DOT drug testing regulations must undergo a return-to-duty test with a verified negative result before performing a safety-sensitive function.

Follow-Up Testing

Employees who violate DOT drug-testing regulations and have a drug problem, as diagnosed by a substance abuse professional, are subject to random follow-up testing for up to five years after returning to duty.

Consequences for Violation of DOT Drug-Testing Regulations

Employees who receive verified positive test results or otherwise violate the regulations must be immediately removed from safety-sensitive positions. Such employees **may not** return to duty until after they undergo evaluation and treatment or pass medical tests. The employees are then subject to random follow-up tests.

Employees who refuse to be tested or engage in conduct that clearly obstructs the testing process are subject to the same consequences as employees who test positive.

DOT regulations neither mandate nor forbid the imposition of additional discipline (such as discharge) by an employer for violating DOT rules. Employers are free to impose additional consequences on their own authority, subject to the legal obligations and limitations previously discussed.

Additional DOT Drug-Testing Requirements

The DOT regulations also require and authorize the following:

- ♦ Testing only for marijuana, cocaine, opiates, amphetamines, and PCP.

- ♦ Testing only by labs certified by the U.S. Department of Health and Human Services (HHS).

- ♦ A medical review officer (MRO) must assess test results. The MRO must determine whether there was a legitimate explanation for positive tests and whether lab the results were scientifically reliable.

- ♦ Employers must use the split-sample method of urine testing. Under this method, the urine sample provided at the testing site is divided into a primary sample and a split sample. Employees and applicants who receive verified positive results or verified adulterated or substituted results on the primary sample may request that the split-sample be sent to another certified lab for testing.

DOT Alcohol Testing

All employers covered by the DOT drug-testing regulations are also required to have an alcohol-testing program complying with DOT standards.

The alcohol rules provide for breath testing using trained technicians and evidential breath-testing devices. The breath-testing devices must be federally approved. The regulations allow the option of using saliva tests or nonevidential breath-testing devices for screening tests only.

Note: Confirmation tests must be conducted with evidential breath-testing devices.

Consequences for Violation of DOT Alcohol-Testing Regulations

Employees with a confirmation test result indicating a blood alcohol concentration (BAC) of 0.04 or greater or who otherwise violate the DOT alcohol regulations must be immediately removed from performing safety-sensitive duties. They **may not** return to such duties until they are evaluated by a substance abuse professional and undergo a successful return-to-duty test. Such employees are also subject to follow-up testing and must successfully complete any prescribed treatment program.

Employees who refuse to be tested or obstruct testing are subject to the same consequences as employees testing 0.04 BAC or above. As with DOT drug testing, employers may impose additional discipline subject to the other legal obligations and limitations previously discussed.

Employees with a BAC between 0.02 and 0.39 are not deemed to be in violation of the regulations, but must be temporarily removed from safety-sensitive duty for 24 hours.

DOT-Required Alcohol Tests

The DOT regulations generally require covered employers to conduct the following types of alcohol tests:

- ♦ Post-accident.
- ♦ Reasonable suspicion.
- ♦ Return to duty.
- ♦ Follow-up.
- ♦ Random.

The DOT regulations require that random testing be conducted annually and, according to 49 C.F.R. § 655.45, DOT employers in the motor carrier and mass transit industries must conduct a number of random alcohol tests each year equal to 10 percent of covered employees.

DOT Policy Requirement

Employers are required to prepare and distribute a policy explaining the requirements of DOT regulations to all covered employees. Each employee must sign a statement certifying receipt of the policy.

Drug-Free Workplace Act

According to the U.S. Department of Labor, millions of Americans use illicit drugs and nearly 75 percent of these users are employed. Companies that have implemented drug-free workplace programs achieve dramatic benefits such as decreased absenteeism, a declining number of accidents, and increased productivity.

Covered Employers

All direct recipients of federal grants and most federal contractors holding a single contract under the federal acquisition regulations that exceeds $100,000, not for the acquisition of commercial goods, and performed in part (or in whole) in the United States must comply with the federal Drug-Free Workplace Act. The act applies to employees and facilities engaged in directly performing work under such contracts and grants. It does not apply to subcontractors or second-tier recipients of pass-through grants, nor does it apply to companies that hold multiple small contracts totaling more than $100,000. A company would be subject to the act only if the value of a single contract is more than $100,000. A company that has several contracts which, when combined, total more than $100,000, is not subject to the act.

Policy

Covered employers are required to retain a drug-free workplace accompanied by both a policy and a drug-free awareness program.

The policy must notify employees performing work under the contract or grant of the following prohibitions and the penalties for convictions:

♦ Employee may not manufacture, distribute, possess, or use controlled substances in the workplace.

♦ Employees must report any criminal convictions for manufacturing, distributing, dispensing, possessing, or using controlled substances in the workplace to the employer within five days.

With respect to employees who report such convictions, employers have 30 days to take appropriate disciplinary action, up to and including discharge, or to require satisfactory participation in an assistance/rehabilitation program. The act gives contractors and grantees discretion to decide what action to take. Contractors must also report any employee convictions for workplace drug crimes of which they have been notified to the contracting agency within 10 days.

The act also requires contractors and grantees to establish drug-free awareness programs informing employees of the employer's drug-free workplace policy, the adverse effects of drug abuse, the penalties that will be imposed for workplace drug violations, and any available drug counseling, rehabilitation, or assistance programs. However, the act does not require that a particular rehabilitation program be provided.

Under the act, drug testing, employee assistance programs, and supervisor training are optional. Such options and the ways unionized employers choose to exercise their discretion under the act are subject to collective bargaining. Thus, such employers may have to bargain over whether treatment will be offered and whether employees will be reassigned to jobs that do not involve the performance of federal contract work instead of being fired.

Grantees and contractors should maintain a current list of the facilities and departments performing federal contract work and have operable programs within 30 days of receiving contracts or grants. Any government audits may include a review of Drug-Free Workplace Act compliance programs.

Department of Defense Regulations

Certain Department of Defense (DOD) contracts involving classified information and national security contain a drug-free workforce clause. DOD contracts should be reviewed individually to see whether they contain such a clause. Ordinarily, contracts to deliver commercial products and contracts to be performed outside the United States are not covered.

The clause requires prime contractors to institute and maintain a drug-free workforce program. Such programs must include the following:

♦ An employee-assistance program (EAP) emphasizing high-level direction, education, counseling, rehabilitation, and coordination with available community resources

♦ Supervisory training to identify and address illegal drug use by employees.

♦ Provisions for self-referrals and supervisory referrals to treatment, with maximum respect for confidentiality consistent with safety and security.

♦ A means of identifying illegal drug users, including drug testing employees in sensitive positions.

♦ The removal of identified drug users from sensitive positions. Contractors who are subject to the clause may not allow employees who use drugs illegally to remain on duty or perform in a sensitive position until the contractor determines that they may properly perform in the position.

Sensitive positions are positions involving access to classified information, national security, health or safety, or requiring a high degree of trust and confidence.

The rule provides that the criteria for testing shall be determined by the contractor based on such factors as the nature of the contract, the employee's job duties, and the risks to health, safety, or national security that could result from an employee's failure to perform the job adequately. Testing is limited to marijuana, cocaine, opiates, PCP, and amphetamines.

In addition, contractors **may** test for the following reasons:

♦ When there is reasonable suspicion of use.

♦ When an employee is involved in an accident or unsafe practice.

♦ As part of treatment or follow-up to rehabilitation.

♦ As part of a voluntary testing program.

♦ As a part of a random testing program imposed without suspicion that a specific individual is using illegal drugs.

Contractors **may** also test applicants. Contractors who are subject to the clause **may not** allow employees who use drugs illegally to remain on duty or perform in a sensitive position until the contractor determines that they may properly perform in the position. Contractors must also adopt appropriate personnel procedures to deal with employees who use drugs illegally.

Considerations When Implementing a Drug- and Alcohol-Testing Program

Employers must consider a variety of factors when implementing a drug-and-alcohol-testing program. The employer should determine the following:

♦ Why the program is being implemented?

♦ Who will be tested?

♦ What types of tests will be given?

♦ What substances will be tested?

♦ Who will give the tests?

♦ The consequences of a positive test.

Reasons to Implement Testing Programs

Testing programs **may** be implemented for the following reasons:

♦ To comply with federal requirements. These include requirements for certain Department of Defense (DOD) contractors, employers subject to the Nuclear Regulatory Commission, and employers subject to Department of Transportation (DOT) testing programs.

♦ To save money. Studies have shown that annually employers lose billions of dollars due to drug abuse among employees. These costs result from lost productivity, increased absenteeism, drug-related accidents, medical claims, and theft.

- To control insurance costs.

- To reduce workers' compensation premiums.

- For employee safety.

- To discourage drug-users from applying for employment. When an employer has a pre-employment drug-testing program, potential applicants who are drug users are less likely to apply for employment.

- To avoid negligent hiring and retention claims. An employer with a drug- and alcohol-testing program may be able to avoid claims of negligence for hiring or retaining employees who the employer knew or should have known had a substance abuse problem.

Employees to Be Tested

Employers must decide which employees will be tested. The options are to test applicants only, all employees, or merely those employees in safety-sensitive or security-sensitive positions. Employers may also decide to test only those employees they reasonably suspect are under the influence of alcohol or are using illegal drugs.

Types of Tests

The types of drug or alcohol tests that can be given include the following:

- **Pre-Employment.** Testing is given before employment to determine if the applicant is using illegal drugs. Most employers do not give pre-employment alcohol tests.

- **Reasonable Suspicion.** An employee may be tested if the employer has a reasonable basis to suspect an employee is using drugs or is at work under the influence of alcohol.

- **Post-Accident.** Testing is given after an employee is involved in an accident. Such testing is generally given if it is provided for in the employer's policy, placing the employee on notice of post-accident testing, and either personal injury is involved or damage to property is estimated at a minimal level.

- **Random.** Testing is given on an unannounced basis and employees are selected for testing on a random basis.

- **Follow-Up.** Testing is given on a scheduled or random basis when an employee returns to work after completing rehabilitation or counseling for substance abuse.

- **Periodic.** Testing is given at specified times. This may be used for employees who have returned to the workforce after testing positive or employees who are in safety- or security-sensitive positions. For example, commercial motor vehicle drivers may be required to submit to an annual test in addition to being subjected to random testing.

Testing for Substance Type

Employers **may** test for the following types of substances:

- Alcohol.

- The five-drug panel required for DOT testing — cocaine, opiates, amphetamines, PCP, and marijuana.

♦ An eight-drug panel or as many substances as a laboratory is capable of accurately testing.

♦ Abused prescription drugs.

The common drugs of abuse are those contained in the five-drug panel required for DOT testing. Employers that test beyond those drugs likely incur an unnecessary expense.

Testing Laboratory

Care should be taken in the selection of a laboratory to analyze the tests. Employers required to test employees under federal drug-testing programs must use laboratories certified for those programs. Even when not required by law, it is preferable to have a laboratory that is certified to perform drug testing in federal programs.

It is important to have a reputable laboratory, experienced and knowledgeable in the proper methods of handling and analyzing urine samples and breath alcohol tests. A good chain of custody is essential to ensure unadulterated samples have been analyzed and that there may be no question as to which sample has been analyzed.

The laboratory should have the highest quality-control standards. A screening test should be used for samples with a confirming test for positive results. The most reliable confirming test is considered to be gas chromatography/mass spectrometry. Laboratory personnel must be willing to defend results and testify in arbitration or court hearings.

Employees should be given notice of test results and an opportunity to establish a legitimate explanation for positive drug-test results to a medical review officer (MRO). Positive drug test results should be verified by the MRO before being reported to the employer.

Consequences of a Positive Test Result

Any drug- and alcohol-policy must have a clear statement as to the consequences of a positive result or for the refusal by an employee to take a required test. The consequences for refusing to be tested should be similar to the penalties for failing a test thereby offering employees an incentive to be cooperative. If an employee assistance program (EAP) is part of the policy, one element should include referral to the EAP.

During policy development, employers must consider the following questions in determining a response to positive test results:

♦ Will there be an opportunity for rehabilitation?

♦ Is the program to be a one-, two-, or three-strike program?

♦ Will an employee be terminated upon their first positive test result?

♦ Will the employee be required to complete or merely enroll in a rehabilitation program before being permitted to return to work?

♦ Will the employee be required to enter into a last-chance agreement?

♦ Will there be a disciplinary suspension or a suspension until the employee is drug-free?

♦ If the employee is in a safety-sensitive or security-sensitive position, will there be a transfer or demotion after a positive test?

♦ Will the transfer or demotion be for a specified period of time or indefinitely?

Other Features of a Good Testing Policy

A good testing policy will provide the following:

- Clearly describe the prohibited conduct and the consequences for such conduct.

- Consider whether to create an EAP.

- Effectively communicate the policy and program to employees and supervisors. Employees should be required to separately sign the policy even if they are already required to sign a general acknowledgment of receipt of a policy handbook.

- Ensure adequate training for supervisors and education for employees.

- Require consent forms for all tests and make clear that refusal to comply will be considered a violation of the policy.

- Ensure an employee's privacy is protected in the testing process and dissemination of test results.

- Document all performance inadequacies.

State Law Considerations Concerning a Drug- and Alcohol-Testing Program

Employers who are not covered by federal laws or regulations must consider whether state or local laws or regulations concerning drug and alcohol testing apply. Some states have mandatory laws governing the conduct of drug and/or alcohol testing. For example, Maine requires employers to submit their drug-and-alcohol-testing policies to the Maine Department of Labor for approval before implementing such policies. Minnesota, Rhode Island, and Boulder, Colorado, require the specimen collection in the testing process, including, but not limited to, blood, urine, bodily fluid, and tissue. Some states, such as Vermont, prohibit company wide and random drug and alcohol testing, unless federal law or regulation requires testing. Other states, for example Oklahoma, require that prior to any drug or alcohol testing, the employer must make an employee assistance program (EAP) available to employees and establish a comprehensive policy which explains all aspects of the testing program. In addition, Maryland, Minnesota, Louisiana, Oklahoma, and North Carolina, among others, have requirements concerning the procedures to be followed in drug and alcohol testing.

When substance abuse testing is not mandated by federal regulations, employers should inquire whether state or local laws restrict their ability to test or offer incentives for certain testing programs.

The Prevalence of Drug Use Among Employees

A survey released by the U.S. Department of Health and Human Services suggests that drug-testing programs may be having a positive effect. The results of the survey indicated that in 2002, there were an estimated 19.5 million illicit drug users (8.3 percent). An estimated 18.2 percent of unemployed adults aged 18 or older were current illicit drug users in 2003 compared with 7.9 percent of those employed full time and 10.7 percent of those employed part time. However, most drug users were employed. Of the 16.7 million illicit drug users aged 18 or older in 2003, 12.4 million (74.3 percent) were employed either full or part time.

Drug and Alcohol Abuse — Performance Indicators

Changes in job performance and in behavior on the job may be indicators that an employee has a problem with drugs or alcohol.

It is vital for employers to objectively and carefully document such changes. Some performance indicators that may indicate an employee has a drug or alcohol problem are the following:

- Frequent tardiness or absences for implausible reasons.
- Unreasonably long lunch, coffee, or bathroom breaks.
- Frequently missed deadlines.
- Disruption of fellow employees.
- Withdrawal from interaction with fellow employees.
- Overreaction to constructive criticism.
- Frequent mistakes related to poor judgment.
- Decreased productivity.
- Great variations in productivity from day to day.
- Inability to concentrate on work.

Guidelines for Supervisors When Confronting a Troubled Employee

The following are actions an employer **should** take if an employee is suspected of drug or alcohol abuse on the job:

- **Do** establish expected levels of work performance.
- **Do** document any and all significant facts and information.
- **Do** be consistent in dealing with the employee.
- **Do** be firm with expectations of the employee and consequences should expectations fail to be met.
- **Do** be prepared to deal with the employee's resistance, denial, defensiveness, and hostility.
- **Do** base confrontation on job performance, and/or on specific, observed behavior including, for example, slurred speech, stumbling gait, bloodshot eyes, and the smell of alcohol on breath.
- **Do** be direct with the employee.
- **Do** provide the information and make appropriate referral according to company policy.
- **Do** take the responsibility to intervene.
- **Do** continue to monitor and document.
- **Do** provide an environment where the employee may be honest and open with perceived troubles.

The following are actions an employer **should not** take if an employee is suspected of drug or alcohol abuse on the job:

- **Do not** be a diagnostician or counselor.
- **Do not** make value judgments or moralize.
- **Do not** allow the employee to pit a supervisor against higher management or the union.
- **Do not** make idle disciplinary threats.
- **Do not** discuss drinking of alcohol unless it occurs on the job.
- **Do not** treat employees differently.
- **Do not** ignore the problem.

Additional Information

Contact Information

Center for Substance Abuse Prevention

The Center for Substance Abuse Prevention (CSAP) was established to help guide the federal government's alcohol, tobacco, and other drug prevention and intervention programs. CSAP administers prevention programs including Community Partnership, High-Risk Youth, National Clearinghouse for Alcohol and Drug Information (NCADI), and the Drug-Free Workplace Helpline. The Helpline provides information and consultation regarding the development and implementation of a workplace substance abuse program.

Center for Substance Abuse Prevention (CSAP)
Division of Workplace Programs, Substance Abuse and Mental Health Services Administration
Room #2-1035
1 Choke Cherry Road
Rockville, MD 20857

Telephone Help-Line: 301-443-6780
Toll-Free: 800-WORKPLACE
Email: DWP@SAMHSA.GOV
Internet: *www.drugfreeworkplace.gov*

Note: For printed information, such as booklets, pamphlets, monographs, workplace kits, video tapes, and tips contact the (NCADI) at the following:

Telephone (Toll-Free): 800-729-6686
Email: INFO@HEALTH.ORG
Internet: *www.health.org*

Employee Assistance Professionals Association

The Employee Assistance Professionals Association (EAPA) represents over 7,000 employee assistance program (EAP) professionals including labor representatives, consultants, and internal and external providers. The EAPA provides information on how to select EAPs, the value they can provide, the theory behind them, and how they operate, as well as contact information for those who wish to get in touch with local EAPs. The EAPA also publishes brochures, books, and research publications on prevention, treatment, and education.

Employee Assistance Professionals Association (EAPA)
2101 Wilson Boulevard, Suite 500
Arlington, VA 22201-3062

Telephone: 703-387-1000 or 703-522-6272
Fax: 703-522-4585
Internet: *www.eapassn.org*

Working Partners for an Alcohol- and Drug-Free Workplace

Working Partners strives to build a drug-free workforce by equipping businesses and communities with tools and information to effectively address drug and alcohol problems.

Working Partners for an Alcohol- and Drug-Free Workplace
200 Constitution Avenue, Room S-2312
Washington, DC 20210

Telephone: 202-693-5919
Fax: 202-693-5961
Email: webwp@dol.gov
Internet: *www.dol.gov/workingpartners*

U.S. Drug Enforcement Administration

The federal Drug Enforcement Administration (DEA) is responsible for the enforcement of federal drug laws and regulations.

The DEA conducts prevention programs in conjunction with numerous national organizations through its Demand Reduction Program. The DEA also develops and distributes a variety of publications and videos on prevention.

U.S. Drug Enforcement Administration (DEA)
Mailstop: AXS
2401 Jefferson Davis Highway
Alexandria, VA 22301

Telephone: 202-307-7936
Internet: *www.usdoj.gov/dea*

U.S. Department of Health and Human Services

The federal **Department of Health and Human Services (HHS)** is the United States government's principal agency for protecting the health of all Americans and providing essential human services, especially for those who are least able to help themselves. The department includes more than 300 programs, covering a wide spectrum of activities including substance abuse treatment and prevention.

U.S. Department of Health and Human Services (HHS)
200 Independence Avenue, SW
Washington, DC 20201

Telephone: 202-619-0257
Toll-Free: 877-696-6775
Internet: *www.hhs.gov*

Chapter 9
Personnel Files

General Principle

Employers are constantly faced with questions regarding employee personnel records. For example, how long should an employer maintain an employee's personnel records and who should be permitted access to such records?

Employers must be aware that state and federal laws provide mandatory retention periods for certain personnel records, while privacy issues regularly play a deciding factor in access and record retention methods.

Recordkeeping Time Requirements

Between state and federal regulations there are numerous laws mandating various lengths of time different employment records should be kept. Many employers create a personnel file in which they keep the majority of an employee's records. Typically this employee file is kept for the period of employment, **plus** an additional four years. This practice is acceptable and covers nearly every recordkeeping law, except for a few extenuating records.

Before disposal of an employee's file, the following records must be removed from the personnel file and further maintained for a specific amount of time:

♦ Pension and welfare benefit plan information must be kept for six years.

♦ First-aid records of job injuries causing loss of work time must be kept for five years.

♦ Safety and toxic/chemical exposure records, including *Mineral Data Safety Sheets*, must be kept for 30 years.

Additionally, employers must maintain the medical records of an employee who worked with toxic/chemical substances for the duration of employment, plus 30 years.

Contents of a Personnel File

Employers often keep a variety of records, forms, and other documents in their employee personnel files.

A personnel file should contain a **minimum** of the following items:

♦ Application for employment.

♦ Employment agreement.

♦ Education verification.

♦ Background verification.

- Personal data changes.

- Records of transfers.

- Salary changes.

- Performance reviews.

- Disciplinary notes and memos.

- Letters of commendation or complaint.

- Signed acknowledgments of receipt of the employee handbook and key policies, such as antiharassment policy.

- Signed waivers.

- Security clearance status.

- Attendance records.

- Separation documentation.

- Correction of records.

Record Retention

Employers should maintain individual personnel files safely and securely within the place of business. Access to these records should only be granted on a limited and restricted basis.

Strict access guidelines are necessary due to the sensitive nature and the private information personnel files often contain and about the individual. Employers should appoint one person to assure the privacy of the file, who must give authorization to others prior to any viewing of personnel files.

As confidentiality is key, records should be kept in a secure, locked location. Although most employee documents and records may be retained in a single personnel file, the subsequent types of documents discussed in this chapter must be kept separately.

Medical Records

Employers must ensure that all employee medical records and medical information remains confidential and protected in a secure location from unauthorized use and disclosure and kept separately from other personnel files.

Medical records may include any of the following:

- Family and medical leave request forms when an employee voluntarily discloses the nature of an illness on the form.

- Return to work releases.

- Workers' compensation records.

- Information about any disabilities that require accommodated provided under the Americans with Disabilities Act (ADA).

- Any other records that relate in any way to an employee's medical history.

Employee Classification Information

Employers with 15 or more employees are required by the Equal Employment Opportunity Commission (EEOC) to maintain records of the sex, race, and national origin of all applicants and employees separate from employee personnel files. These records must be kept as a demonstration of the employer's attempt to recruit and develop a workforce that accurately reflects the community's ethnic profile.

Employers should keep these records in a common file instead of each employee's personnel file in case a situation arises requiring an employer to expeditiously produce this data.

Employment Eligibility Verifications

All forms and information that verify the employee's right to work in the United States should be kept in a separate file apart from each employee's personnel file. These forms and information most commonly consists of the Forms I-9 and photocopies of verification documents.

Maintaining this information in a separate file and location ensures easy access to the information should the employer be required to produce such information for an audit by immigration or labor officials. Additionally, employers can easily review all the forms and information on a regular basis to determine whether it is necessary to verify any expired or expiring documents.

Employee Access to Personnel Files

Many states have laws governing access by employees and former employees to their personnel files. Because the degree and conditions of access vary within each, state employers should familiarize themselves with all applicable laws before implementing a company policy.

Third-Party Requests to Review a Personnel File

In the absence of a valid subpoena or the employee's permission, an employer's disclosure of the contents of any employee's personnel file to third parties may subject the employer to a lawsuit for violating the employee's right to privacy. Importantly, employers should beware that disclosure to a third party, albeit in response to a valid subpoena, may nonetheless lead to potential liability from a subsequent lawsuit.

General Principles

Discipline of employees often gives rise to employment litigation. The following general guidelines for managing employees with disciplinary problems may help employers avoid litigation.

Employers must have clear disciplinary standards and evidence that employees were given notice of the standards. In implementation, the standards must be applied uniformly. Additionally, the organization should retain the right to determine the discipline that will be imposed in each individual situation. Employers must create a discipline policy that will not limit their right to enforce appropriate disciplinary measures.

A disciplinary procedure should follow these four rules:

♦ The employee must know the nature of the problem.

♦ The employee must know what to do to fix the problem.

♦ The employee must have a reasonable period of time in which to fix the problem.

♦ The employee must understand the consequences of inaction.

Progressive Discipline

Companies should consider using a progressive discipline system. The progressive discipline system generally begins with the recruitment process and continues through orientation, training, performance evaluations, and daily supervision. A progressive discipline system consists of the following:

♦ Verbal warning.

♦ Written warning.

♦ Suspension.

♦ Termination.

Elements of Due Process

An employer must demonstrate that affirmative steps were taken to rehabilitate a problematic employee. Progressive discipline is due process, or the necessary steps toward rehabilitation, for the employee.

Knowledge

Employees have the right to know employer expectations and the consequences of the failure to meet these expectations.

Consistency

Employees have the right to consistent and predictable employer responses when a rule is violated. Violations must not be corrected on an ad hoc basis, because the employer will be perceived as arbitrary, unreasonable, and discriminatory.

Appropriate

The discipline chosen for a particular problem must be appropriate. Occasional poor performance, tardiness, and absenteeism are certainly actionable, but probably not cause for termination. An employee's performance record and previous disciplinary record must be taken into account.

Opportunity

An employer must allow an employee to respond to allegations of misconduct before administering discipline. In a system structured for rehabilitation, failure to allow an employee a chance to offer a defense or alternate position may be cause for litigation.

Time Limit Reasonable

Progressive discipline must allow employees a reasonable period of time to improve their performance.

Investigating Employees

When employers investigate employee misconduct in the workplace, they are often caught in a "catch-22." For example, on one hand employers must conduct inquiries into employee performance and allegations of rules violations or misconduct because the Supreme Court has held that failure to promptly and thoroughly investigate reported employee misconduct may disqualify an employer from an "affirmative defense" against liability for workplace discrimination and subject the employer to punitive damages. (See *Burlington Indus., Inc. v. Ellerth*, 524 U.S. 742 (1998) and *Faragher v. City of Boca Raton*, 524 U.S. 775 and 789 (1998).)

On the other hand, investigating employee misconduct creates the possibility of exposure to legal liability. For example, employers conducting workplace investigations often are subject to requirements of the Fair Credit Reporting Act (FCRA), which since 1999 had been interpreted to govern such an investigatory process if third parties were used. (See *Federal Trade Commission Staff Opinion Letter* Vail, April 5, 1999 and *www.ftc.gov/os/statutes/fcra/vail.htm*.)

Under that interpretation, the Federal Trade Commission (FTC) required employers using third-party investigators to notify employees suspected of misconduct before conducting an investigation, to obtain the employee's prior consent before commencing the investigation, and to fully disclose investigative reports before taking any adverse action against an employee. Such stringent requirements made workplace investigations extremely difficult while increasing the risk of liability, especially the vulnerability to claims of retaliation actions.

As one can see, applying the requirements of the FCRA to an investigation of a typical case leads to an absurd result. If an impartial third party is used to conduct an investigation, the employer would have to comply with the act's requirements as follows:

- Have the alleged harasser's written consent before it could begin the investigation.

- Provide the alleged harasser with a copy of the resulting investigative report before taking any adverse action.

- Disclose to the alleged harasser the name of the alleged victim, the investigator's identity, and the names of all persons interviewed during the investigation.

With the cloak of anonymity absent, victims and witnesses were less likely to provide the most accurate accounts of incidents, and employers were left in uncertainty.

With the enactment of the Fair and Accurate Credit Transactions Act (FACT Act), on March 31, 2004, employers have enjoyed relief from the FCRA's stringent investigation requirements. Although the FACT Act reincorporates the majority of the FCRA's provisions, it lessens the investigative burdens on employers by countering the 1999 FTC opinion letter. Specifically, the FACT Act eliminates the need for prior consent before third parties conduct workplace investigations and removes the pre-adverse action disclosure to the employee being investigated for the alleged misconduct if communication of the third-party investigator's report is limited to the employer or an agent of the employer. As a practical matter, the report should not be disclosed to the complaining party; doing so may bring it within the scope of an investigative "consumer report" otherwise triggering the disclosure requirements.

In the event adverse action is taken against the employee based on the results of the third-party investigation, the FACT Act still requires the employer to provide the employee a summary of the third-party investigative report. Employers using third parties to conduct internal investigations must therefore remember to provide this summary whenever an adverse action is taken, even if a mere written warning results. The summary, however, does not need to identify the individuals interviewed or identify other sources of information. If employers follow the FACT Act's requirements regarding third-party investigations, they will eliminate the "catch-22" created by the FCRA under the FTC's interpretation.

Rehabilitation

The purpose of progressive discipline systems is to rehabilitate, and employers must try to assist employees in solving their problems.

Employers should document their efforts by performing the following procedures when disciplinary action occurs:

- Clearly state in writing the nature of the problem and how the employee's performance or conduct damaged the organization.

- Provide a clear and unequivocal warning that the employee's failure to improve will result in discipline, up to and including termination.

- Prove through progressive disciplinary actions that the employee's poor performance continued despite repeated warnings.

- Demonstrate that discipline was dispensed in a fair and consistent manner, so as to notify any future employee that termination under similar circumstances may be reasonably expected.

Warnings

The typical progressive discipline formula begins with a verbal warning and progresses to a written and then a final written warning before termination. Usually the impetus that moves the process from one stage to the next is a repeated violation of the same rule or type of rule (for example, repeated tardiness or unexcused absences). Disciplinary actions include the following oral and written warnings, suspension, and discharge.

Oral Warnings

When giving an oral warning, the employer should speak privately with the employee. Oral warnings are proper for infractions of a relatively minor degree. The supervisor should inform the employee at all times that the employee is receiving an oral warning and that the employee is being given an opportunity to correct the behavior. It is important the employee be notified of the following:

♦ The number of days the warning will continue.

♦ That failure to correct the behavior will result in more severe disciplinary measures.

A written record of the oral warning should be completed and placed in the employee's personnel file.

Written Warnings

If the employee continues to disregard the oral warning or if the infraction is severe, the supervisor should issue a written warning. The supervisor should give a detailed description of the infraction in the warning and sign the written notice of infraction. An employer should take the following steps when issuing a written warning:

♦ Discuss the warning with the employee.

♦ Confirm that the employee understands the reasons for the disciplinary action.

♦ Inform the employee of the number of days the warning will operate.

♦ Provide the employee with a copy of the warning at the time of the discussion.

♦ Obtain the employee's signature, with the current date, on the warning copy acknowledging the employee's receipt.

♦ Place the original warning in the employee's personnel file.

Example:

Date: _____

Employee Name: _____

Any further violations (more absences, tardiness).

Within the next _____ (days, months).

Will result in _____ (next step in disciplinary process).

Employee Signature: _____

Supervisor Signature: _____

Suspension

Suspension is the most severe form of discipline — short of termination — given by a supervisor. Supervisors should reserve suspension for severe infractions of a rule, standards, or for excessive violations. Usually, the employee has already received a written warning and has made little or no effort to improve performance or behavior. Suspension should be utilized only after a thorough evaluation by the supervisor. Employers should follow these steps when imposing a suspension:

- Present all the facts that initiated the reason for the disciplinary suspension and the duration of the suspension.

- Inform the employee of the reasons for the disciplinary action and give the employee an opportunity to respond before the suspension is imposed.

- The original notice of suspension should be placed in the employee's personnel file.

After the employee returns from a period of disciplinary suspension, the supervisor should make certain that the employee may return to the workplace without injury to the employee's dignity or self-worth.

Discharge

If the employee fails to improve after the supervisor has issued a suspension, the last option available to the employer is termination. When the supervisor is unsure whether termination is proper, the "last chance" letter should be considered. This last chance letter alerts the employee that they should be terminated, however the employer is willing to offer the employee one more chance to rectify the actions that may lead to termination. However, any future form of misconduct will result in an immediate discharge.

Summary Discharge

Progressive discipline is an employee benefit. However, employers are not required to offer progressive discipline to someone whose actions are unlawful. If an employee engages in illegal activity or other egregious conduct (such as gross insubordination, gross negligence, or drug use on company premises), employers may be justified in the prompt termination of the individual.

Note: An employer may place an employee on "investigatory" suspension pending further review and final decision.

Employers need to remember that discipline must be administered fairly and justly. The application of discipline should be logically and sequentially follow upon previous disciplinary actions documented in the employee's file.

Protected-Class Employees

Employers must be especially careful about documentation when dealing with protected-class persons. Special attention should be paid to the following when dealing with protected-class employees:

- Uniformity.

- Absence of evidence of discriminatory intent.

- Use of "last chance" technique (*See* **Warnings: Discharge** section).

Categories for Discipline

Situations that necessitate discipline fall into the following two broad categories and require different approaches, for example:

- **Misconduct.** Employees are doing something they should not be doing.

- **Poor Performance.** Employees are not doing something they should be doing.

Caution: Managers or supervisors should never use a confrontational, blaming approach with an employee who is not performing up to standard.

Misconduct

Examples of misconduct include the following:

- Violation of work rules.

- Sexual harassment.

- Intoxication.

- Sleeping on the job.

- Smoking on the job or jobsite.

- Conducting personal business on the job.

Of course, extreme examples include criminal behavior, such as drug dealing, rape, and murder. In every case the supervisor must act — rather than react — with as much control as possible. However, when someone or something is in danger, a quick reaction is necessary.

Some forms of conduct for which discipline may be necessary include the following:

- Illegal conduct.

- Intentionally false representations on a job application.

- Insubordination.

- Poor interactions with subordinates and/or co-workers.

- Failure to meet new policy standards.

Poor Performance

Poor performance should always be handled with a combination of coaching and progressive discipline. Initially, employees who are not correctly performing their duties should be presumed to be in need of coaching or counseling. Should this approach be ineffective, the employer may begin the progressive discipline. If the employee does not or cannot make the changes necessary for proper performance, the employee may be terminated. The important elements are as follows:

- Treating everyone fairly and consistently.

- Documenting any warnings given.

- Documenting any failure to improve performance.

Absenteeism and Tardiness

A widespread discipline problem for employers is absenteeism and tardiness. Some employers have established programs designed to minimize absenteeism and tardiness. Effective programs must be communicated to employees. Employees must know what the attendance policies are and what attendance records will merit incentives or discipline.

Small employers may find a combination of approaches to be most effective.

Incentives

A reward policy will usually work better than a penalty policy.

The following suggested incentives might improve attendance and punctuality in the workplace:

- ♦ Departmental competitions that award a small bonus to the department with the best attendance record for a month or quarter.

- ♦ Using an employee's attendance record as a factor in granting salary increases.

- ♦ Offering attendance awards in the form of cash, extra leave, or recognition at a special lunch for employees who meet certain attendance standards.

- ♦ Paying for unused sick leave time at the year's end or upon termination.

- ♦ Allowing employees to annually carry over unused sick leave or convert the unused leave to vacation or personal days.

Additionally, some employers use the concept of "personal days." Each employee receives a number of personal days, rather than sick days, each year. Employees may take personal days at any time, for any reason (with proper notice where possible). This practice may greatly improve employee morale, as the employees are granted more freedom in their workplace decisions.

Discipline

Establishing clear standards for attendance may involve designating steps for discipline, such as the following:

- ♦ An employee who is absent or tardy for _____ days within a day period will get a verbal warning.

- ♦ An employee who is absent or tardy for _____ days within a _____ day period, after the verbal warning, will receive a written warning.

- ♦ An employee who is absent or tardy for _____ days within a _____ day period, after the written warning, will be suspended without pay.

- ♦ An employee who is absent or tardy for _____ days within a _____ day period after suspension will be terminated.

Note: Employers should carefully monitor their attendance policy. Adherence to a strict attendance policy may be unlawful if giving an employee time off would be a reasonable accommodation for an employee's disability under the Americans with Disabilities Act (ADA).

Types of Work Rules

The following is a list of the areas in which many employers have developed work rules. However, every employer should not have rules on all of the listed topics. Most small employers have written rules on only a few areas that are either important to the organization or chronic problems in the particular workplace, industry, locale, or labor pool from which the employer hires.

- Attendance.

- Punctuality.

- Telephone usage costs.

- Confidential information.

- Visitor rules.

- Access to premises.

- Smoking.

- Moonlighting.

- Off-the-job conduct.

- Personal appearance and dress.

- Employee records.

- Gifts and gratuities.

- Ethical business conduct.

- Customer service.

- Insubordination.

- Poor interactions with subordinates or co-workers.

- Intentional false misrepresentations on a job application or about reasons for absences.

- Sexual harassment.

- Substance abuse.

- Personal use of company equipment.

- Personal phone calls.

- Email policy.

- Privacy policy.

- Reference policy.

- Personal demeanor.

- Safety and health.

- Solicitations and distribution of literature.

- Use of company bulletin boards.

- Theft and fraud.

- Unauthorized overtime.

- Sleeping on the job.

- Fighting.

- Poor job performance.

- Failure to meet new policy standards.

When an employer lists any violations that may lead to discipline or termination, the employer should also add a disclaimer similar to the following:

Listed are some of our work rules. The list includes types of behavior and conduct that the organization considers inappropriate and which could lead to disciplinary action up to and including termination of employment without prior warning. This list should not be viewed as being all-inclusive. Additionally, management reserves the right to impose discipline up to and including termination for other inappropriate or dangerous actions or misconduct.

Violations

An employer should reserve the right to list what actions are in violation of company policy and the appropriate discipline, if any. The following statement should precede the list of violations incurring actions, "Violations of any of the following performance standards may result in disciplinary action or immediate discharge."

A typical list of actionable violations contains the following:

- Failure or refusal to follow the written or oral instructions of a supervisor or manager.

- Insubordination.

- Neglecting job duties and responsibilities.

- Engaging in unauthorized personal business during workhours.

- Falsifying or misrepresenting company or employment records.

- Discourtesy or rudeness in dealing with employees, representatives of clients, or prospects.

- Failure to give proper notice when unable to report for or continue work as scheduled.

- Unexcused or excessive absenteeism.

- Abuse of sick leave privileges.

- Theft, abuse, or misuse of company property, materials, or supplies.

- Unauthorized use of company property and equipment, including telephones, copy machines, and mail service.

- Threatening, harassing, or inflicting bodily harm to fellow employees.

- Making false and malicious statements concerning employees or the organization.

♦ Intentionally discriminating against employees in violation of applicable laws and engaging in harassment of any employee.

♦ Possession, use, purchase, consumption, transfer, or sale of alcoholic beverages, controlled substances, or illegal drugs at any time during working hours, on company premises, while representing the organization, or reporting to work under the influence of alcohol, controlled substances, or illegal drugs.

♦ Violating any company policies, rules, regulations, or practices.

Off-Duty Time

A conflict may develop between an employee's freedom to spend off-duty time free from employer restrictions and the employer's ability to discipline an employee based on off-duty conduct. Generally, the employer may not regulate an employee's conduct or actions outside the scope of the workplace.

An employee that is terminated or disciplined for off-duty conduct may successfully assert an invasion of privacy claim based on a theory of unreasonable intrusion into private affairs. To limit exposure to possible liability, employers may consider discipline only when the employee's off-duty conduct directly interferes with the employer's business operations and interests and only in the context of consistent and careful application of its rules and policies.

Preventive Measures

All employers will have situations involving employees with poor attitudes, poor work habits, poor job performance, and absenteeism or tardiness. It is essential that an employer appropriately respond to a problematic employee by helping to correct behavior or by engaging in disciplinary procedures.

Supervisors should review employee performance regularly. Whenever problems develop, the supervisor should discuss the problem with the employee as soon as possible and suggest ways of correcting the problem. Discussions should be documented and placed in an employee's file. Oral and written warnings should be given to the employee whenever specific problems occur. A progressive discipline procedure should be followed in all cases except serious misconduct.

If unacceptable behavior continues, the supervisor should contact the personnel or human resources department and provide a detailed explanation of the problem. A specific meeting between human resources personnel and the employee should be arranged. At that time the precise aspects of work behavior that are unacceptable should be explained to the employee and the employee should be specifically told, in writing, what action or activity must be corrected. The employee also should be told that failure to comply with these requirements will result in discharge.

Checklist

An employer should customarily follow a basic checklist whenever disciplining or terminating an employee. Employers should never discipline an employee unless they can answer in the affirmative to all of the following:

♦ Has the following analysis been applied:

• The employee knew of the rule or performance standard.

- The rule or standard is reasonable and that its enforcement would be reasonable under all the circumstances.

- Review of all relevant materials including employee handbooks, contracts, policy statements, the employee's disciplinary history, evaluations, and attendance records.

- All employees or third parties who may know of or were involved in the misconduct have been interviewed.

- Accurate notes have been taken from all interviews and investigations about who, what, where, when, and why.

- The employee was confronted about the misconduct.

- The employee was given a fair opportunity to explain or deny the misconduct.

- Based upon the interviews, records, and the investigation process the employer has confidence that all the necessary facts (who, what, where, when, why, and how) have been revealed.

- The proposed disciplinary action has been reviewed to ensure accuracy, consistency, and completeness.

- The disciplinary action is consistent with how other employees have been disciplined for the same or similar conduct.

- The disciplinary action is the proper corrective measure under applicable policies and the employee's disciplinary history.

- The discipline memo or provided notice is accurate and complete and states the following:

  - Date of violation.

  - Specific rule violated.

  - Number of prior warnings.

  - Detailed description of misconduct.

  - Corrective action and penalty.

  - Date and signature of supervisor.

- Personnel have approved the proposed disciplinary action.

- Arrangements for the presence of a reliable management witness if an employer is concerned about how the employee may react.

♦ During a private conference with the supervisor and employee, has the following been completed:

- Review of the disciplinary notice/memorandum with the employee.

- Review of the facts with the employee.

- Explanation of the following:

  - The employee's misconduct and why the misconduct is unacceptable.

  - The penalty given.

  - The penalty that will result if the misconduct is repeated.

  - How to improve performance/conduct.

- If the employee is to be discharged, the supervisor must provide the employee written notice (a copy of which should be kept in the employee's personnel file) of the effective time and date of the discharge.

♦ After the disciplinary conference, the supervisor must immediately make the necessary entries in the personnel file and other applicable records.

Note: Although an employer has the right to regulate and monitor workplace conduct, employers should seek an attorney when considering disciplining employees for conduct or social behavior that occurs off the premises and during nonwork time. This is advisable no matter how serious the conduct may be (for instance, arrest, or conviction for sexual offenses or drug possession).

Limitations on Right to Terminate

Employers using disciplinary policies that list "cardinal offenses" that result in termination may limit their right to terminate for offenses not listed. A 2000 Ninth Circuit Court of Appeals decision also discusses when termination for "just cause" might not be permitted when an employer uses the list procedure.

In this case the employer was subject to a collective-bargaining agreement prohibiting termination without a written warning within the previous nine months for the same type of offense. The agreement also listed seven "cardinal offenses" which allowed immediate termination without first receiving a warning. The employee was terminated for conduct not in the agreement. After an arbitrator ruled for the employer, the Ninth Circuit reversed, holding that if an employee has not committed a cardinal offense and has not received the required warning notice, the employer may not terminate the employee even for just cause. Although in the present case, the "cardinal offenses" policy was in a collective-bargaining agreement, the same conclusion could be reached based on the same policy in an employee handbook.

Employee Right to Co-Worker Presence in Disciplinary Procedures

Employers must remember to allow nonunion employees to bring along a co-worker for a disciplinary or investigatory meeting with supervisors. A 2000 National Labor Relations Board decision expanded this previously union-only right to nonunion employees.

Co-workers are not limited to mere observation and may assist and counsel workers in such meetings. Employees must make a clear request for representation before or during the meeting and under no circumstances can they be punished for making the request. The employer has three options after receiving the request as follows:

♦ Grant the request and suspend the meeting until the co-worker arrives and has had a chance to consult with the employee.

♦ Deny the request and terminate the meeting immediately.

♦ Give the employee a choice of having the interview without representation or ending the meeting.

Employers are not required to inform employees of this new right. However, employers should review personnel policies, grievance procedures and work rules to confirm they do not interfere with these employee rights. Finally, employers should train all supervisors and managers to make sure they know how to handle employee requests for representation.

Chapter 11

Termination

At-Will Employment

Several centuries ago, the law assumed that when an employer hired an employee the employee was being hired to work for a full year. Unless the employer and employee reached a different specific agreement as to the length of employment, both could assume that the job would last for a year. As time passed, this legal assumption changed as many states restricted an employer's ability to discipline or discharge an employee. Today, an employment relationship for no specific duration may generally be terminated at any time, for any reason or for no reason at all.

The phrase "at will" is just another way of saying "at the will of either party." In other words, *at-will employment* means, "the job will last as long as both parties wish it to continue and it will end when either party wants it to end." Accordingly, under at-will employment, the employee is not guaranteed a job for any specific period of time. The employment contract between the employer and the employee (any agreement regarding the job, pay, benefits, duties, etc.) can end at any time. Simply put, the employer may terminate the employee at any time, and the employee may quit at any time.

Exceptions to Employment-at-Will

This rule contains several recognized exceptions and legal limitations. Although employers may terminate at will employees at any time, they cannot fire employees for an illegal reason. For example, discharge or termination may not be legal in the following instances:

- ♦ Employees working under a union contract generally can be terminated only for "just cause." *Just cause* is defined in one of the following two categories:
    - • **Misconduct.** Although the following list is not exhaustive, misconduct includes the following:
        - ▪ Theft.
        - ▪ Workplace violence.
        - ▪ Being intoxicated while at work.
        - ▪ Bringing firearms to work.
        - ▪ Engaging in serious forms of sexual or racial harassment.
    - • **Unsatisfactory performance.** Examples of unsatisfactory performance amounting to just cause have included the following:
        - ▪ Excessive absenteeism.
        - ▪ Poor quality of work.
        - ▪ Failure to meet numerical production standards.

    Note: Serious misconduct is often subject to immediate dismissal, even under a union contract. However, unsatisfactory performance generally will not result in discharge until the employee has received a progression of discipline and failed to improve.

- ◆ Employers may not illegally discriminate against at will employees and fire them based on any of the following:

  - Race.
  - Creed.
  - Sex or sexual orientation.
  - Color.
  - National origin.
  - Religion.
  - Age.
  - Marital status.
  - Physical or mental disability.
  - Union activity.
  - Pregnancy.
  - Medical condition.
  - Parental status.
  - Military status.

If they do, the employees may sue for wrongful discharge. Basically, employers may fire at will employees for no reason or for a good reason, but not for an illegal reason. Many laws also specifically prohibit retaliation against employees for exercising rights protected by statute. For example, such statutes prohibit retaliation against employees filing a workers' compensation claim, a discrimination charge, or reporting the employer for some workplace violation.

Some written employment contracts may specifically limit the circumstances an employee may be terminated. In some circumstances, a contract may imply that the employee can be terminated only for "good cause." In this situation, the employer needs to have a reasonable justification to validate discharge. Situations of "good cause" termination are employee's absenteeism, other discipline problems, or a corporate restructuring that requires layoffs. Contracts of this nature are enforceable in court.

Federal Laws Limiting Employment-at-Will

Various federal and state laws provide limitations on employment-at-will. The following lists applicable federal laws:

- ◆ **Age Discrimination in Employment Act** (29 U.S.C.A. § 621).
  Prohibits employment discrimination against employees ages 40 or older, bars retaliation against persons exercising ADEA rights.

- ◆ **ADA** (42 U.S.C.A. § 12101).
  Prohibits employment discrimination against qualified persons with disabilities; bars retaliation against persons exercising ADA rights.

- ◆ **Bankruptcy Code** (11 U.S.C.A. § 525).
  Prohibits employers from discriminating against or terminating an individual solely because the person has filed for bankruptcy.

- ◆ **Civil Service Reform Act of 1978** (5 U.S.C.A. § 7513(a)).
  Permits removing federal civil service employees only for efficiency-related causes.

- **Civil Rights Act of 1964, Title VII** (42 U.S.C.A. §§ 2000e-2 and 2000e-3(a)).
  Prohibits discharge based on race, color, religion, sex, or national origin and reprisal for exercising rights under the act.

- **Clean Air Act** (42 U.S.C.A. § 7622).
  Prohibits firing employees who assist in any proceeding under the act.

- **Consumer Credit Protection Act** (15 U.S.C.A. § 1674(a)).
  Prohibits firing employees because of garnishment of wages for any one indebtedness.

- **Employee Retirement Income Security Act of 1974** (29 U.S.C.A. §§ 1140 and 1141).
  Prohibits terminating employees to prevent them from attaining vested pension rights.

- **Energy Reorganization Act of 1974** (42 U.S.C.A. § 5851).
  Prohibits firing employees who assist in any proceeding under the act.

- **Fair Labor Standards Act** (29 U.S.C.A. §§ 215(a)(3) and 216(b)).
  Prohibits discharge for exercising FLSA rights.

- **Federal Water Pollution Control Act** (33 U.S.C.A. § 1367).
  Prohibits firing employees who assist in any proceeding under the act.

- **Immigration Reform and Control Act of 1968** (8 U.S.C.A. § 1324b).
  Prohibits employment discrimination against individuals, except unauthorized aliens, because of national origin and against U.S. citizens or aliens eligible for citizenship because of citizenship status.

- **Judiciary and Judicial Procedure Act** (28 U.S.C.A. § 1875).
  Prohibits firing employees for service on grand or petit jury.

- **Labor Management Relations Act** (29 U.S.C.A. §§ 158(a)(1), 158(a)(3), and 158(a)(4)).
  Prohibits termination for union activity, protected concerted activity, or filing charges or giving testimony under the act.

- **Occupational Safety and Health Act of 1970** (29 U.S.C.A. § 660(c)).
  Prohibits firing employees for exercising OSHA rights.

- **Railroad Safety Act** (45 U.S.C.A. §§ 441(a) and 441(b)(1)).
  Prohibits firing employees who assist in any proceeding under the act.

- **Rehabilitation Act of 1973** (29 U.S.C.A. §§ 793 and 794).
  Prohibits federal contractors or any program or activity receiving federal financial assistance from discriminating against persons with disabilities.

- **Veterans' Re-Employment Rights Act** (38 U.S.C.A. §§ 4321 – 4327).
  Requires reinstatement of and protects returning veterans for a limited time against discharge without just cause.

Activities Protected By Law

An employer may not terminate an employee for participating in activities that are protected by law. Examples of such activities include the following:

- Garnishments.

- Disclosure or refusal to disclose wages.

- Voluntary participation in alcohol or drug rehabilitation programs.

- Refusal to authorize disclosure of medical history or records.

- Jury duty.

- Political activity or serving as election officer on Election Day.

- Military service.

- Volunteer firefighting.

- Refusal to patronize an employer.

- Refusal to commit illegal activity.

- Absenteeism caused by attendance at child's school regarding a suspension or for a child's school or child care activities.

- Domestic violence victim taking time off to obtain a restraining order, receive care or counseling, or to relocate.

- Refusal to disclose arrest records that do not lead to convictions.

- Refusal to take a polygraph test.

- Enrollment in an adult literacy program.

- Refusal to participate in abortions.

- Consideration for employment without regard to results of blood tests for AIDS.

- Health care employees' exercise of statutory duty to report apparent victims of abuse or neglect, without suffering discharge or discipline.

Wrongful Discharge

A *wrongful discharge* occurs when an employee is terminated for a wrong reason or in the wrong way.

A *termination* occurs when an employee is either of the following:

- Fired.

- Laid off.

- Suspended for an unreasonably long period.

- Constructively discharged.

When employees are "at-will" employees, an employer does not really need a reason to justify a termination. These employees may be fired for any reason or for no reason. Still, they cannot be fired for an illegal reason, such as unlawful discrimination, refusing a supervisor's sexual advances, or for their other protected characteristics and activities as outlined above.

Some employees are not at-will and are promised some type of job security. If employees have been promised that they will not be fired unless certain conditions are met, the employer must comply with these promises or face a claim for wrongful discharge. Similarly, a discharge may be "wrongful" when an employer violates an employee's procedural rights. For instance, some employers promise employees a formal hearing, a certain number of written warnings, or some other process before they are finally terminated. If an employer fails to carry out these preliminary procedures before firing an employee, the firing may be considered a wrongful discharge.

The courts also limit employers' rights to terminate employees at will. There are several instances as follows where employers are not able to terminate an employee at will:

- Discharges in violation of public policy.

- Discharges that violate the "good faith and fair dealing" principle.

- Discharges that involve breach of contract.

- Discharges for employee seeking rights under applicable law.

- Discharges for cooperation with any investigation.

- Discharges for testifying or future testimony in any action brought under appropriate law.

Termination under these circumstances is wrongful and often results in a wrongful discharge suit.

Discharges in Violation of Public Policy

A number of courts have held employers liable for employee discharges that violate *public policy*. Cases falling under this category include discriminatory discharge and retaliatory discharge.

Specific examples of public policy retaliatory discharge lawsuits involve employees who claim they were terminated for any of the following:

- *Whistleblowing.* This term refers to reporting unlawful activities by the employer to law enforcement official or as simple as complaining to another employee or the media.

- Filing a workers' compensation claim.

- Refusing to perform illegal, unethical, or unsafe activities on behalf of an employer.

- Fulfilling a legal duty, such as serving on a jury or attending court when subpoenaed as a witness.

- Cooperating in a governmental investigation involving the employer.

Employers must be aware of public policy discharge cases because they are often treated similarly to personal injury cases. In these cases, plaintiffs may actually recover compensation for mental anguish and punitive damages as well. Punitive damages "punish" the defendants by awarding damage amounts that often greatly exceed the actual economic damages of lost wages and benefits.

Under the Federal False Claims Act, employees may file suit against their employers for suspected fraud against the federal government. This law entitles employees to recover a percentage of any amounts received by the government in a settlement or otherwise. Employers doing business with the federal government need to be aware that disgruntled employees have this option available to them. The act also prohibits retaliation against an employee who files an action, testifies, or otherwise assists the government in an investigation under the act.

Good Faith and Fair Dealing

Many state courts have held that employment relationships are contractual in nature and contain an implied promise of good faith and fair dealing.

In theory, one party to the contract must not act in *bad faith,* depriving the other party of the benefits from the agreement. This means decisions should be made on a fair basis, and employees who are similarly situated should be treated in the same manner.

Similarly situated in this case means employees in the same general job categories and with similar seniority and rank.

Most good faith and fair dealing cases involve abusive or highly offensive discharges. They may include the following:

- Termination of an employee to avoid paying a sales commission.

- Retaliation against an employee for refusing to become romantically involved with a supervisor.

- Retaliation for publicizing or alleging wrongdoing on the part of the employer.

Breach of Contract

In the most common wrongful termination lawsuits, plaintiffs claim that their discharge breached a contract — whether formal or informal — not to terminate employment except for good cause. Consequently, employers **must** structure employment documents and policies precisely in case a terminated employee later sues for wrongful termination alleging breach. If the terms of the employment agreement are accurately described, the judge may dismiss the case before it goes to jury. Jury trials pose exceptional dangers for employers because the jury will most likely be comprised of employees rather than employers.

Express Contract/Specific Promises

Express contracts or specific promises to employees are enforceable in many states although they are not formal or in writing. These informal promises are most often by a manager or some other individual within the organization who holds authority.

Typically, employees often think they were discharged unfairly and in breach of a promise made years before. For example, one of the supervisors may have told the employee that the organization would never fire anyone without a good reason to do so. Many courts and juries have treated such informal oral statements like binding contracts.

Implied Contracts

Implied contracts are based upon the length of employment and indicators of job security an employee has received. Indicators of job security include promotions, bonuses, etc., which indicate an employee has been doing a good job and has a right to feel secured in a job.

Even when employers made no specific promises, juries have determined that an implied contract existed, suggesting that employees would not be discharged except for good cause. Often, courts decide that such a promise exists even where the parties themselves clearly did not actually intend to create a contract. Frequently, juries must decide whether the employer had created a reasonable expectation that an employee would be discharged only for good cause.

The following list demonstrates the types of evidence juries have considered:

- Employee handbooks that establish an initial employee probationary period.

- Disciplinary policies that state employees will be discharged only for particular offenses.

- Progressive disciplinary policies that allow employees chances to improve their performance where, in fact, the employee was not given such a chance.

- Handbooks or records that state "fairness" or special consideration will be given employees because of longevity or seniority.

- An employee's work history, which reflects regular merit raises, good performance evaluations, praise, and promotions.

- The employer's practice of discharging employees only for good cause.

- An industry-wide practice that employees are treated fairly or terminated only for good cause.

The employer must affirmatively declare its employer-at-will status to prevent the above- mentioned situations. All employers should review their handbooks, policies, and procedures regularly, even when only supervisory employees receive such material. Employers must make sure that these documents do not contain promises or obligations to which the employer is unwilling to commit. Employers should avoid words such as "will," "shall," and "must" when stating obligations towards employees.

Related Legal Claims

Employees will often allege other claims as part of their wrongful discharge lawsuits. The following list illustrates other types of claims linked with a wrongful discharge lawsuit:

Fraud and Negligent Misrepresentation

Often an employee may discover that a job is not all that it appeared to be during the pre-employment interviews. The job duties may be different, the bonuses may be extremely difficult to earn, or perhaps the boss is more difficult to work with then originally thought. Under these circumstances, the employee may claim to have accepted the job offer because the employer made statements that seemed sincere but were actually statements the employer should have known were not true. This is especially the case when an employee was discharged or came from another highly compensated job.

Intentional Infliction of Emotional Distress

This type of claim includes allegations of an intentional and extremely abusive discharge of the employee. The employee also claims the discharge was conducted in a degrading and humiliating manner.

Employers can reduce emotional distress liability by any of the following:

- ◆ Avoiding anger in administering discipline.

- ◆ Requiring review of a contemplated disciplinary decision by another supervisor or manager who has no personal bias against the employee.

- ◆ Using common sense.

- ◆ Documenting, signing, and dating every critical incident.

Interference with Contractual Relationships

This type of action involves allegations that individual supervisors or managers interfered with the contractual relationship between employees and their employer. An example of such a claim is where a supervisor knowingly communicates false information about an employee to higher management that results in the termination of the employee. Normally these claims are brought against supervisors or managers.

Defamation

Defamation claims are often linked to wrongful termination. A claim of defamation involves allegations by employees that supervisors or co-workers made false statements that injured the employee's reputation. Examples of potential defamation claims include the following:

- ◆ Gross misconduct, theft, embezzlement, or falsification of records.

- ◆ Using or abusing drugs.

♦ Professional incompetence, criminal convictions, or arrests.

♦ Having a communicable or venereal disease.

Note: These claims may be valid only when the employer falsely accuses the employee.

Defamatory claims may be oral or written and may be communicated to individuals inside or outside the organization. Any derogatory statements can be the basis of a defamation action. This applies whether they were written or oral, and whether they were made to individuals within or outside the organization. In some states, even statements made only to a terminated employee may be considered as defamation.

Employers have a right to make derogatory statements about employees to certain persons within the organization who have a need to know, and prospective employers who specifically request information about the employees. Employers can encounter problems if the employee can prove that the statement was made with a reckless disregard for whether it was true. In the employment setting, defamation claims primarily arise from the following two situations:

♦ Discussing an employee's alleged poor performance, misconduct, or reasons for termination beyond those who need to know.

♦ Responses to reference checks.

Employers can frequently avoid defamation claims if they acquire and apply a basic understanding of the law in this sensitive area, and follow a few simple precautions. The following can help employers avoid defamation liability:

♦ Investigating and documenting incidents of employee misconduct thoroughly before imposing discipline, thereby avoiding a claim that the employer acted in "reckless disregard."

♦ Taking care to limit disclosure of the reasons for discipline to those with a legitimate need to know.

♦ Keeping medical data, mainly drug testing results, strictly confidential.

♦ Limiting responses to reference checks to confirmation of dates of employment and positions held.

♦ Obtaining a signed release from an employee before releasing any employment data.

Employer Defenses to Defamation

Employers may put forth a variety of defenses in response to a defamation suit. They include truth, consent, statute of limitations, absolute privilege, and qualified privilege.

Truth

This is a complete defense to a defamation suit because it defeats an essential element of a defamation suit — a false statement. True statements, even if damaging to an employee's reputation, may not give rise to a legal claim.

Consent

When an employee agrees to the publication or communication of the alleged defamatory statement, this also serves as a complete defense to a defamation suit. Courts recognize consent as a defense. They do not want to penalize an employer for relying on an employee's words or actions that lead the employer to believe that it may communicate a potentially defamatory statement.

Statute of Limitations

The statute of limitations can provide a complete defense to a defamation claim. A statute of limitations fixes the time within which a court action must be initiated. If the employee does not bring a claim within the statutorily defined period, the claim is lost and cannot be initiated after the period has expired.

Absolute Privilege

When the allegedly defamatory communication is privileged, an employee may not recover damages for defamation. In order to further the public's interest, courts recognize an absolute privilege in a variety of situations. Statements under the following circumstances will be absolutely privileged:

♦ When they are made by legislators during a legislative proceeding.

♦ When they are made by participants in a judicial or quasi-judicial proceeding.

♦ When there is a legal requirement to make a statement.

Where an absolute privilege exists, the employer has complete immunity from a defamation lawsuit, even if the employer made the remark out of malice.

Qualified Privilege

A qualified privilege exists when otherwise defamatory statements are made under circumstances where the person making the statement has a legitimate and reasonable justification to communicate. Typically, this happens when a meeting is held specifically to discuss the employee's conduct and negative comments are made.

Note: The qualified privilege does not totally protect an employer from defamation liability. When the employer abuses the privilege — by spreading the statements beyond any legitimate business justification, or by making false statements of fact with a bad motive — the employer may lose the qualified privilege.

Invasion of Privacy

Recently, employees have raised invasion of privacy claims in the context of employment litigation. Invasion of privacy claims are usually based on one of the three following theories:

♦ Unreasonable intrusion into an individual's personal affairs.

♦ Placing an individual in a false light by publicizing facts that are literally true but that give a false and negative impression of the individual.

♦ Public disclosure of embarrassing and private facts.

The following examples illustrate employment-related situations where this issue is likely to occur:

♦ Checking of references.

♦ Drug testing.

♦ Disclosure of employee records.

♦ Disclosure of discipline or misconduct.

♦ Searches of purses, lunchboxes, packages, lockers, automobiles, or the employee's person.

♦ Electronic transmission of data.

Employers can avoid liability from invasion of privacy by simply removing an expectation of privacy. An employer can establish, distribute, and post policies stating that personal items, lockers, purses, and automobiles are subject to search and that drug testing may be required under certain circumstances during employment.

Employers should also consider the following:

- ◆ Inform employees with email access that the email is not private and may be read by anyone having access to the system including the employer.

- ◆ Obtain consent to provide employment references, search employee property and persons, or perform drug testing.

- ◆ Protect the confidentiality of employee performance evaluations, medical records, and disciplinary records.

- ◆ Limit undercover investigations to workplace surveillance.

Constructive Discharge

Sometimes employees quit, but not voluntarily. When employees are forced or coerced into quitting, it is called a "constructive discharge." Employees may claim in these circumstances that the resignation was not really voluntary, but rather was forced by the employer's actions or the employer's failure to correct an intolerable work environment. For example, an employee who is victimized by her supervisor's constant sexual harassment may feel compelled to quit. The employee's leaving will be a constructive discharge. In this situation, the employee may sue for wrongful discharge (and harassment), even though the employee "quit." Generally, a discharge is considered constructive if the following apply:

- ◆ The employer created or condoned working conditions for the employee that a reasonable person in the employee's position would find intolerable.

- ◆ Any reasonable employee would quit rather than endure the situation.

Other than harassment, employees may be constructively (unfairly) discharged due to any of the following:

- ◆ Discrimination.

- ◆ Dangerous duties.

- ◆ Hazardous situations.

- ◆ Demeaning or malicious assignments.

- ◆ Even because of an employer's failure to give the employee any work to do.

Prevent Constructive Discharge

A sincere "open door" policy may be an employer's best defense against constructive discharges claims. Employers should document and appropriately address all employee concerns. When an employee quits after complaining of intolerable work conditions, the employer should immediately investigate to verify the employee's claim and, if appropriate, remedy the situation. If the employer wishes to retain the employee, the employer should offer the employee unconditional, immediate reinstatement. The employer should assure the employee that the intolerable conditions have been addressed and corrected. This approach can reduce potential liability and severely undercut a claim of constructive discharge.

Guidelines for Discharging Employees

Improperly handled discharges not only raise important legal issues, but also undermine employee morale and productivity.

Retain Employees When Possible

Of course, if discharges can be avoided in the first place, improper discharges become a moot point. Therefore, the following suggestions should be considered before discharging any employee:

♦ Employers should establish fair and reasonable work rules and apply them uniformly to all employees. Fair and reasonable rules foster good employee morale because the employees know what is expected of them. The work rules should also be related to valid business interests.

♦ When employees perform or behave inappropriately, an employer must respond with corrective or disciplinary procedures.

When Discharge is Unavoidable

Sometimes, discharge is unavoidable. However, employers will minimize the risk of liability, retain an element of control, and maintain employee dignity if they take the following steps:

♦ The executive in charge should make the final decision to discharge, based upon the recommendation of lower line management and a human resources executive.

♦ Consider the timing of the termination — do not meet before birthdays, holidays, etc.

♦ Two managers or a manager and human resource representative should be present.

♦ Be sure to pre-plan what will be said in the meeting.

♦ Document the meeting.

♦ Maintain control over the situation. If employees are involved in the termination process, they may feel that they control the outcome.

♦ Make any severance package consistent with what other employees have been offered.

♦ Make the firing a statement of fact and not open to discussion. Keep any termination discussion focused and to the point. Communicate all the reasons for the decision. Allow the employee an opportunity to respond.

♦ Try to balance the negative with positive statements about other aspects of the employee's performance. Explain the decision while acknowledging the employee's strengths and contributions.

♦ Focus on the employee's future and not encourage thinking that the termination is the end of the line. An employer might consider showing the discharged employee a written termination statement for dissemination to future employers. Properly worded, such a statement can minimize the employee's fears about the future.

♦ Provide job counseling for terminated employees.

♦ Collect keys and other security-sensitive employer belongings.

♦ If circumstances warrant, have the employee escorted off the premises.

Termination by Telephone or Letter

The law does not require an employer to terminate an employee in person. An employer may terminate an employee by telephone, letter, or any other means of effective communication. Employers must remember that regardless of the means of the communicating the termination, the laws for final wage payment applies. All final wages are due and payable immediately upon termination. Employees terminated other than in person must have all wages available at the normal place wages are paid.

Termination Decision Checklist

Sometimes problems become so significant that an organization has no choice but to terminate one of its employees. Possibly the conduct is so serious that it warrants immediate termination. The following termination checklist provides guidance to employers who must discharge employees:

♦ When the employee is a member of a protected group, treat the employee the same as members of nonprotected groups.

♦ Make sure the rule that the employee violated was published and be able to document how, where, and when it was published.

♦ Confirm that the employee received a written copy of the work rules. To prove this, distribute employee handbooks upon hiring.

♦ Apply rules and standards of conduct consistently. If different employees have violated the same rule, take the same disciplinary action with each.

♦ When the termination is for poor performance, confirm that the employee was given a notice of poor performance and an opportunity to improve.

♦ When a written contract exists, carefully read the contract before a termination decision.

♦ Review the length of employment for the employee in question.

♦ If the employee has filed any kind of claim against the organization — workers' compensation, benefits pay claim, or discrimination charge — the employer must take care to avoid a retaliatory discharge claim.

♦ Review the employee file for complaints about company policies and concerns about company activities the employee perceived to be illegal or immoral.

♦ Always consider alternatives to discharge. For example, consider last- chance agreements, demotion, option to resign, or settlement agreements.

♦ Take special care with reviews for employees with recognizable disabilities.

♦ Review the employee file for previous documented violations of the same rule or standard of conduct. Always consider who wrote the document.

♦ Evaluate the previous twelve months of written reviews. Consider any disciplinary actions.

♦ Make sure the event triggering disciplinary action was thoroughly investigated and that the employee had an opportunity to give his or her version.

♦ Ensure that all evidence includes names of witnesses, dates, times, places and other pertinent information on all past violations.

♦ Ensure that the degree of discipline imposed on the employee reflects the seriousness of the proven offense.

♦ Consider the extent, if any, that the organization contributed to the problem.

Final Decision

The termination checklist summarizes the most important considerations in the termination process. Before any final decision to discharge, the personnel or human resources department should become involved. In fact, the human resource manager should review the termination. This type of review is necessary to confirm that the discharge followed and that other company employees in similar circumstances received the same treatment.

Note: It is not sufficient simply for a department head to review a supervisor's decision. The human resources department should check for oversights, assuring uniform and consistent treatment of all employees.

Communicating the Decision

Communicating the termination decision to the employee being terminated is also an important part of the process. The employee should understand the organization's rationale for the decision to discharge. The individual who performs this function should document carefully what was said to the employee and by the employee.

Avoid the late Friday afternoon notice and try to lessen the severity by making the news not unexpected. In most situations the employee will already be on probation or possibly expecting termination. Employers deciding to terminate an employee should give notice in the early part or middle of the week. The notice should be brief and candid. Accent the positive, but do not make the message inconsistent with the decision. No apologies are necessary. However be mindful that the event is traumatic and treat the employee with dignity and respect.

Notice to Employee of Change in Relationship

Employers are required to give immediate written notice to employees when there is a change in the employment relationship. This includes discharge, layoff, leaves of absence, and change in status from employee to independent contractor.

There is no specific notice required and employers can create their own. Employers must give a copy to the employee and should retain one for their records. The employee's signature of acknowledgement is not required by law but should be requested by the employer. This notice may serve as evidence to challenge the granting of unemployment insurance or other employee benefits.

Termination Procedure Checklist

Certain employer obligations arise upon termination. The termination procedure should meet these obligations. Employers should also anticipate and avoid practical problems. The termination conference is critical because employers often mishandle the final interview. For instance, the employer will sometimes make illegal statements or employees will become angry and hostile. Therefore, several guidelines should be followed.

The following checklist includes many of the points to consider and implement in the interview:

- ♦ The employer should review the employee's employment history, commenting on specific problems that have occurred and the attempts to correct those problems.

- ♦ The employee should be told immediately that the individual is being terminated. Do not drag out the ultimate announcement.

- ♦ Explain the decision briefly and clearly.

- ♦ Avoid counseling at this point, as it should have already occurred.

- ♦ Avoid compliments in an effort not to hurt the employee's feelings.

- ♦ Always give a truthful explanation for termination. The stated reason for termination can be critical if litigation occurs. In some cases, courts have held that failing to state the true reason for the termination or stating reasons that are inconsistent constitutes discrimination.

- ♦ Carefully complete any documentation to avoid saying too much or too little. When terminations involve complicated or controversial matters, the employer should obtain legal advice concerning what to say in the separation notice.

- ♦ Explain fully any benefits — including insurance and unemployment compensation — that the employee is entitled to. Tell the employee when the benefits will be received. When the employee will not receive certain benefits, the employer should explain why.

- ♦ Give the employee an opportunity to have a say. Avoid argument and justification.

- ♦ Do not base the decision to terminate an employee on a discriminatory reason. The reasons should be business- related.

    Caution: Terminating the following types of employees is especially sensitive:

    - A pregnant employee.
    - An older employee.
    - A minority employee.
    - Any other employee who may claim discrimination.

    Warning: With these types of employees, the potential problem of a subsequent claim or lawsuit is obvious. Take special care with these employees not to make any reference to anything which could be considered discriminatory. This is essential.

- ♦ The termination interview should never contain references to sex, age, race, religion, national origin, or disability.

- ♦ If employers are prepared and organized, they exhibit confidence that the right decision has been made.

- ♦ Try to obtain an employee's agreement that the job performance has not been satisfactory.

- ♦ Take brief notes during the meeting. After the meeting, write notes detailing what the employee has been told and what the employee said. Each employer representative attending the interview should sign the document.

- ♦ Another managerial employee should be present at the time of actual discharge.

- ♦ Arrange for the return of materials, documents, tools, or other company property in the personal possession of the employee.

♦ Establish a procedure to help the employee clean out lockers, desks, etc.

♦ Establish a procedure to retrieve ID's, delete passwords, change locks, and handle other security matters. If physical security preparations might be needed, plan in advance.

♦ Remind the employee of any noncompete or confidentiality requirements.

♦ Always consider seeking a release of liability.

♦ Solicit suggestions about the exit interview process from the exiting employee. For employees who exit without an interview or who abandon the job, the employer may want to solicit suggestions by mail.

♦ With a voluntary resignation, try to get a signed resignation stating the reason(s) for leaving. This discourages former employees from later deciding that their termination was not really voluntary; it also offers protection from unemployment compensation claims.

♦ Allow the employee to physically leave with as much dignity and self-esteem as possible. In the case of discharge, employers should consider transportation arrangements, especially when the employee's motor skills are impaired in any way.

♦ All employment-related documents should be up-to-date, complete, and accurate, signed, dated, and approved appropriately, as should the termination checklist.

♦ Conduct the employee termination and exit procedure according to current business or industry practices and conventions.

Unemployment Compensation

Employers should handle unemployment compensation claims carefully and meticulously. Often the employee states a different reason for termination than the employer's. An unemployment compensation hearing provides a useful opportunity to ascertain the former employee's position. An unemployment compensation decision which favors the employer may help persuade the employee not to pursue the matter further. It may also help persuade the EEOC or a court that the employee's claim is not valid.

Replacing a Terminated Employee

Pay special attention when replacing a terminated employee. Of course, employers should seek the most qualified employee. However, employers will better insulate themselves from discrimination charges by choosing another person of the same race, sex, national origin, or age.

Separation Agreements

Sometimes an employer has reason to believe that an employee, if discharged, may file a lawsuit. In these situations, consider a separation agreement with the employee. A separation agreement consists of two essential elements as follows:

♦ The employer must give some additional valuable consideration to the employee — such as additional pay or enhanced retirement benefits — to which the employee was not otherwise entitled.

♦ The employee, in turn, must give a general release and covenant not to sue.

Note: Employers must allow employees appropriate time to review the terms of the agreement with a representative of the employee's choosing, including an attorney.

Separation agreements contain general releases that are knowingly and voluntarily entered into. These reduce the risk of litigation. If properly prepared and executed, these agreements may provide a strong defense against employment claims covered by the release.

However, depending on applicable state law, a separation agreement may be ineffective or may even backfire because of any of the following:

♦ The employee's release was based upon the company's payment of — such as vacation pay or severance pay — that the discharged employee would have received even without a separation agreement.

♦ The employer submits the agreement to an employee before the individual challenges the discharge; the employee then rejects the agreement and uses it as evidence of wrongful termination.

♦ The language of the agreement is too general and fails to identify specifically what claims the employee is agreeing not to pursue.

♦ The release is based on certain promises not contained in the written agreement, and the agreement fails to specify that the document contains the parties' complete agreement in the specific matter.

♦ The agreement does not describe in enough detail the employer's rights if the employee fails to follow the agreement — normally a promise not to sue, a promise not to publicize the agreement, and a promise not to re-apply for employment.

An employer might want to provide expressly for the consequences if the employee breaks a promise.

The agreement might provide that the employee:

♦ Will be liable for all legal expenses that result from breaking the promise not to sue.

♦ Will be liable for liquidated damages for breaking the promise not to publicize.

♦ Will be denied employment without legal recourse for breaking the promise not to re-apply for employment.

Noncompetition Agreements and Trade Secrets

When employer relationships end, the employer has many more concerns beyond the loss of an employee. While employed with an organization, employees gain valuable techniques, information, and relationships that make them competition for their former employer. Employees who have received confidential and proprietary information through the course of employment or who were the organization's principal contact for customers have the ability to seriously affect the confidentiality of that information and the customer relationships.

Unfortunately, employees with no written contract for employment are free to move among jobs even within the same field or among competitors. Additionally, employees are free to use their knowledge and expertise even in competition with former employers.

Employers are not entirely defenseless if they take certain measures in advance the terminated employment relationship. Even absent these advance precautions employers have some protections. Employees who gain access to their employer's trade secrets remain under a legal obligation not to disclose or abuse those trade secrets, even where there is no written contract.

Confidentiality Agreement

The next provision (depending on the corporate culture and the employer's level of concern) is a secrecy or confidentiality provision. The confidentiality/secrecy provision should prohibit the disclosure of any such secret or confidential information while employed and for a period after employment.

Alternative 1: "Employee understands and agrees that in the course of his/her employment, he/she will receive and become aware of information, projects, practices, customer contacts, and potential customers which are sensitive and confidential in nature. Employee agrees to keep all such information strictly confidential, and further agrees that he/she will not communicate, disclose, divulge, or otherwise use, directly or indirectly, such confidential and/or sensitive information."

Alternative 2: "Employee agrees to maintain the strict confidence of Employer's trade secrets and customer information both during and after the term of this agreement."

Nonsolicitation Agreement

In the alternative the employee can agree that the individual will not engage in certain specified competitive activities, such as soliciting the former employer's customers or, more specifically, those customers that the employee had direct contact with. Such an agreement is referred to as a *nonsolicitation agreement*.

Limited Protections

Employers have some legally recognized limited protections against unfair competition, disloyal employees, and overreaching competitors. Employers must carefully review their legal rights and responsibilities and have knowledge of conflicting public policies.

A covenant not to compete is a contractual restriction upon an individual's ability to compete with another person or entity following the termination of a transaction or relationship. Many employers seek to protect their business by requiring employees to sign agreements not to compete with the employer should the employee be terminated. These agreements were normally reserved for high-level executives, researchers, and outside sales personnel, but are currently being increasingly used for mid-level managers, technical staff, and other employees whose departure could create a competitive disadvantage.

Note: Unlike the common law duty of loyalty, a noncompete agreement prohibits conduct taking place after the employment relationship has ended.

Duty of Loyalty

Company employees are under a duty of loyalty to the organization. Generally, employees are not permitted to induce current customers, suppliers, or other employees to leave the organization, nor are they allowed to operate a competing business when employed by the organization. If an employee breaches this duty, the employer may be entitled to collect lost profits, punitive damages, and even out-of-pocket expenses in finding and training replacement employees.

Employees who are found to have breached this duty may be forced to forfeit their salaries and relinquish any profits gained as a result of the disloyal conduct. Additionally, a court may issue an injunction prohibiting similar conduct in the future. In essences, the duty of loyalty prohibits an individual from using trade secrets or proprietary information gained from a former or current employer to the detriment of that employer. Since the law recognizes this duty, the employer does not need to do anything special to create it. In addition, the employees are not required to sign any agreement to be covered by the duty. However, the employer does have the responsibility to prove in court that the information protected meets the appropriate standards and that everything was done to keep the information secret.

Restrictions on Noncompete Agreements

Courts generally do not like noncompete agreements and welcome the opportunity to limit or eliminate them. The dislike stems from a desire to allow individuals to earn a living in the field of their choice and unwillingness to let employers coerce their employees. Broad agreements are usually tossed out or rewritten by the court in those state that allow such an option. Courts will consider the following factors in determining whether to enforce a restrictive covenant:

♦ **Is there a legitimate employer interest in being protected from a particular employee's competitive activity?**

Even if such an interest is present, courts may refuse to enforce a restriction that is too broadly drafted.

♦ **Is the restriction reasonable in light of all the circumstances?**

The restriction must be no more than necessary to protect the employer's legitimate business interests.

♦ **Is the restriction reasonably limited in time and geography?**

The time limit must be reasonable based on such factors as the time to train a new employee and for customers to become familiar with the new employee. The geographical limitation must be to areas necessary to protect the employer's interests.

♦ **Does enforcing the restriction hurt the public interest or adversely affect public policy?**

This is usually not a significant concern since such restrictions do not result in such a major impact.

♦ **Is there reasonable consideration in exchange for the restriction being signed?**

Most states require noncompete restrictions to be signed in exchange for the employee receiving something of value. Normally this means the initial job offer, a raise promotion, or extra benefits upon leaving the organization.

♦ **What triggers the noncompete agreement?**

Some noncompete agreements apply automatically regardless of whether the termination was for cause, without cause, or as part of a layoff or reduction in force. Others apply only when the employee resigns or is terminated for cause, while some limit the period of restricted activity to the time severance benefits are being paid. The employee is therefore free to forego severance payments to accept employment.

Summary

Employment-related litigation is becoming more common, and employees are recovering larger and larger verdicts. Employers should regularly review all of their personnel policies and procedures, as well as employee handbooks and other written personnel documents, to ensure that no promises or statements are being made that could be construed as a binding employment contract. All employers should publish written disclaimers that preserve the employment-at-will relationship. Finally, when terminating employees, an employer should confirm that its action is uniform, consistent, and fair. Whenever possible an employee should be given advance warning that particular behavior or continued misconduct could result in termination. Fairness, honesty, and candor with employees are the keys to defending against or successfully avoiding employment-related lawsuits.

Separation Agreement and Release
Individual Employee
(Sample)

This SEPARATION AGREEMENT AND RELEASE is made this _____ day of _____, 20___ by and between _____ ["Employer"] and _____ ["Employee"], residing at _____ [employee's address].

WHEREAS, Employee and Employer mutually desire to terminate their employment relationship;

NOW, THEREFORE, in consideration of the mutual promises and covenants set forth in the Agreement, the parties agree as follows:

1. Separation from employment. Employee will terminate employment with Employer effective _____ [termination date]. On or before this date, Employee agrees to return to Employer any and all employer property acquired during the term of employment.

2. Consideration for signing. In consideration for Employee signing this SEPARATION AGREEMENT AND RELEASE, Employee shall receive:

Payment of two weeks' salary as severance in the amount of _____ [amount], less withholdings under federal, state, or local law, in one lump sum payment.

Payment of additional severance in the amount of _____ [amount], less withholdings under federal, state, or local law, in one lump sum. This represents one week of additional severance pay for each of Employee's _____ [number] years of service.

Coverage under Employer's health insurance plan through the end of the month of Employee's termination. Thereafter, Employee shall be entitled to exercise COBRA rights in accordance with federal law, provided Employee makes timely COBRA payments to Employer. (The Employee has separately received a notice of COBRA rights.)

(If applicable) The attached Letter of Reference.

3. No additional benefits. Employee acknowledges and agrees that the individual shall receive no benefits additional to those set forth above.

4. Compliance with employment agreement [as applicable]. Employee agrees to abide by all terms and conditions set forth in the Employment Agreement with Employer dated _____ [date].

5. Release of claims. Employee stipulates, agrees, and understands that in consideration of the payments set forth in paragraph 2 above, that being good and valuable consideration, Employee hereby acting of his or her own free will, voluntarily and on behalf of himself/herself, his or her heirs, administrators, executors, successors and assigns, releases Employer and its subsidiaries, affiliates, directors, officers, employees, and agents, and each of them ("Releases"), from any and all debts, obligations, claims, demands, judgments, or causes of action of any kind whatsoever, in tort, contract, by statute, or on any other basis, for compensatory, punitive, or other damages, expenses, reimbursements, or costs of any kind, including but not limited to any and all claims, demands, rights, and/or causes of action arising out of the written Employment Agreement with Employer or any alleged oral modification [if no written employment agreement, a modification might state, "out of his or her employment with Employer or any employment contract, where applicable"], or relating to purported employment discrimination or violations of civil rights, such as, but not limited to, those arising under Title VII of the Civil Rights Act of 1964, the Civil Rights Act of 1991, the Civil Rights Acts of 1866 and/or 1867, the Age Discrimination in Employment Act of 1967, the ADA of 1990, Executive Order 11246, the Equal Pay Act of 1963, the Rehabilitation Act of 1973, [add names of relevant state or local fair employment statutes], or any other applicable federal, state, or local employment discrimination statute or ordinance or any other claim, whether statutory or based on common law, arising: (1) by reason of employment with employer or the termination of that employment or circumstances related thereto; or (2) by reason of any other matter, cause, or thing whatsoever, for the first date of employment to the date or execution of the SEPARATION AGREEMENT AND RELEASE.

Note: This is a generic sample policy and does not necessarily reflect the employment laws in any or all of the 50 U.S. states. Before establishing any company policy, one should review the applicable state laws or seek guidance from legal counsel.

Chapter 12

Alternative Dispute Resolution

Introduction

In the past 20 years there has been a tremendous increase in the amount of employment discrimination litigation. Antidiscrimination laws — for example, the Americans with Disabilities Act (ADA) and the Civil Rights Act — provide enhanced rights (jury trials) and remedies (compensatory and punitive damages) for plaintiffs, while unlimited awards of damages and attorneys' fees are available under Sec. 1981.

The Equal Employment Opportunity Commission (EEOC) reported that over the past 10 years there has been a dramatic increase in sexual harassment complaints that have raised the consciousness of employees and the ante for employers. Additionally, over 170,000 charges have been filed under the ADA during the past 10 years.

The employment relationship is changing as a result of these social and legal developments. To accommodate these changes, many progressive companies have made a commitment to encourage employee involvement and empowerment. For example, many companies have adopted participative dispute resolution procedures.

These procedures include a variety of methodologies that are often successfully used in combination. They include the following:

- ◆ Arbitration agreements.

- ◆ Complaint resolution procedures.

- ◆ Peer review and peer review panels.

- ◆ Employee involvement groups.

- ◆ Participative management strategies.

Companies adopting participative dispute resolution procedures have recognized the value of employee input and peer judgment. Moreover, in a report by the federally funded Commission on the Future of Worker Management Relations the value of employee participation as a vital element in preserving competitiveness in the global marketplace was recognized. The commission recently reported that private dispute resolution, such as mediation and arbitration, as well as newer, more informal employee participation and alternative dispute resolution (ADR) systems, are not being used to their full potential for dealing with workplace issues.

There has also been judicial approval of ADR procedures to resolve disputes. In 1991, the U.S. Supreme Court granted approval to mandatory arbitration clauses in the employment relationship in the case of *Gilmer v. Interstate/Johnson Lane Corp.* Other federal and state courts have upheld mandatory arbitration outside of a collective-bargaining relationship to resolve claims of sexual harassment; sex, age, and race discrimination; state law discrimination; and wrongful discharge claims.

The ADA, the Civil Rights Act, and other statutes specifically encourage parties to use mediation, conciliation, and arbitration to resolve disputes. Government agencies, such as the EEOC, are encouraging the use of mediation and arbitration. For example, the EEOC has established dispute resolution centers to review employment discrimination complaints filed with the commission. The EEOC has also employed mediation and voluntary arbitration as the cornerstones of the agency's new case processing procedures. Additionally, the U.S. Department of Labor has adopted an ADR program. Evidenced by agency policies and procedures, employment discrimination legislation has continuously encouraged employers to implement the use of ADR.

Types of ADR Solutions

Many employers are unaware that they already practice ADR. The simple principle underlying ADR is that disputes are best settled quickly before they intensify, thus avoiding litigation. A model ADR program is designed to immediately bring disputes to the attention of key decision-makers in an effort to settle the issue as soon as possible. The goal of ADR is to provide a forum for the parties themselves to work toward a voluntary, consensual agreement, as opposed to having a judge or other authority decide the case. Principal ADR solutions include open-door policies, internal mediation, and arbitration.

Open-Door Policies

Open-door policies offer a quick resolution to disputes by encouraging employees to bring grievances to their immediate supervisors. An open-door policy requires a commitment by managers to listen and react to employees. Managers must be trained to identify particular problems that may require a particular investigational procedure. For example, allegations of sexual harassment or safety concerns should be referred immediately to senior management for appropriate investigation and resolution.

When the immediate supervisor is the cause of the problem or lacks authority to resolve the problem, successful open-door policies allow employees to take their grievances to different levels within the organization.

Open-door policies may prevent litigation by correcting problems before someone is injured or a discontented employee becomes embittered and retains a lawyer. Should an employee bring suit against an employer, the records from a good-faith open-door policy may demonstrate that an employer was attempting to accommodate employees with a venue to amicably handle concerns and grievances.

Of course, a disgruntled employee may still pursue litigation after exhausting options within an open-door policy. Employers should be careful in dealing with chronic troublemakers who may use open-door meetings as a basis for court complaints.

Internal Mediation

A more formal method to resolve complaints is to designate one, specific individual to whom employees submit complaints. Sometimes called an **ombudsman**, this type of mediator functions as a go-between in trying to resolve the dispute.

When a personality conflict exists between the employee and manager or when an employee is embarrassed to submit a complaint, the intervention of a mediator may be more successful than an open-door policy. A good mediator can help all parties involved in the dispute to view issues objectively and reach a mutually satisfactory solution.

A system of internal mediation will succeed or fail based on the skill and credibility of the mediator. Careful selection of the individual who will fill the important role of mediator is crucial. Employees must trust the mediator to keep their confidences and feel that the mediator has enough influence with management to effect change. Additionally, key decision-makers must publicly support the mediation process so that supervisors will respect the process and the mediator.

Internal mediation also conserves resources better than an open-door policy because only one individual is working on the disputes, rather than several managers. A mediator may be likely to investigate complaints more promptly and thoroughly due to the mediator's fewer operational responsibilities in comparison to line supervisors or managers.

At worst, if mediation fails, the employer has the opportunity to clarify an employee's complaint and assess the merit of the organization's position. If the employee chooses to go to court, the employer will already have much of the information necessary to defend itself.

Ombudsman

As previously stated, an ombudsman is a person who is authorized by an employer to confidentially receive complaints or questions about alleged acts, omissions, improprieties, and broader systemic problems within the ombudsman's defined jurisdiction. The ombudsman is also charged with the duty to address, investigate, or otherwise examine these issues independently and impartially. It is essential that the procedures used are fair in order to ensure a just resolution of the matter.

An ombudsman may make formal or informal reports regarding the results of a review or investigation. They may also make recommendations regarding how disputes should be resolved. Additionally, based on an agreement with the employer, an ombudsman may go as far as initiating litigation to enforce or protect the authority of the office.

Peer Review

Based on recent surveys, 90 percent of human resource executives report that their companies have adopted an open-door policy as the primary method for handling nonunion employee complaints.

However, these same executives report that 75 percent of the time employees with complaints bypass the open-door policy and consult an attorney, file a discrimination charge, write letters to company executives, contact the press, or seek help from a union.

Realistically, a gap exists between the theory that employees will use the company open-door policy and the path employee's follow when they have complaints or grievances. Peer review offers a viable alternative to the open-door policy by providing employees a system that they feel confident will produce equitable results.

An employer may opt to use a peer review panel to review and resolve employee disputes, at least concerning disciplinary action or discharge. The panel consists of a mix of employees and managers (some employers use peer review panels consisting exclusively of employees) who hear and evaluate employee appeals from disciplinary or other actions.

While these peer review panel decisions are not final, binding, or a legal deterrent to filing suit, as a practical matter they unquestionably reduce the risk of employment litigation. The reduced risk is based upon the employees' perception that the employer has treated them fairly, the fact that employees receive a form of due process in reviewing the disciplinary action, and plaintiffs' attorneys recognize that a decision by the employees' peers reduces the sympathy factor in an employment lawsuit.

Although peer review is primarily used for handling employee disciplinary complaints, with properly trained panelists it may also be designed to cover other workplace issues. However, matters such as compensation, performance reviews, benefits, layoffs, and company policy would normally be excluded from their consideration. Additionally, groups acting in a true peer review capacity are generally excluded from the National Labor Relations Act's (NLRA) proscription on dominated labor organizations, which may affect the legitimacy of employee committees.

Peer review panels do not deal with the employer within the realm of the ban by making proposals to management, which the employer accepts or rejects; rather, they act in a decision-making capacity. (The availability of further review by top management does not alter the fundamental nature of their role.)

The Elements of an Internal Peer Review System

An employer would determine an employee's eligibility for peer review. This determination would be based upon how to maximize the benefits to be achieved from a peer review system. Many times, employers view employee eligibility for the peer review process in the same way as other employment benefits. For example, eligibility might include all regular full-time and part-time employees who have completed a specified length of service with the organization, excluding probationary or temporary employees.

In order to achieve the greatest return for implementing peer review, the option for peer review should be treated as an additional employment benefit.

Peer review should be capable of handling a range of employee complaints from discipline to termination. With a properly trained group of panelists, it may also be designed to cover discrimination issues, including sexual harassment. Matters that would probably be excluded from peer review are compensation issues, performance reviews, benefits, layoffs, and company policy.

Initially, employees with a complaint would be encouraged to resolve the dispute by following the existing procedure of using the chain of command, including the open door policy when appropriate. If the dispute is not resolved at this point, the employee has the options of either bringing the complaint to the attention of a designated senior executive for a final and binding decision or taking the matter to a review panel under the peer review process.

If a review panel is chosen, the employee selects one facilitator from a list of trained facilitators. The chosen facilitator then coordinates the panel's selection, meeting, and actions.

Generally, about 10 percent of the employer's total workforce should be trained as potential panelists. The facilitator arranges for the employee to randomly draw names for panelists. If it is a panel of five, the employee draws six names, keeping three for the panel with one alternate for each panelist. The employee then draws the names of four management representatives, keeping three for the panel with one alternate.

The facilitator collaborates with the employee focusing on the employee's presentation and ensures that the employee obtains all appropriate documents for the panel. At the meeting of the panel, the facilitator plays a significant role in making sure the employee and the panel carry out their respective roles.

The Benefits of Internal Peer Review

Experience shows that peer review has many lasting benefits including, but not limited to, the following:

♦ **Management Development.** Participation by managers trained to act as panelists and facilitators improves management skills, particularly in the area of problem solving.

♦ **Litigation Avoidance.** Employees refrain from seeking legal counsel, filing a discrimination charge or lawsuit, writing directly to executives, or seeking a union. Additionally, there is a reduced likelihood that an attorney will take the case if the panel affirmed management's actions.

♦ **Due Process.** Employees have an opportunity to air their grievances. In addition, peer review instills a perception of fairness in the workplace.

♦ **Reduction in Costs.** There is generally a reduction in employee calls and letters to the home office and in discrimination charges and lawsuits, all of which result in a reduction of legal expenses and costs.

♦ **Union Avoidance.** A union's major sales pitch or benefit regarding union membership — a formal grievance procedure — has lost all value.

♦ **Employee Development and Empowerment.** Training panelists and involving employees in the implementation of the program enhances their range of skills and promotes the feeling of being able to make a difference.

♦ **Training.** Collecting and recording grievances for a library of real-life situations is an effective tool for future training.

Peer review is a valuable resolution program that allows employees to present complaints in a nonthreatening forum. When implemented, peer review has successfully resolved employee complaints, improved morale, reduced legal and operational costs, and avoided employment litigation.

Arbitration

Final binding arbitration is the most formal ADR method. In an arbitration agreement, employees and employers agree to submit their dispute to a neutral third party, an arbitrator, and agree to abide by the arbitrator's decision. While arbitration hearings are not as formal as court proceedings, they usually involve the presentation of witnesses, evidence, and arguments.

Employers may also use nonbinding arbitration. This option is the same as binding arbitration except that the parties may reject the arbitrator's decision. Rarely does nonbinding arbitration offer more advantages than binding arbitration.

Advantages of Arbitration

Arbitration has several advantages over traditional litigation as follows:

♦ The parties have more influence over the selection of the arbitrator than they would over the selection of a judge.

♦ Arbitrators are less likely to award excessive actual or punitive damages than are judges.

♦ Arbitrators tend to be less influenced by passion or prejudice than are juries.

♦ The discovery process in arbitration is generally more streamlined, thus the administrative cost, time restraint, and inconvenience of preparing for an arbitrated case is less extensive than preparing a case in state or federal court.

♦ Arbitration generally takes less time than a traditional court action.

Disadvantages of Arbitration

Of course, arbitration does have some disadvantages, including the following:

♦ Unlike a trial court decision that can be appealed to a higher court, arbitration decisions cannot generally be appealed on their merits.

♦ Judges dismiss many employment cases based on pretrial motions to dismiss or for summary judgment. Some cases may proceed further in arbitration than they would in court because arbitrators traditionally reserve judgment until after a hearing.

♦ Because many employers are implementing the ADR process, some arbitrators may be unfamiliar with the exact legal standard to be applied in each employment action.

♦ Traditionally, arbitrators are more lenient in admitting evidence than courts. Consequently, damaging evidence may come to light in an arbitration that would otherwise be excluded from a court procedure.

♦ Some arbitrators may try to satisfy both sides by issuing split decisions reinstating employees without awarding them damages.

Arbitration to Avoid Civil Litigation

The U.S. Supreme Court has ruled that binding mandatory arbitration is lawful and enforceable as a substitute for civil litigation based on fair employment practice laws. Employers are including arbitration clauses in employment agreements, requiring the employer and employee to submit any disputes arising from the employment relationship to binding arbitration; for example, wrongful discharge disputes, infliction of emotional distress, discrimination, and harassment.

The U.S. Supreme Court considered the enforceability of such agreements under the Federal Arbitration Act (FAA) in *Circuit City Stores, Inc. v. Adams*. In the case, the Supreme Court held that employment agreements containing arbitration provisions are enforceable under federal law, settling conflicting opinions among the lower courts as to whether employers could require employees to submit disputes to arbitration rather than file lawsuits. Employers now have a reliable alternative to courtroom litigation as a means to redress employee complaints.

In another recent arbitration case, *EEOC v. Waffle House*, the Supreme Court found that an agreement between an employer and an employee to arbitrate employment-related disputes does not bar the EEOC from pursuing victim-specific judicial relief — such as backpay, reinstatement, and damages — in an ADA enforcement action.

The court explained that because the EEOC is not a party to the contract and has not agreed to arbitrate its claims, the FAA's pro-arbitration policy goals do not require the agency to relinquish its statutory authority to pursue victim-specific relief, regardless of the forum that the employer and employee have chosen to resolve their disputes.

Terms of Arbitration Clauses

An arbitration agreement should explicitly set forth certain terms, since the employer must comply whenever the employee requests arbitration pursuant to the contract. The specific terms should consist of the following:

◆ The kinds of claims required to be submitted to arbitration.

◆ The rules to govern the arbitration. Various organizations such as the American Arbitration Association and the Federal Mediation and Conciliation Service publish standard rules for arbitration, including the availability of pre-hearing discovery. These organizations can be used to supply lists of arbitrators and procedures for selecting the arbitrator.

◆ The types of remedies the arbitrator can award. For purposes of avoiding parallel litigation, the awards should be defined broadly enough to include the kinds of legal and equitable remedies available in a court. Remedies should include such things as actual damages, including front pay and backpay, as well as punitive damages, attorneys' fees, and arbitration costs.

◆ The responsibility for the payment of the costs of arbitration. Employees cannot be expected to bear substantial administrative or arbitrator fees.

In a recent decision, the Supreme Court re-emphasized the rule that arbitration clauses must be particularly clear. Accordingly, when drafting such a clause, employers should be as detailed as possible.

ADR Advantages and Disadvantages

Advantages to Using ADR

Should ADR fail to avoid litigation, the existence of such a system enhances the appearance and reality of fairness within the organization. Additionally, the system may deflate a litigant's chances if the organization's ADR findings were in favor of management.

Courts may recognize ADR as final and binding if the system incorporates elements of notice, due process, fact, and issue specificity, finality, and other guarantees of impartiality and fairness. The evidentiary value of ADR proceedings in subsequent litigation is substantial. In addition, litigants may be expected to exhaust internal remedies before beginning litigation. Finally, emotional distress claims may be rebutted based on the availability of a fair and consistent dispute resolution system.

When the subject matter involved in the dispute is sensitive, ADR may protect the privacy interests of the parties and keep the nature of the matter confidential. For example, the facts and allegations surrounding charges of sexual harassment may be extremely sensitive, and the parties may wish to avoid the public attention that may result from litigation in the courts, where documents and files are matters of public record. For this same reason, ADR procedures are being used to resolve disputes involving trade secrets and other highly confidential matters.

ADR can also be used to achieve zero-litigation goals. For example, peer review may be used as an adjudicatory forum similar to a trial by a jury of peers. Another method to avoid litigation is use of an ombudsman, who functions as a neutral open door option for the resolution of complaints. Similarly, the mediation process centers around a neutral referee who guides the parties to an acceptable compromise on the issues.

More formal options such as fact-finding and arbitration present an adjudicatory forum similar to a hearing before a trial examiner who has the responsibility to perform the following:

♦ Gather, evaluate, and weigh evidence.

♦ Analyze issues and applicable rules.

♦ Issue a binding decision on the merits of the case in favor of one of the parties, including remedies and/or penalties.

ADR can also reduce vulnerability to union organizing because a procedure to resolve complaints internally eliminates the need for union intervention. It also helps to achieve an issue-free workplace. ADR mechanisms enhance employees' sense of empowerment, value, authority in the workplace and with management. Employees also perceive management to be fair, consistent, and respectful to employees. Moreover, employees have access to a mechanism similar to grievance and arbitration of disputes under a collective-bargaining agreement.

Disadvantages

Of course, arbitration does have some disadvantages, such as the following:

♦ Unlike a trial court decision that can be appealed to a higher court, arbitration decisions cannot generally be appealed on their merits.

♦ Judges dismiss many employment cases based on pretrial motions to dismiss or for summary judgment. In contrast, arbitrators traditionally reserve judgment until after a hearing so some cases may proceed further in arbitration than would have in court.

♦ Because many employers are utilizing of this form of ADR, some arbitrators may be unfamiliar with the exact legal standard to be applied in each employment action.

♦ Arbitrators are traditionally more lax in admitting evidence than courts; as a result damaging evidence may be presented in an arbitration that would be excluded from a court procedure.

♦ Some arbitrators try to satisfy both sides by issuing split decisions reinstating employees without awarding them damages.

Formal Policy Considerations

Use of employment mediation is increasing rapidly. Time and again conflicts are resolved promptly, at modest cost, through the intervention of a skillful mediator.

When a terminated or current employee asserts a claim against the employer, it frequently is in the interests of both sides to attempt to resolve the matter early through mediation for a number of reasons as follows:

♦ The procedure gives the employee the opportunity to be heard and vent emotions.

♦ Resolutions are usually prompt, but if the case cannot be settled, other options are not ruled out.

♦ The resolution is likely to be more mutually beneficial than one fashioned by a court or jury.

♦ Lingering animosity is likely to be lessened.

- The parties retain control over the outcome.

- Legal fees and other costs are modest.

- The procedure is private and confidential.

Nevertheless, there are several impediments to the use of mediation in this area, such as the following:

- Many attorneys representing employers or employees are still unfamiliar with, and consequently skeptical of, mediation.

- Many attorneys are reluctant to be the first to propose mediation for fear that their proposal may be seen as a sign of weakness.

- Some employee disputes are not suitable for mediation (for example, disputes involving misappropriation of trade secrets).

- Some attorneys are predisposed against mediation until after formal discovery has concluded.

When a former or existing employee first asserts a claim, the employer often believes that the claim is without merit and must be defended vigorously. Nevertheless with management approval, most lawsuits are settled before they ever reach the courtroom, but only after the costs and burdens of trial preparation have been incurred.

It is recommended that, at the outset of a case, the employer's in-house attorney or outside counsel engage in a dialogue with the responsible executive to analyze the case and to reach a well-considered decision as to whether the case must be tried to judgment — at considerable expense — or whether the employer is willing to settle on reasonable terms. If the case is susceptible to settlement at any stage, serious consideration should be given to proposing mediation in the hope of achieving an early settlement; thus, saving the employer the high costs and burdens of full-scale litigation or arbitration.

Private Arbitration of Employment Disputes Upheld

The U.S. Supreme Court has made it easier for employers to resolve workplace disputes through the use of arbitration procedures rather than the courts.

In a ruling on March 2, 2001 (*Circuit City Stores, Inc. v. Adams*) the Supreme Court held that employment agreements containing arbitration provisions are enforceable under federal law. This decision settled conflicting opinions among the lower courts as to whether employers could require employees to submit disputes to arbitration rather than file lawsuits.

Employers now have a reliable alternative to courtroom litigation as a means to redress employee complaints. Among the points favoring arbitration over courtroom litigation are the following:

- Disputes may be resolved more quickly and efficiently.

- Proceeding through arbitration is generally less costly.

- Arbitrators are believed to be expert decision-makers bringing specific knowledge and experience to the table, as opposed to lay jurors.

- Arbitration may provide a user-friendly vehicle for both the employee and employer.

- Arbitration may provide a system that ensures fairness and due process.

Among the concerns an employer may have about arbitration are the following:

- ♦ A fear of a rise in employee disputes.

- ♦ Difficulty in overturning an arbitrator's unfavorable decision.

- ♦ A tendency among arbitrators to appease all parties in order to resolve the dispute.

- ♦ Inclusion of evidence that normally would be excluded from a court proceeding.

Although the Supreme Court has now said that arbitration agreements are enforceable, it did not address the practical issues regarding implementation. Employers must make certain their arbitration provisions are carefully drafted.

Arbitration Agreement and an EEOC Suit for Victim-Specific Remedies

As previously discussed, in a recent U.S. Supreme Court case, *EEOC v. Waffle House*, the court found that an agreement between an employer and an employee to arbitrate employment-related disputes does not bar the EEOC from pursuing relief. The lawsuit must be brought under the EEOC's own name and pursue victim-specific judicial relief, such as backpay, reinstatement, and damages, in an Americans with Disabilities Act (ADA) enforcement action.

The court explained that because the EEOC was not a party to the contract and did not agree to arbitrate the claims, the EEOC was in no way constrained by the private agreement. The Federal Arbitration Act's (FAA) pro-arbitration policy goals do not require the agency to relinquish its statutory authority in order to pursue victim-specific relief, regardless of which forum the employer and employee have chosen to resolve their disputes.

Although, an employee's conduct may effectively limit the relief the EEOC can obtain in court. For example, if the employee fails to mitigate damages or accepts a monetary settlement. In the *EEOC v. Waffle House* case the employee had not sought arbitration, nor was there any indication that settlement negotiations were entered into with the employer.

Sample Policies

Communicating New Policies

The presentation of the employer's decision to implement employment dispute resolution procedures is vital to the acceptance of those procedures by its employees. Employees as well as management should feel that these procedures are fair and protect their interests. In addition, both parties must understand the legal consequences of agreeing to a binding arbitration.

In an effort to achieve this end, the sample policy that follows outlines the process and its benefits.

Alternative Dispute Resolution Policy (Sample)

Policy Statement

When a current or former employee asserts a claim against the employer, it is often in the mutual interests of both parties to avoid the costs, delays, uncertainty of outcome, and animosity of a full-scale litigation.

Policy Overview

Voluntary Mediation Provisions

In most cases, it is the employer's policy to propose or agree to mediation of an employment dispute. Mediation can be a highly effective procedure for bringing about settlement for many types of disputes — particularly employment-related disputes. However, mediation may not be appropriate where the employer has determined the need for a judicial determination to enforce the employer's rights or to offer protection against unfair competition or misappropriation of intellectual or other property or breach of restrictive covenants. Mediation also may not be appropriate when the dispute involves a modest amount of money.

The success of mediation depends on the qualifications and skill of the mediator and on the confidence both parties have in that individual. The mediator will be selected by agreement of both parties. If they do not agree, both will rank order a list of candidates. The candidate with the best-combined score will be the mediator.

Normally, the meditation fees are divided equally between the parties. However, in appropriate cases the employer may agree to bear more than one-half the cost.

To maximize the chances that the mediation will be successful, both the employee and a senior manager of the employer must agree to personally participate in each mediation session, unless excused by the mediator. Each party may also be represented by an attorney, or other person of their choice, and must voluntarily provide information needed for the mediator to evaluate the claim.

The procedure requires parties to suspend litigation activities while the mediation is ongoing, and each party is free to withdraw from the mediation after the first session. Additionally, the mediation process may be subject to reasonable time limits.

Arbitration Options
Voluntary Post-Dispute Arbitration

In an attempt to resolve a dispute where mediation is unsuccessful, or in lieu of mediation, the employer will not rule out the binding arbitration of disputes with present or former employees. On a case-by-case basis, the employer will determine whether to agree to binding arbitration.

Mandatory Pre-Dispute Arbitration

Although mediation is not binding and the chances of success are high, mediation may still fail to resolve the dispute. Where mediation fails, it is the employer's policy to resolve the dispute through binding arbitration. Upon an employer's issuance of a policy to resolve employment disputes via arbitration, all employees who remain employed for 90 days or more after its issuance, along with all new employees, will be bound by this policy.

The employer instituting this policy is convinced that the arbitration procedure is evenhanded, fair to both sides, and has significant mutual advantages. For example, it is likely to be more expeditious, more economical, and less burdensome or adversarial than litigation. Arbitration is private and the results are final. Arbitration does not change either party's substantive legal rights, but merely changes the forum in which those rights are adjudicated.

Addition to Mandatory Binding Arbitration

Employees find arbitration to be much more palatable if they are not bound by an adverse result and are free to go to court after the arbitrator's award is handed down. While non-binding arbitration may grant the employee "a second bite at the apple," in most cases an employee who lost in a fair arbitration proceeding will accept the award. Additionally, in any subsequent court action the arbitration award may be introduced in evidence.

Dispute Resolution Procedure

Due to the high costs of lawsuits, perpetual life disruptions, and delay of litigation in the courts the employer has advocated the use of negotiation, mediation, and other forms of alternative dispute resolution, including arbitration. The litigation process is highly unsatisfactory for both the employer and employee as the process is adversarial from the beginning, the outcome of trial is uncertain, and is not final until all appeals are concluded.

Certainly, most problems are solved through discussions with a supervisor, with a human resources representative, or through other internal procedures. Where these procedures do not produce a satisfactory result, however, the employer would like to offer a more efficient, less adversarial alternative to filing a lawsuit. The employer believes ADR to be mutually beneficial in resolving employee disputes that are not solved through other means.

Adopting a multi-step ADR program offers the possibility of using mediation as a first step to try to find a mutually agreeable way to resolve employment disputes. If agreement is not reached in mediation, the employer or employee may use arbitration to resolve such disputes. A brief summary of each procedure follows. The employee should note, however, that the actual provisions of the procedures, and not any summary, will govern.

Mediation

Although mediation is strongly favored for the most significant employment disputes, this step may not always be suitable. In mediation, an experienced neutral third party is first selected by agreement and then meets with the parties to help resolve their differences. The mediator accomplishes this by helping the parties open communications, focusing on the parties real interests, and attempting to find a satisfactory resolution for both participants. Mediation is a non-binding process — there is no requirement that either party accept any recommendation the mediator might make for settlement. The settlement and its terms are entirely subject to party agreement. Both parties are entitled to be represented by an attorney or any other individual of their choice.

Key Advantages of Mediation

Mediation has proven successful in the great majority of cases. It offers the following advantages:

- Provides the opportunity for all parties to narrate their version of the dispute in a non-aggressive atmosphere.

- Facilitates listening.

- Helps reduce feelings of hostility.

- Helps separate emotional issues from factual issues.

- Promotes discussion of solutions rather than focusing on one party winning and the other losing.

- Aids parties in reaching a resolution rather than letting a third party hand down a finding.

- Offers an opportunity for a solution that is agreeable for both the employee and the employer.

While an employer may have a policy to agree to mediation, it is important to remember that mediation is voluntary.

Requesting Mediation

The employee may request mediation orally or in writing if internal procedures have not resolved a dispute. The employer will generally agree, unless the employer concludes that the dispute is not suitable for mediation. Any employee may suggest the name of a mediator they consider to be fair, impartial, and experienced. If the employer does not readily agree with the employee in regard to a mediator, the employer will submit a short list of candidates. The employer and employee will then either agree on one of these candidates or each party will rank order the candidates. The candidate with the best-combined score will be the mediator. Both parties will then sign a submission agreement to begin the mediation process.

Conducting the Mediation

The employee may propose modifications; however the mediation will be conducted under currently accepted procedures. An attorney or other person of their choice may represent the employee. If an attorney represents the employee, an attorney also may represent the employer. The employee and the employer representative must attend each mediation session.

The mediator will guide the discussion and help settle differences. The mediator is likely to meet privately with each side to develop a better understanding of the problem.

When the employee and the employer agree on the terms of a settlement, both will sign a written settlement agreement.

Expenses of Mediation

Actual mediation meetings frequently take between 6 and 15 hours. Mediators usually charge between $250 and $350 per hour. Normally, the mediator's fee will be divided equally, however the employee may request that the employer pay more than one-half of the fee. The employee will typically bear the cost of any attorney or other representative the employee retained.

Arbitration

If either the employer or employee does not agree to or cannot resolve the dispute through mediation, either party may request the other to submit the claim to arbitration. Arbitration must be used by the parties rather than litigation or instituting an administrative agency's authority.

The Procedure

Arbitration is a process in which a dispute is presented to a neutral third party, the ***arbitrator***.

The arbitrator makes a decision after both sides present their arguments at the hearing. There is no jury. If the employee prevails, the employee can be awarded anything the employee might seek through a court of law. Though arbitration is much less formal than a court trial, it is an orderly proceeding, governed by rules of procedure and legal standards of conduct.

Advantages

The arbitration process offers several of the following mutual advantages to the employer and to the employee:

♦ **Speed.** Court proceedings are cumbersome, lengthy, and frequently leave neither party with an acceptable result.

The arbitration process will normally be completed within a number of months, permitting the arbitrator to resolve disputes quickly and fairly. If the arbitrator finds that the employee is entitled to compensation or other relief, it is likely to be received much sooner than court awarded compensation. Although arbitration statutes allow very limited modification for issues, such as bias or fraud by the arbitrator, the ability to appeal an arbitrator's award is not available.

♦ **Reduced Cost.** All parties will save money by avoiding the significant legal fees and other costs of court proceedings.

♦ **Experienced Decision-Makers.** Courts do not specialize in resolving employment disputes; however, arbitrators do.

♦ **Confidentiality and Privacy.** Claims are resolved in a more agreeable fashion when both sides have the protection of confidentiality.

Requesting Arbitration

An employee must provide the appropriate departmental manager with written notice to initiate arbitration. Such notice must be provided within the applicable period required by law.

If in doubt, the employee may determine that period by consulting either their or the employer's representative. The employee's notice will state their claim, the relevant facts, and the remedies being sought. The notice must be accompanied by documents in support of the employee's claim.

Selecting an Arbitrator

The employee and the employer will attempt to agree on a neutral arbitrator. If the employer or employee cannot promptly agree, both may submit a list of qualified candidates from which one may be selected.

Expenses of the Arbitration

The employee's share of the arbitrator's fees and related expenses will not exceed two days' gross compensation or one-half of such expenses — whichever is less. In case of demonstrated hardship, the arbitrator may relieve an employee of the obligation to contribute to their fee and related expenses. The employee may voluntarily elect to pay one-half of all such expenses. The employee will typically bear the employee's own attorney's fees and the costs of producing their evidence.

Note: This is a generic sample policy and does not necessarily reflect the employment laws in any or all of the 50 U.S. states. Before establishing any company policy, one should review the applicable state laws or seek guidance from legal counsel.

Model Contractual Provision for Mediation Policy (Sample)

Proposal of Mediation

Any party to an alleged employment dispute may initiate mediation at such time as the party becomes aware there is an alleged dispute. A *party* is defined for purposes of this provision as a complainant employee or employer.

The party initiating the mediation must give written notice to all parties to the mediation. This notice must indicate that a response — either accepting or declining mediation — must be given within 14 days. Any party wishing not to mediate must waive, in writing, the right to mediation. Any party filing an EEOC complaint or Title VII suit will be considered as having constructively waived their right to mediate. Neither this document nor an agreement to mediate waives any substantive legal right or responsibility of any party. By choosing to mediate, no party is at any time waiving the right to file suit in court, go to arbitration, or file an EEOC complaint.

The Mediation Process

The mediation sessions will aim to reach an agreement about the future conduct and relationship of the parties. The mediator's role is to facilitate agreement; the mediator is not a judge or an arbitrator and does not rule on the merits of this case. The power to resolve the dispute resides solely with the parties, not the mediator. Before beginning the mediation session, all parties must read the description of the mediation process accompanying this policy and must acknowledge in writing that they have read the description.

The mediator has complete control over the procedures used during the sessions, including the frequency and duration of caucusing, the use of the initial joint session, and the scheduling of the sessions.

The choice to participate in mediation is voluntary. Any party may terminate the mediation at any time for any reason simply by giving written notice of the termination to the mediator and to each of the other parties to the mediation. Filing an EEOC complaint or Title VII suit will be considered termination, for purposes of this policy.

The mediation sessions are confidential. Neither the mediator nor any party to the mediation may disclose any information about or from the mediation process to anyone. Each party and the mediator shall sign a confidentiality agreement before the beginning of the first mediation session.

All parties shall attend the mediation sessions and make a good-faith effort to mediate. At least one of the individuals present on behalf of each party must have authority to settle the dispute. Each party to the mediation is encouraged to bring counsel to the mediation sessions. Counsel shall function, however, as advisors rather than advocates.

The parties' remedies are not limited to cash settlements. Exploration of other potential remedies is strongly encouraged.

Selection of a Mediator

The mediator must meet the following criteria:

- ◆ Be neutral and impartial.

- ◆ Be knowledgeable in the area of sexual harassment.

- ◆ Be certified by an organization that requires the following:

  - • Supervised training in the mediation process.

  - • Adherence of the mediator to standards of conduct.

The mediator shall immediately disclose any potential conflict of interest to all parties.

An organization certifying mediators shall provide a list of three suggested mediators who meet the qualifications previously listed. Additionally, any party to the mediation may suggest another qualified mediator, although all parties must be in agreement to utilizing this individual.

If the parties cannot agree on a mediator within 14 days after mediation has begun, the organization supplying the mediator will suggest one appropriate individual. No party may then object to the suggested mediator unless the mediator has a conflict of interest.

The mediation shall begin within 21 days from the date on which the mediator was chosen.

Costs

The cost of the mediator will be split as follows:

- ◆ The employer is responsible for 90 percent of the mediator's fees.

- ◆ The complainant employee is responsible for 10 percent.

Inability of the employee to pay the 10 percent will not, however, prevent a complainant employee from pursuing mediation. In such cases, the employer shall pay the full amount and make arrangements with the complainant employee for repayment, up to the 10 percent, on a reasonable schedule.

The human resources department or similar office of the employer shall set the amount to be paid and the repayment schedule. Furthermore, the employer shall pay the cost of counsel for the complainant employee, up to and including the cost of 25 billable hours or $3,000 — whichever is less. The complainant employee is responsible for choosing individual counsel. This counsel, if paid for by the employer, must be present at the mediation.

Settlement

Any settlement reached must contain a liquidated damages clause, providing a set amount to be paid should a party breach the contractual agreement. Once settlement has been reached, the mediator or counsel for one of the parties shall draft a written settlement document incorporating the terms of the settlement. If the mediator does not draft the settlement agreement, the mediator shall review the agreement before it is given to the parties for signature.

This draft shall be given to all parties, reviewed, changed if appropriate, and executed.

Note: This is a generic sample policy and does not necessarily reflect the employment laws in any or all of the 50 U.S. states. Before establishing any company policy, one should review the applicable state laws or seek guidance from legal counsel.

Chapter 13
Telecommuting

Introduction

A growing number of employers are allowing their employees to choose whether to work at home or from an alternative worksite. Because the practice often involves computer and telecommunications technology, it is known as ***telecommuting***. Reports indicate that almost 11.1 million employees telecommuted in 1997. Today, more than two-thirds of Fortune 1000 companies have telecommuting programs in place. The volume of telecommuters is expected to double over the next 10 years.

Before implementing a telecommuting policy, management should consider the benefits for and concerns of both the employer and the potential telecommuting employee. In addition, the legal consequences of telecommuting must be considered.

Companies should formulate policies or guidelines that define criteria for evaluating positions eligible for telecommuting. Obviously, some employees will always be needed in an office to support co-workers or coordinate telecommuters in the field. Clear criteria can help employers determine whether telecommuting is right for them and distinguish which positions are suitable for home performance and which should remain traditional office or workplace jobs.

Benefits for Employers

Employers offer alternative workplace arrangements for many reasons. Based on a number of recent studies and surveys, an employer considering telecommuting as a workplace option might expect the following benefits:

♦ **Improves the quality of work and increases productivity.** Employees concentrate on the project itself with less distraction from the office environment.

♦ **Improves morale and reduces stress** giving employees more options to balance work and family demands.

♦ **Saves hours of commuting time**, allowing the employee to spend more time on projects, completing them with a higher quality of work in a timelier manner.

♦ **Employer/supervisor can concentrate on the outcome and quality of the project at hand** rather than tracking hours an employee is present in the actual office. This enhances teamwork and communication in the office.

♦ **Mental health concerns are alleviated through telework opportunities.** The employee reduces the frustration and fatigue resulting from commuting to the official office.

- **Provides a valuable tool for recruitment of new employees** as well as retention incentive for experienced employees to stay with the government instead of opting for retirement.

- **Environmental issues,** including traffic congestion, air quality, energy issues, limited parking availability, etc., are significantly improved by reducing commuter traffic via telework programs.

- **Expands the location and availability of employees,** thereby increasing access by the customer. For instance, in large metropolitan areas it may be difficult for customers to get to a central office "downtown"; however, telework centers located in surrounding suburbs are easier to access.

- **May be used to provide services when the duty station office is closed.** For example, after a natural disaster, inclement weather, etc.

- **Extends employment opportunities to people with disabilities**, including employees who have partially recovered from work-related injuries who can perform their job from a remote location.

- **Accommodates employees who have temporary or continuing health problems** or who might otherwise have to retire on disability.

Jobs Adaptable to Telecommuting

Employers should consider their own circumstances and requirements to determine the likelihood of successfully implementing telecommuting in their organization. What job categories would be appropriate for telecommuting? What job functions or tasks can be accomplished away from the office? As a general rule of thumb, if an employee can close the office door for up to eight hours and effectively accomplish the job without the need for face-to-face contact with other employees, that employee's job is adaptable for telecommuting.

Job tasks that have been proven to be suited to telecommuting include the following:

- Tasks that are easily measured. Jobs that have countable or observable output with obvious beginning and ending points are a better choice than those that are not as clearly defined. This would include unit-oriented jobs such as data-entry jobs, as well as project-oriented jobs such as accounting, auditing, designing, and writing.

- Tasks that require very little unscheduled face-to-face contact. Most of the employee's contacts can be done via telephone or electronic mail or can occur at scheduled meetings. The job should require few, if any, critical face-to-face meetings.

- Tasks that do not require frequent access to files, equipment, or supplies that cannot easily or economically be moved to the employee's home or other telecommuting site.

Establish Thresholds

The first thing an employer should do is to establish threshold requirements that employees must meet before they can even apply for telecommuting arrangements. Some criteria to consider are as follows:

- **Disciplinary Record.** Because it is more difficult to monitor employees who work at home, trust is crucial to an effective telecommuting arrangement. Employees who have had recent disciplinary problems have not earned that trust and probably should not be allowed to apply for telecommuting privileges.

♦ **Length of Employment.** Individuals who have worked for an employer for less than a specified period of time, such as one year, should be ruled out. The employer probably will not know enough about new employees to assess whether they can be trusted, and the employees probably will not know enough about the organization's inner workings to function effectively at home.

Employers may wish to develop a list of positions that *per se* are ineligible for telecommuting. If an individual's request to perform one of those jobs at home is denied, the existence of this list will make it clear that the request was denied because of the nature of the employee's position, not because of the employee's gender, age, etc.

Selecting Between Applicants

At this point an employer has established general prerequisites that will weed out the positions and employees who should not even apply for telecommuting privileges. Next an employer will need some criteria for choosing among eligible applicants.

These factors may include the following:

♦ Specific requirements of the employee's job.

♦ The amount of interaction with supervisors, other employees, customers, vendors, etc., required.

♦ The necessary amount of day-to-day supervision.

♦ The company's business, both current and projected.

♦ Availability of other qualified personnel on site.

♦ The duration of the requested telecommuting arrangement.

♦ The reason for the request (medical, personal, etc.).

♦ The nature of the position (full-time or part-time).

In articulating the criteria, an employer should make clear that the organization reserves the right to determine how it will weigh each factor.

Making and Documenting the Decision

While it is important to establish the criteria for deciding who can telecommute, it is equally important to determine who will apply those factors. Effective implementation of a telecommuting policy requires input from both the employee's manager and the organization's senior human resource professional.

Having the would-be telecommuter's manager approve the arrangement is desirable to ensure that the setup makes tactical and strategic sense. The approval of the senior HR professional helps to guarantee consistency in the application of the criteria.

The basis for whatever decision is made should be documented, for a number of reasons. First, the documentation can help to promote consistency. In the absence of records, inconsistencies are inevitable. Second, documenting the nondiscriminatory reasons for treating employees differently is important. If an employee claims to have been unlawfully denied a telecommuting arrangement that was offered to another employee, the employer can use the documentation to show the lawful factors that distinguish the two situations.

Finally, documentation may be helpful when an organization denies a request for telecommuting as an accommodation for a disability. Although an employer can make a strong argument that telecommuting is not a reasonable accommodation, it will be less convincing if the organization has allowed telecommuting for nondisabled employees. However, if the documentation clearly shows the business reasons for allowing employees to telecommute and if those reasons are not present in the case of the disabled worker, the employer will be in a much stronger position.

Terms and Conditions of Leave

Upon deciding to permit telecommuting, employers should provide employees with a memo explaining the terms and conditions of the arrangement. Although the organization's telecommuting policy should generally address these conditions, the memo for each employee should be more specific.

Below are some terms and conditions that the memo should address.

Right to Discontinue

The memo should make clear that the organization reserves the sole discretion to terminate the telecommuting relationship at any time. Even if an employer has the right to terminate an employment relationship at-will, the employer may risk creating a legal claim by failing to make clear the at-will nature of the telecommuting relationship.

Trial Period

An employer may wish to subject the telecommuting relationship to a 90-day trial period. This would be similar to the introductory period at the beginning of most employment relationships. Although not legally necessary, as a practical matter the telecommuting trial period should give the employer an opportunity to focus closely on whether the relationship works.

The employer also should make clear that the employee's successful completion of the trial period does not restrict the employer's at-will right to terminate the telecommuting relationship at a later date. The employer's failure to expressly state this may result, by negative implication, in its waiver of this right.

Wage and Hour Issues

One of the biggest risks in telecommuting involves the recording of hours worked. Simply put, an employee can claim to have worked more hours than actually worked.

Employers should have a general idea of how long a telecommuting employee will need to complete an assigned task. However, an employee who works with above-average speed may be able to charge an employer for time in excess of that needed to complete the work.

A related risk is that the employee will accrue substantial overtime. Employees subject to the Fair Labor Standards Act's wage-and-hour requirements must be paid one and-a-half times their regular hourly rates for all hours worked over 40 in a week.

To minimize the chances of having to pay excessive overtime compensation, employers should require that telecommuters keep track of the hours they actually work per week and submit weekly time records. If an employee submits time records and later claims to have worked overtime in excess of the hours noted on the records, the claims will be suspect.

The employer also may wish to make it clear that an employee who telecommutes cannot work more than 40 hours in a given week without written or electronic permission from a supervisor for that week. To ensure that the employee does not work more than the agreed-upon number of hours, the employer should review time records regularly. Because the law defines ***employ*** as "suffer or permit to work," an employer must compensate a telecommuter for unauthorized work if the employer allowed or acquiesced in the work.

Finally, the employer may wish to require that the telecommuter sign in and out with a supervisor by telephone, email or other means. Employees who use a computer could be required to track time worked through computer-generated time reports that show log-on and log-off times. This not only may help in terms of wage-and-hour issues but also should reinforce the nature of the supervisory relationship, even if there are no face-to-face interactions.

Equipment

Most employees who telecommute will need the use of a computer and related equipment and services. This obviously raises the issue of who pays for the hardware, the software, and any special monthly charges. These issues should be resolved up front. If the employer provides equipment to the telecommuter, the employee should be required to promise, in writing, to return the equipment upon request or automatically upon termination. The agreement also should provide — to the extent permitted by applicable laws, which vary from state to state — that the employee's failure to return the equipment at the agreed-upon time constitutes authorization for the organization to withhold wages otherwise due.

The employer also may wish to restate in the memo with greater specificity what already should be in its general search policy: The organization reserves the right to monitor any documents or messages sent, received, or stored on the employer's information systems. This specific reiteration for telecommuters is recommended to debunk any increased expectation of privacy that the employee may have simply because some or all of the hardware, software, or documentation is located within the residence.

Finally, telecommuting obviously creates greater risks in terms of unauthorized access and/or use of confidential information. Telecommuters should be required to sign a special confidentiality agreement that covers access, use, and dissemination of confidential information.

Statutory Notices

Under federal and state laws, an employer must post certain abstracts of statutes in the place of employment. Some laws specify that these notices must be posted not only at an employer's main office but also at each worksite.

For purposes of some posting requirements, a telecommuting employee's home may constitute a separate worksite. Yet it is hard to imagine that any employee would not object to having a Family and Medical Leave Act notice, for example, posted in the living room. While this may seem like a minor technical issue, it can have significant consequences in terms of the applicable statute of limitations. If a notice is not posted where it should be, the period for filing claims may be unlimited.

The memo that the employee receives upon the commencement of the arrangement should make clear where the statutory abstracts are to be posted and should remind the telecommuter to review them when on the company's physical premises. For this and other reasons it is recommended that the employer consider requiring that the employee be physically present at the employer's worksite on a regular basis, whether it be weekly, monthly or quarterly.

Promotional Opportunities

An employee who requests the option to telecommute later may complain about feeling left out of the career advancement loop. Because an employee who is not physically present at the worksite has less contact with supervisors, the employee may be less likely to be considered for a vacant position. Employees should be told in the memos that telecommuting limits the potential for promotional opportunities. They also should be told that the burden is upon telecommuting employees to come to the primary worksites to see if vacancies have been posted.

Legal Concerns

A policy should contain guidelines to limit the organization's legal risks and the employer should follow the guidelines if telecommuting is put into practice.

Occupational Safety and Health Act

Employers are required by law to maintain a safe workplace for employees, even if it is at home. Based on recent policy announcements, the Occupational Safety and Health Administration (OSHA) generally will not inspect, nor require employers to inspect, the home worksites of employees engaged in telecommuting. However, if employees are engaged in manufacturing or other physical activities at home in the interest of their employers, which may pose safety or health hazards to them (for example, making lead molds), then OSHA may seek to inspect the work areas upon a complaint.

In any event, employers subject to recordkeeping requirements must record the occupational injuries and illnesses of all home workers and may need to take feasible measures to comply with relevant OSHA standards at least to the extent that they do not involve controlling the worksite.

Workers' Compensation

Another key legal consideration in telecommuting is workers' compensation. An employee who is injured while working at home may be eligible for workers' compensation, even though the employer has no effective control over the conditions of the employee's home.

Worse yet, the employee may claim to have been injured while telecommuting, even though the injury occurred while out of the home or not when working. At the very least this is an issue of fact for a workers' compensation referee.

However, most telecommuting work is sedentary so it is unlikely that an employee will be injured while working at home or that an allegation that the employee was injured while doing so will be credible.

When an employee has been injured while telecommuting, it is unlikely that the injury will result in total disability. Most telecommuting intrinsically is light duty, at least in terms of the physical demands.

To minimize the workers' compensation risks an employer should require that an employee notify a designated manager immediately if the employee is injured at home. While this will minimize the risk, it will not eliminate it. Again, it comes down to a matter of trust.

 In addition, the employer may wish to inspect the employee's home office to ensure that it is an ergonomically healthy environment and preclude the employee, at least on paper, from changing the environment without the employer's permission. Of course, any visitor to the employee's home must give due regard to the telecommuter's privacy rights.

Finally, as part of the pre-telecommuting arrangement, an employer should secure a release from the employee allowing the employer to come in and inspect the employee's worksite immediately after any accident or injury. While such actions will not stop all fraudulent claims, they will help employers to better address such claims.

Fair Labor Standards Act

Telecommuting policies and procedures must remain within acceptable limits of federal and state wage-and-hour laws. The regulations do not contain any unique requirements or exceptions for telecommuters. Wage-and-hour requirements that apply to on-site employees also apply to off-site employees. If an employee is not exempt from the Fair Labor Standards Act (FLSA) the employer still has the obligation of maintaining time records for the employee, as minimum wage and overtime restrictions are still applicable. This may be done by having the employees fill out time sheets or log on and off a computer or telephone at the beginning and ending of their workhours. Employers concerned about potential exaggeration of time records should develop methods for verification.

When establishing a system for evaluating the productivity of exempt or salaried employees, employers must take care not to compromise the employees' exempt status under the FLSA. The system should not undermine the fact that they are paid on a salary basis.

Americans with Disabilities Act

The Americans with Disabilities Act (ADA) requires employers to offer reasonable accommodation for qualified applicants and employees with disabilities. Reasonable accommodation is any change in the work environment or in the way things are customarily done that enables an individual with a disability to apply for a job, perform a job, or gain equal access to the benefits and privileges of a job. According to the Equal Employment Opportunity Commission (EEOC), allowing an individual with a disability to work at home may be a form of reasonable accommodation.

Although the ADA does not require an employer to offer a telework program, if an employer does offer telework it must allow employees with disabilities an equal opportunity to participate in the program. An employer may be required to waive certain eligibility requirements or otherwise modify its telework program for someone with a disability who needs to work at home. For example, an employer may generally require employees to work at least one year before they are eligible to participate in a telework program. If a new employee needs to work at home because of a disability, and the job can be performed at home, the employer may have to waive its one-year rule for this individual.

If an employer does not allow employees to telecommute, changing the location where work is performed may fall under the ADA's reasonable accommodation requirement of modifying the workplace policies. Alternatively, the employer may select any effective accommodation, even if it is not the one preferred by the employee.

Reasonable accommodations include adjustments or changes to the workplace for the ease of comfort of individuals with disabilities, such as the following:

- Providing devices or modifying equipment.
- Making workplaces accessible (installing a ramp).
- Restructuring jobs.
- Modifying work schedules and policies.
- Providing qualified readers or sign language interpreters.

An employer may provide an alternative method of reasonable accommodations, or a combination of them, to permit an employee to remain in the workplace. For example, a disabled employee who needs to use paratransit requests to work at home because the paratransit schedule does not permit employee to arrive before 10 a.m., two hours after the normal starting time. If this may be coordinated with the paratransit schedule, the employer may allow the employee to begin the work shift at 10 a.m., rather than granting the request to work at home.

The ADA recommends an employer determine an employee's need to work at home through a flexible, interactive process between the employer and the employee. Initially, the employee must request to work at home by notifying employer that a medical condition interferes with employee's ability to do the job. Then, the employer and the employee should conduct an open discussion detailing why the employee needs to work from home, the employee's medical condition, available accommodations, and all reasonable options. The employer may request information about the employee's medical condition (including reasonable documentation) if it is unclear whether the employee's disability is within the parameters of the ADA. As the dialogue continues, the employer and the employee must determine whether a particular job may be performed at home. First, the employer and the employee should identify and review all of the essential job functions (that is, those tasks that are fundamental to performing a specific job). Second, the employer and the employee should determine the feasibility of working at home, including the employer's ability to supervise the employee adequately and whether any duties require the use of certain equipment or tools or require face-to-face time that cannot be replicated at home. If the employer determines that some job duties must be performed in the workplace, the employer and the employee must consider whether working part time at home and part time in the workplace will meet their needs.

The frequency the disabled employee may work at home is only to the extent that the employee's disability necessitates the reasonable accommodation. As part of the interactive process, the employer should discuss with the employee the nature of the disability and reach an agreement meeting both of their needs. Not all persons with disabilities want to work at home and not all jobs can be performed at home. However, allowing an employee to work at home may be a reasonable accommodation if the employee's disability prevents the employee from successfully performing the job on-site.

Insurance and General Liability Issues

Before implementing a telecommuting policy, an employer must determine how to handle certain insurance issues. Work injuries and workers' compensation have already been discussed. The employer and the telecommuter should consider other insurance and liability issues before telecommuting begins. For example, it needs to be determined who will be responsible for theft or damage to equipment. Will it be the employee's obligation to provide insurance coverage for such incidents or will the organization provide the insurance coverage? Likewise, who shall provide insurance coverage if third parties are injured at the telecommuter's home? It is unlikely that injuries to individuals at the telecommuter's home for social or personal reasons will be the employer's responsibility. However, injuries that are related to the telecommuter's work or equipment may be found to be the employer's responsibility.

Note: Preventive steps should be taken to lessen the chance of liability and insurance concerns. The employer and the employee should understand from the beginning where the liability for each begins and ends in the working relationship.

Zoning

Local zoning codes may prohibit home-based work at the telecommuter's home. Employers should ensure that zoning codes permit home-based work at the employee's location before investing time and equipment in setting up the employee's residence for work.

Telecommuting Written Agreement

To clarify expectations and obligations, employers and employees should enter into written agreements covering telecommuting arrangements. Important subjects for an agreement would include the following:

- The employee's coverage for workers' compensation while working at the alternative jobsite.
- The employer's (or employee's) provision of necessary equipment.
- The maintenance of the employee's alternative workspace to the same standards as required for the onsite office. The employer may retain the right, subject to reasonable notice, to inspect the alternative worksite during scheduled workhours.
- The employee's responsibility to secure any equipment provided by the employer.
- Responsibility for the cost of utilities.
- Clarification of the employer's policy regarding dependent care during workhours.
- The employee's ability, accessibility, and/or flexibility for and the location of meetings.
- The employee's duty to make reports to the employer's office or to report in periodically.

Conclusion

More employers are coming to recognize that telecommuting offers a unique opportunity to cut costs and retain valuable employees. Management support is essential for a program to succeed. Managers must be trained to supervise telecommuting employees and policies and procedures must be developed to accommodate the telecommuter while limiting the risks to the employer. Clearly defined procedures and guidelines not only allow both employers and employees to know what is expected of them, but also reduce the likelihood of unexpected employment issues or lawsuits. Samples of a telecommuting policy, agreement, and time sheet are provided at the end of this chapter.

Contact Information

Equal Employment Opportunity Commission
1801 L Street, NW
Washington, DC 20507

Telephone: 202-663-4900
Toll-Free: 800-669-4000
TTY: 202-663-4494
Toll-Free: 800-669-6820
Internet: *www.eeoc.gov*

Job Accommodation Network
P.O. Box 6080
Morgantown, WV 26506-6080

Telephone (Toll-Free): 800-526-7234 or 800-ADA-WORK
Fax: 304-293-5407
Email: jan@jan.wvu.edu
Internet: *www.jan.wvu.edu*

Note: Calls are answered from 8 a.m. to 8 p.m. Eastern Time, Monday through Thursday, and on Fridays from 8 a.m. to 7 p.m. Machines answer after-hours calls.

Telecommuting Policy
(Sample)

The Company considers telecommuting to be a viable alternative work arrangement in cases where individual, job, and supervisor characteristics are best suited to such an arrangement. Telecommuting allows employees to work at home, on the road, or in a satellite location for all or part of their regular workweek. Telecommuting is a voluntary work alternative that may be appropriate for some employees and some jobs. It is not an entitlement and it is not a company-wide benefit. Telecommuting in no way changes the terms and conditions of employment with the Company.

Procedure

1. Either an employee or a supervisor can suggest telecommuting as a possible work arrangement.

2. Telecommuting can be informal, such as working from home for a short-term project or on the road during business travel, or formal, as will be described below. Other informal, short-term arrangements may be made for employees on family or medical leave to the extent practical for the employee and the organization and with the consent of the employee's health care provider, if appropriate. All informal telecommuting arrangements are made on a case-by-case basis, focusing on the business needs of the organization first. Such informal arrangements are not the focus of this policy.

3. Individuals requesting formal telecommuting arrangements must have been employed with the Company for a minimum of 12 months of continuous, regular employment and must have exhibited above-average performance, in accordance with the company's performance appraisal process.

4. Any telecommuting arrangement made will be on a trial basis for the first three months and may be discontinued, at will, at any time at the request of either the telecommuter or the organization.

5. The Company will determine, with information supplied by the employee and the supervisor, the appropriate equipment needs (including hardware, software, modems, phone and data lines, facsimile equipment or software, photocopiers, etc.) for each telecommuting arrangement on a case-by-case basis. The human resource and information system departments will serve as resources in this matter. Equipment supplied by the organization will be maintained by the organization. Equipment supplied by the employee, if deemed appropriate by the organization, will be maintained by the employee. The Company accepts no responsibility for damage or repairs to employee-owned equipment. The Company reserves the right to make determinations as to appropriate equipment, subject to change at any time. Equipment supplied by the organization is to be used for business purposes only. The telecommuter should sign an inventory of all office property and agrees to take appropriate action to protect the items from damage or theft. Upon termination of employment all company property will be returned to the company, unless other arrangements have been made.

6. Consistent with the organization's expectations of information asset security for employees working at the office full-time, telecommuting employees will be expected to ensure the protection of proprietary company and customer information accessible from their home office. Steps include, but are not limited to, the use of locked file cabinets, disk boxes, and desks, as well as regular password maintenance and any other steps appropriate for the job and the environment.

7. The employee will establish an appropriate work environment within their home for work purposes. The Company will not be responsible for costs associated with initial setup of the employee's home office such as remodeling, furniture, or lighting, nor for repairs or modifications to the home office space. Employees will be offered appropriate assistance in setting up a workstation designed for safe, comfortable work.

8. After equipment has been delivered, a designated representative of the Company will visit the employee's worksite to inspect for possible work hazards and suggest modifications. Repeat inspections will occur on an as-needed basis. Injuries sustained by the employee while at their home work location and in conjunction with their regular work duties are normally covered by the company's workers' compensation policy. Telecommuting employees are responsible for notifying the employer of such injuries in accordance with company workers' compensation procedures. The employee is liable for any injuries sustained by visitors to the worksite.

9. The Company will supply the employee with appropriate office supplies (pens, paper, etc.) for successful completion of job responsibilities. The organization will also reimburse the employee for all other business-related expenses such as phone calls, shipping costs, etc. that are reasonably incurred in accordance with job responsibilities.

10. The employee and manager will agree on the number of days of telecommuting allowed each week, the work schedule the employee will customarily maintain, and the manner and frequency of communication. The employee agrees to be accessible by phone or modem within a reasonable time period during the agreed upon work schedule.

11. Telecommuting employees who are not exempt from the overtime requirements of the Fair Labor Standards Act will be required to record all hours worked in a manner designated by the organization. Telecommuting employees will be held to a higher standard of compliance than office-based employees due to the nature of the work arrangement. Hours worked in excess of those specified per day and per workweek will, in accordance with state and federal requirements, require the advance approval of the supervisor. Failure to comply with this requirement can result in the immediate cessation of the telecommuting agreement.

12. Before entering into any telecommuting agreement, the employee and manager, with the assistance of the human resource department, will evaluate the suitability of such an arrangement, paying particular attention to the following areas:

- Employee Suitability. The employee and manager will assess the needs and work habits of the employee, compared to traits customarily recognized as appropriate for successful telecommuters.

- Job Responsibilities. The employee and manager will discuss the job responsibilities and determine if the job is appropriate for a telecommuting arrangement.

- Workplace Adaptability. Equipment needs for out of office work, workspace design considerations, and scheduling issues.

13. Tax and other legal implications for the business use of the employee's home based on IRS and state and local government restrictions. Responsibility for fulfilling all obligations in this area rests solely with the employee.

14. If the employee and manager agree, and the human resource department concurs, a draft telecommuting agreement will be prepared and signed by all parties and a three-month trial period will commence.

15. Evaluation of telecommuter performance during the trial period will include daily interaction by phone and email between the employee and the manager, and weekly face-to-face meetings to discuss work progress and problems. At the conclusion of the trial period the employee and manager will each complete an evaluation of the arrangement and make recommendations for continuance or modifications. Evaluation of telecommuter performance beyond the trial period will be consistent with that received by employees working at the office in both content and frequency but will focus on work output and completion of objectives rather than time-based performance.

16. An appropriate level of communication between the telecommuter and supervisor will be agreed to as part of the discussion process and will be more formal during the trial period. After conclusion of the trial period, the manager and telecommuter will communicate at a level consistent with employees working at the office or in a manner and frequency that seems appropriate for the job and the individuals involved.

17. Telecommuting is NOT designed to be a replacement for appropriate child care. Although an individual employee's schedule may be modified to accommodate child care needs, the focus of the arrangement must remain on job performance and meeting business demands. Prospective telecommuters are encouraged to discuss expectations of telecommuting with family members prior to entering into a trial period.

18. Employees entering into a telecommuting agreement may be required to forfeit use of a personal office or workstation in favor of a shared arrangement to maximize organization office space needs.

19. In certain limited circumstances, the Company may contract with an office space provider to meet the needs of employees who wish to telecommute but who do not have appropriate home office space, or for groups of employees whose proximity to the organization and to each other makes such an arrangement feasible.

The availability of telecommuting as a flexible work arrangement for employees of the Company can be discontinued at any time at the discretion of the employer. Every effort will be made to provide 30 days notice of such a change to accommodate commuting, child care, and other problems that may arise from such a change. There may be instances, however, where no notice is possible.

Note: This is a generic sample policy and does not necessarily reflect the employment laws in any or all of the 50 U.S. states. Before establishing any company policy, one should review the applicable state laws or seek guidance from legal counsel.

Telecommuting Agreement
(Sample)

This is an agreement between *{Employer}* and *{Employee}* and shall cover the period from *{Beginning date}* through *{End date}*.

This agreement establishes the terms and conditions of telecommuting.

The employee volunteers to participate in the telecommuting program and to follow the applicable guidelines and policies. The employer agrees with the employee's participation.

Duration: This agreement will be valid until canceled by either party.

Workhours: Workhours and location are specified as part of this agreement.

Pay and Attendance: All pay, leave and travel entitlement will be based on the employee's official duty station. The employee's time and attendance will be recorded as if the employee is performing official duties at the office.

Leave: Employees must obtain supervisory approval before taking leave in accordance with established office procedures. The employee agrees to follow established procedures for requesting and obtaining approval of leave.

Overtime: The employee will continue to work in pay status while working at the home office. An employee working overtime that is ordered and approved in advance will be compensated in accordance with applicable law and rules. The employee understands that the supervisor will not accept work products resulting from unapproved overtime. The employee agrees that failing to obtain proper approval for overtime work may result in removal from the telecommuting program or other appropriate action.

Equipment: The supervisor and the employee must agree upon the equipment to be used in telecommuting. The Company is not required to provide equipment for the home office; however, with the approval of the supervisor, the telecommuter may be provided employer owned equipment necessary to perform work assignments. *Please fill out the provided equipment inventory slip.*

Maintenance of Equipment: Equipment provided by the employer must be protected against damage and unauthorized use. Employer-owned equipment will be serviced and maintained by the employer. Equipment provided by the employee will be at no cost to the employer and will be maintained by the employee.

Cost: The employer will not be responsible for operating costs, home maintenance, or any other incidental costs (such as utilities) associated with the use of the employee's residence. The employee does not give up any reimbursement for authorized expenses incurred while conducting official business for the employer.

Liability: The employer will not be liable for damages to the employee's property resulting from participation in the telecommuting program. In signing this document the employee agrees to hold the Company harmless against any and all claims, excluding workers' compensation claims.

Workers' Compensation: The employee is covered by workers' compensation if injured in the course of performing official duties at the telecommuting location.

Verification of Home Safety: In signing this agreement the employee verifies that the home office provides work space that is free of safety and fire hazards.

Work Assignments: The employee will meet with the supervisor to receive assignments and to review completed work. The employee will complete all assigned work according to procedures mutually agreed upon with the supervisor.

Evaluation: The evaluation of the employee's job performance will be based on established standards. Performance must remain satisfactory to remain a telecommuter. Employees will not be allowed to telecommute while on a performance improvement plan (PIP).

Records: The employee will apply safeguards which are approved by the employer to protect records from unauthorized disclosure or damage. All records, papers, and correspondence must be safeguarded for their return to the office.

Participation in Evaluation: The employee and supervisor agree to promptly complete and submit telecommuting evaluation materials and to attend periodic group meetings for the telecommuting program.

Curtailment of the Agreement: The employee may stop participating in this program at any time. Management has the right to remove the employee from the program if participation fails to benefit organizational needs.

The employee agrees to work at the office or telecommuting location and not from another unapproved site. Failure to comply with this provision may result in termination of the agreement and/or other appropriate disciplinary action.

Workhours and Location: The following are the working hours and locations which are agreed to as a part of the Telecommuting Agreement:

Official Work Location: *{Place name and location}*

Telecommuting Location: *{Place name and location}*

General Workhours:

Day	Date	Hours	Location O=Official Office T=Telecommuting
Monday:			
Tuesday:			
Wednesday:			
Thursday:			
Friday:			
Saturday:			
Sunday:			

Telecommuting Work Plan: (Include a description of duties, how work output will be reviewed and monitored, and how supervision will be provided.)

We agree to abide by the terms and conditions of this agreement.

Employee: _____ **Date:** _____ *{Date}* _____

Supervisor: _____ **Date:** _____ *{Date}* _____

Approving Authority: _____ **Date:** _____ *{Date}* _____

Note: This is a generic sample policy and does not necessarily reflect the employment laws in any or all of the 50 U.S. states. Before establishing any company policy, one should review the applicable state laws or seek guidance from legal counsel.

Company-Owned Equipment Inventory (Sample)

(Please include all provided equipment including telecommunication services):

{List items individually}	*{List items individually}*
{List items individually}	*{List items individually}*
{List items individually}	*{List items individually}*
{List items individually}	*{List items individually}*

Note: This is a generic sample policy and does not necessarily reflect the employment laws in any or all of the 50 U.S. states. Before establishing any company policy, one should review the applicable state laws or seek guidance from legal counsel.

Self-Certification Safety Checklist for Home-Based Telecommuters (Sample)

Name: _____

Organization: _____

Address: _____

City/State: _____

Business Telephone: _____

Telecommuting Coordinator: _____

Dear Telecommuter:

The following checklist is designed to assess the overall safety of your alternate duty station. Please read and complete the self-certification safety checklist. Upon completion, you and your supervisor should sign and date the checklist in the spaces provided.

The alternate duty station is _____.

Describe the designated work area in the alternate duty station:

_____.

A. Workplace Environment

1. Are temperature, noise, ventilation, and lighting levels adequate for maintaining your normal level of job performance? Yes ___ No ___

2. Are all stairs with four or more steps equipped with handrails? Yes ___ No ___

3. Are all circuit breakers and/or fuses in the electrical panel labeled as to intended service? Yes ___ No ___

4. Do circuit breakers clearly indicate if they are in an open or closed position? Yes ___ No ___

5. Is all electrical equipment free of recognized hazards that would cause physical harm (frayed wires, bare conductors, loose wires, flexible wires running through walls, exposed wires to the ceiling)? Yes ___ No ___

6. Will the building's electrical system permit grounding electrical equipment? Yes ___ No ___

7. Are aisles, doorways, and corners free of obstructions to permit visibility and movement? Yes ___ No ___

8. Are file cabinets and storage closets arranged so drawers and doors do not open into walkways?   Yes ___ No ___

9. Do chairs have any loose casters (wheels) and are the rungs and legs of the chairs sturdy?   Yes ___ No ___

10. Are the phone lines, electrical cords, and extension wires secured under a desk or alongside a baseboard?   Yes ___ No ___

11. Is the office space neat, clean, and free of excessive amounts of combustibles?   Yes ___ No ___

12. Are floor surfaces clean, dry, level, and free of worn or frayed seams?   Yes ___ No ___

13. Are carpets well secured to the floor and free of frayed or worn seams?   Yes ___ No ___

14. Is there enough light for reading?   Yes ___ No ___

B. Computer Workstation (If Applicable)

1. Is your chair adjustable?   Yes ___ No ___

2. Do you know how to adjust your chair?   Yes ___ No ___

3. Is your back adequately supported by a backrest?   Yes ___ No ___

4. Are your feet on the floor or fully supported by a footrest?   Yes ___ No ___

5. Are you satisfied with the placement of your VDT and keyboard?   Yes ___ No ___

6. Is it easy to read the text on your screen?   Yes ___ No ___

7. Do you need a document holder?   Yes ___ No ___

8. Do you have enough leg room at your desk?   Yes ___ No ___

9. Is the VDT screen free from noticeable glare?   Yes ___ No ___

10. Is the top of the VDT screen eye level?   Yes ___ No ___

11. Is there space to rest the arms while not keying?   Yes ___ No ___

12. When keying, are your forearms close to parallel with the floor?   Yes ___ No ___

13. Are your wrists fairly straight when keying?   Yes ___ No ___

_____
Employee's Signature/Date

_____
Immediate Supervisor's Signature/Date

Approved [ ] Disapproved [ ]

Note: This is a generic sample policy and does not necessarily reflect the employment laws in any or all of the 50 U.S. states. Before establishing any company policy, one should review the applicable state laws or seek guidance from legal counsel.

Supervisory - Employee Checkout List (Sample)

The following checklist is designed to ensure that your telecommuting employee is properly oriented to the policies and procedures of the telecommuting program.

Name of Employee: _____

Name of Immediate Supervisor: _____

Action Completed: **Date:**

Employee has read guidelines outlining policies and procedures of
the pilot program.   _____

Employee has been provided with a schedule of core hours.   _____

Employee has been issued equipment.   _____

Equipment issued by the agency is documented.   _____

Check as applicable, Yes or No:

Computer...   Yes ___   No ___

Printer...   Yes ___   No ___

Modem..   Yes ___   No ___

Fax Machine...   Yes ___   No ___

Copy Machine...   Yes ___   No ___

Telephone...   Yes ___   No ___

Desk..   Yes ___   No ___

Chair...   Yes ___   No ___

Other...   Yes ___   No ___

Please initial when completed:

Policies and procedures for care of equipment issued by the agency   _____
have been explained and are clearly understood.

Policies and procedures covering classified, secure, or privacy act
data have been discussed, and are clearly understood.   _____

Requirements for an adequate and safe office space and/or area
have been discussed, and the employee certifies those requirements   _____
are met.

Performance expectations have been discussed and are clearly
understood.   _____

Employee understands that the supervisor may terminate employee
participation at any time, in accordance with established   _____
administrative procedures and union negotiated agreements.

Employee has participated in training for Federal telecommuters.   _____

_____

Supervisor Signature

_____

Employee Signature

Note: This is a generic sample policy and does not necessarily reflect the employment laws in any or all of the 50 U.S. states. Before establishing any company policy, one should review the applicable state laws or seek guidance from legal counsel.

Index

B

C

D

E

F

G

H

M

N

O

P

R

T

U

V

W

Z